AF522625

THE ESSENTIAL
U. R. ANANTHAMURTHY

THE ESSENTIAL U. R. ANANTHAMURTHY

EDITED BY N. MANU CHAKRAVARTHY
AND CHANDAN GOWDA

ALEPH

ALEPH BOOK COMPANY
An independent publishing firm
promoted by ***Rupa Publications India***

First published in India in 2023
by Aleph Book Company
7/16 Ansari Road, Daryaganj
New Delhi 110 002

Copyright in the pieces in the original Kannada © Esther Ananthamurthy
Anthology copyright © Aleph Book Company 2023
Introduction copyright © N. Manu Chakravarthy and Chandan Gowda 2023
Copyright in translated pieces vests in respective authors/translators/proprietors.
Acknowledgements on pp. 297 are an extension of the copyright page.

All rights reserved.

This is a work of fiction. Names, characters, places, and incidents are either the product of the authors' imagination or are used fictitiously and any resemblance to any actual persons, living or dead, events, or locales is entirely coincidental.

The views and opinions expressed in this book are those of the author and the facts are as reported by him, which have been verified to the extent possible, and the publisher is not in any way liable for the same.

No part of this publication may be reproduced, transmitted, or stored in a retrieval system, in any form or by any means, without permission in writing from Aleph Book Company.

ISBN: 978-93-93852-90-8

1 3 5 7 9 10 8 6 4 2

For sale in the Indian subcontinent only.

Printed in India.

This book is sold subject to the condition that it shall not, by way of trade or otherwise, be lent, resold, hired out, or otherwise circulated without the publisher's prior consent in any form of binding or cover other than that in which it is published.

CONTENTS

EDITORS' INTRODUCTION

Born into a Madhva Brahmin family in Thirthahalli, Shivamogga district, in 1932, U. R. Ananthamurthy (URA) spent his boyhood in an agrahara. His father was a village accountant who wanted his son to become a mathematician. Several of URA's stories and memoir writings convey the formative influence of his childhood experiences. The novels of Shivarama Karanth and Kuvempu excited him during his high school days. His encounter with the thoughts of Ram Manohar Lohia and his involvement in the Kagodu farmers' satyagraha in the early 1950s, through the socialist leader and his close mentor, Gopala Gowda, proved an enduring influence: the ideal of caste equality, the primacy of Indian languages for intellectual creativity, and the value of a decentralized polity were among his lifelong passions.

URA did his BA and MA in English literature at the University of Mysore. Professor C. D. Narasimhaiah, the reputed literary scholar associated with the founding discussions of Commonwealth Literature, was among his teachers. Mysore was a major hub of intellectual discussions at that time. Kuvempu, the great Kannada novelist, taught Kannada literature at the University of Mysore. Gopalakrishna Adiga, the famous modernist Kannada poet and an important interlocutor for URA, taught at a college in Mysore. R. K. Narayan also lived in Mysore in this period.

Following his studies in Mysore, URA taught English literature at colleges in Shivamogga and Hassan. In 1963, he left for the University of Birmingham to pursue his PhD. Although he was interested in doing his doctoral research on D. H. Lawrence, his advisor, Malcolm Bradbury, the novelist, suggested he work instead on the English fiction of the 1930s, the period that saw the rise of fascism in Europe. URA's research focused on the work of Christopher Isherwood and Edward Upward, who had both fallen out of communism for different reasons.

After completing his PhD in 1966, URA returned to teach English literature at the University of Mysore. He was to work here till his retirement in 1992. During his entire academic career, he wrote little by way of literary criticism in English. The world of Kannada literature and criticism was his home.

As a teacher, writer, critic, and, later, administrator, URA engaged with a vast number of individuals and was a public intellectual in a capacious sense. He had a special place among Indian writers for his steady embrace of the intellectual and political significance of Indian language writing. Major political figures, farmers' activists, Dalit activists, and environmental activists were among his friends. He lent consistent support to the activist efforts towards the promotion of caste equality and an anti-communal culture. In 2001, he even led a successful campaign to stop mining activities in Kudremukh. His contribution to the shaping of democratic sensibilities of the Kannada readers is truly immense.

URA wrote his first novel, *Samskara,* in 1965, while he was a student in Birmingham. Though his previously published short fiction had established him as a promising writer, this novel proved to be a landmark of literary modernism (Navya) in Kannada. Its ruthless depiction of the decadent aspects of Brahmin society invited instant controversy in Karnataka. The selfhood of Praneshacharya, an austere, self-denying scholar and arbiter of orthodox Madhva morality, is destabilized following the death of a heterodox fellow Brahmin. Did the defiant deeds of the latter disqualify him for traditional funeral rites? Seeking an answer to this question lands Praneshacharya in radical self-doubt and also leads him to new sensory pleasures and to the world outside the confined milieu of his agrahara, putting him on the path of self-awakening.

Samskara affirms the need to seek truth outside prevalent moral frames, the value of scepticism in the face of community orthodoxy, the sensual pleasures of the body, among others. Lohia's vision of caste equality, D. H. Lawrence's celebration of the instinctual life and disdain for the life-negating stance of Christian morality, Jiddu Krishnamurti's insistence that individual awareness be freed from existing knowledge: all of these seem to have mattered for this novel which broke from the Kannada literary ethos of the time.

A persistent suspicion of how ideology limits the scope of human experience and pre-empts the search for truth is an abiding concern in URA's work. Praneschacharya realizes that his search for God was routed through a prior commitment to Madhva philosophy and therefore was not really a quest. URA's next novel, *Bharathipura* (1974), hauls up the main protagonist, Jagannatha, for routing his reformist imagination of caste inequality and religious superstition through a liberal ideology rather than in any grounded engagement with the local world of caste and religious practices.

While *Bharathipura* had its admirers, many critics dismissed it as a novel of ideas. Signifying a decided shift in URA's intellectual orientation, this novel departs from *Samskara*'s suspicion of traditional society as a limiting force towards individual experience, and directs scepticism towards the modern imagination of caste equality and social reform. Jagannath's efforts at reforming the practices of untouchability and local beliefs in God, which are rooted in liberal ideas of equality and modern rationalism, are constantly frustrated. Indeed, he becomes contemptuous of the Dalits when they do not share his understanding of their problem and loses his humanity. The novel's suggestion that reformist critique and political creativity are better fashioned from grounds internal to the world of lived experience and not from the abstract ideals of freedom and equality from the outside resurfaces in many of URA's subsequent writings. His concern to show the limitations of Western liberal and Marxist thought for evolving a critique of Indian society, which powerfully anticipate the central preoccupations of 'post-colonial' discussions found in academia two decades later, stayed unwavering till the end.

Based on the life of Gopala Gowda, *Avasthe* (1978), URA's third novel, mulls over the fate of political idealism within a manipulative electoral democracy and the existential challenges that non-rational, erotic, and mystical experiences pose for rational individuals. Tired of political cynicism and ideological thought, the socialist leader, the main protagonist, longs to realize two intertwined aims: to relive the luminous quotidian life that he had experienced is his younger days and to see how best to stir anger among the vulnerable people that could destroy the pettiness inside a social order that only works for the already secure people ('those who have reached the shore').

URA's next novel, *Bhava* (1994), plays with the double sense of the title Sanskrit term, i.e., being as well as becoming, to raise questions about the nature of the self and its place in the world. It brings into play characters whose outward selves are at odds with their inner selves with those where such a conflict is absent. Spiritually barren, the former seek release from the acts of becoming, and wish to attain a self that experiences 'stillness in motion', a self that is freed of the desire towards kin and material attachments (samsara).

Preeti, Mrutyu, Bhaya (Love, Death, Fear), URA's unfinished novel from 1959 that was published in 2012, gives a glimpse of the modernist imagination of the youthful writer. Shekhar, a writer enmeshed in troubled family and romantic relationships, longs for an undivided self which is in harmony with nature. Moving between first and third person accounts, this novel, where the shadows of T. S. Eliot, the French existentialists, as well as the Kannada modernist writers are seen, shows URA's unique style of being preoccupied with an alienated self and its overcoming.

A distinct style of URA's social realism is to put the social world on hold to glance inside a protagonist's inner self, in the form of a soliloquy or an emotional state, among others, and then return to reality, as it were, with unsettled certitudes and transformations in the self. And, in letting the readers feel the angst, the turmoil of such inner states, metaphors often do valuable work.

Intense, ambitious and suspenseful, URA's short stories exhibit a heterogeneity of thematic concerns. Consider the ones found in this book. 'Ghatashraddha' (1962), an early short story, delineates the violence of a tradition that does not take kindly to a young Brahmin widow who has become pregnant. Narrated by a young boy, the story also offers glimpses of the decline and corruption seen in a Brahmin agrahara in modern times. In 'Mouni' (1966), which was written in Birmingham, an areca nut farmer sits down in silent protest after having been defeated through the machinations of a rival farmer and the heartlessness of the local creditors. A tacit plea for morality in economic relations, the silent protest stirs the conscience of the rival farmer in the end. The story places an earnest faith in the power of non-violent dissent to transform the hearts and minds of those on the opposite side. 'Kamaroopi' (1995) centres around a chance airport encounter of a well-known political scientist with an amoral wheeler-dealer, who offers him a glimpse into the sinister entanglements running the Indian polity. A rumination on the crookedness inherent in the running of political empires, whose violence disappears into the folds of time or, at times, acquires respectability later on, it also brings up close the elastic personality of a schemer fully at ease with the illicit twists of the polity.

Many stories of URA bring together two contrasting forces in what he termed 'dialectical opposition' and let the narrative emerge in the space of this charged relation. 'Jaratkaru' (1995) offers an empathetic regard for the devout whose ritual commitments do not entail, as is often presumed by secular thought, a closed mind or an insensitivity towards others. Indeed, the orthodox mother of the protagonist, a modern writer who actively disavows any sense of the sacred, shows herself to be far more considerate and understanding than her hubris-filled son.

A few of URA's later short stories host binaristic interactions between epic themes: Western versus Indian rationality, ideology versus experiential knowledge. Such oppositions set off mutual provocations which leave one of the paired protagonists transformed and ambivalent. 'Stallion of the Sun' (1995) is a high energy depiction of an encounter between a modern and a non-modern self. Ananthu, a successful and widely travelled professor, runs into Venkata, a close boyhood friend who is now a priest. The academic's view of his friend as a simpleton living a circumscribed, small-town life slowly gets unravelled through the latter's spontaneous acts of kindness and hospitality and his well-meaning curiosity amidst his straitened circumstances. While giving the narrator an oil massage, Venkata asks him to imagine entering a forest and lays out a rhythmic, exuberant description of the trees, plants, birds, fruits, and their colours, among others, disclosing to him a way of thought, a cosmology, which goes unnoticed in the modern world. In delineating such an intellectually humbling event, URA is less interested in pushing a revivalist stance than in making space for non-modern knowledges as sources of creativity and self-expansion and for keeping the future open with plural possibilities.

'Akkayya' (1995) also throws into relief the narrow modern self of the narrator, a professor of English in Philadelphia, through the figure of his elder sister, a woman taken to be an imbecile, but whose selflessness, compassion, and care towards the people and animals around her are unmatched in the family. Her mode of being, which allows her to perceive—in her visions of her previous births—a loving kinship with a cow and a Dalit man, reveals a unique consciousness and knowledge of the world, which modern society dismisses as abnormal.

Between 1970 and 2009, URA wrote four volumes of poetry and later published his translations of Lao Tzu's *Tao Te Ching* and the poetry of Bertolt Brecht, Rainer Maria Rilke, William Wordsworth, and W. B. Yeats. He loved poetry and took delight in parsing their meaning. URA's poetry has not found the critical attention that his prose has; his poetry moves across the realms of spirituality, politics, history and quotidian life in a free-flowing minimalist manner without embellishments, making for an intimate poetic experience. His poem 'Mithuna', for example, effortlessly blends the realms of the erotic, the transcendental and the everyday and even suggesting their inseparability. Poems such as 'Dalai Lama and History', 'Gandhi's Chappals', and 'Gandhi and Henry VIII' illustrate the philosophical themes of patience, non-violence and political care through evocative metaphors.

Collected in over a dozen volumes, URA's essays convey the range of his literary and political passions. Showing a sustained engagement with modern Kannada literature and a multi-faceted concern for democratic culture, they take on big themes: the civilizational significance of bhasha literatures, the relevance of tradition for creativity, the necessity of interpreting Indian society outside frames of western rationality.

URA has acknowledged the decisive influence of the Centre for Contemporary Cultural Studies at Birmingham, where he took part in discussions led by Richard Hoggart, Stuart Hall, and Raymond Williams, among others, on his evolution as a critic. While this centre's passion for analysing culture alongside historical and economic forces stayed with him, the inability of secular theories to properly understand the life worlds of non-Western societies was never lost on him. India could not and should not modernize in the same manner as the modern West: he had evolved this certitude. The cultural autonomy of communities in India was of paramount importance. In his striving to break free from the intellectual dominance of Western knowledges, the writings of Lohia, and later, Gandhi mattered greatly.

URA wrote passionately about how a modern Indian writer ought to understand the minds of non-modern Indians with whom he or she shared their languages. Being a 'critical insider' who engages with a society's cultural conversations (or, tradition) and transforms them, mattered greatly to him. Bhakti and Sufi poets and saints and more recent figures like Gandhi, for him, were critical insiders. Being a critical insider did not mean an avoidance of non-Indian thought since tradition often accommodated newness from outside sources and could open itself up to new experiences*.

Like Gandhi and Tagore, URA viewed India not as a nation, but as a civilization that had been formed across centuries through the interaction of a multiplicity of faiths, philosophies, and languages. While the necessity of a secular constitution for India was never in doubt, a secular politics, he felt, would fail to adequately engage a multi-faith society like India.

In the mid-1980s, the Karnataka government decided to ban the practice of offering nude worship by Dalit women in Chandragutti, Shivamogga district, as it saw it as an exploitative practice. URA was alone in asking that the devotees be allowed to practice their faith even if that seemed offensive to modern sensibilities. The state, he argued, was only obliged to ensure that commercial exploitation of the devotees and the violation of their privacy did not occur. He did not see his support for the autonomy of Dalit women to worship in the nude as being at odds with his support for affirmative action for the Dalits and tribals or, indeed, for the ideals of the Indian Constitution.

The ecological fate of mankind, the dangers of the Hindu right and the ravages of neoliberal development preoccupied URA in his later years. In the last few weeks of his life, he worked feverishly to complete a political tract titled 'Hindutva or Hind Swaraj?' (2014) It shares his worry that Gandhi's ideals of a decentralized economy,

*For a discussion of URA's views on newness in tradition, see Chandan Gowda, 'A Writer's Horizon', *Seminar*, No. 666, 2015.

a soft state, and religious pluralism might be caving in to Savarkar's violent wish to turn India into a highly centralized and militarized state with exclusive space for Hindus.

URA's writings are those of a modern Indian striving to come to terms—intellectual, aesthetic, and normative—with a complex entity called Indian civilization. *The Essential U. R. Ananthamurthy* is an attempt to convey a sense of his magisterial endeavour.

NOVELS

He bathed Bhagirathi's body, a dried-up wasted pea pod, and wrapped a fresh sari around it; then he offered food and flowers to the gods as he did every day, put some flowers in her hair, and gave her holy water. She touched his feet, he blessed her. Then he brought her a bowlful of cracked wheat porridge from the kitchen. Bhagirathi said in a low voice, 'You finish your meal first.'

'No, no. Finish your porridge. That first.'

The words were part of a twenty-year-old routine between them. A routine that began with the bath at dawn, twilight prayers, cooking, medicines for his wife, and crossing the stream again to the Maruti temple for worship. That was the unfailing daily routine. After their meals, the Brahmins of the agrahara would come to the front of his house, one by one, and gather there to listen to his recitation of sacred legends, always new and always dear to them and to him. In the evening he would take another bath, say more twilight prayers, make porridge for his wife, cook, and eat dinner. Then there would be more recitations for the Brahmins who gathered again on the veranda.

Now and then Bhagirathi would say: 'Being married to me is no joy. A house needs a child. Why don't you just get married again?' Praneshacharya would laugh aloud. 'A wedding for an old man….'

'Come now, what kind of an old man are you? You haven't touched forty yet. Any father would love to give you his girl and bless her with wedding water. You studied Sanskrit in Kashi…. A house needs a child to make it home. You've had no joy in this marriage.'

Praneshacharya would not answer. He would smile and pat his wife who was trying to get up, and ask her to try and go to sleep. Didn't Lord Krishna say: Do what's to be done with no thought of fruit? The Lord definitely means to test him on his way to salvation; that's why He has given him a Brahmin birth this time and set him up in this kind of family. The Acharya is filled with pleasure and a sense of worth as sweet as the five-fold nectar of holy days; he is filled with compassion for his ailing wife. He proudly swells a little at his lot, thinking, 'By marrying an invalid, I get ripe and ready.'

Before he sat down to his meal, he picked up the fodder for Gowri, the cow, on a banana leaf and placed it in front of Gowri, who was grazing in the backyard. Worshipfully he caressed the cow's body, till the hair on her hide rose in pleasure. In a gesture of respect, he touched his own eyes with the hand that had touched the holy animal. As he came in, he heard a woman's voice calling out, 'Acharya, Acharya.'

It sounded like Chandri's voice. Chandri was Naranappa's concubine. If the Acharya talked to her, he would be polluted; he would have to bathe again before his meal. But how can a morsel go through the gullet with a woman waiting in the yard?

He came out. Chandri quickly pulled the end of her sari over her head, blanched, and stood there afraid.

'What's the matter?'

'He...He....'

Chandri shivered; words stuck in her mouth. She held on to the pillar.

'What? Naranappa? What happened?'

'Gone....'

She covered her face with her hands.

'Narayana, Narayana—when was that?'

'Just now.'

Between sobs, Chandri answered:

'He came back from Shivamogga and took to bed in a fever. Four days of fever, that's all. He had a painful lump on his side, the kind they get with fever.'

'Narayana.'

Praneshacharya, still wrapped in the ritual raw silk, ran to Garudacharya's house and went straight to the kitchen calling out, 'Garuda, Garuda!'

The dead Naranappa had been related to Garuda for five generations. Naranappa's great-grandfather's grandmother and Garuda's great-grandfather's grandmother were sisters.

Garudacharya was in the act of raising a handful of rice mixed with saaru to his mouth when Praneshacharya entered, wiping the sweat of midday from his face, and said, 'Narayana. Don't. Garuda, don't eat. I hear Naranappa is dead.' Dumbstruck, Garuda threw down the mixed rice in his hand on the leaf before him, took a gulp of consecrated water, and rose from his seat. He couldn't eat, even though he had quarrelled with Naranappa, severed all relations with him, and shed his kinship long ago. His wife, Sitadevi, stood there motion less, ladle in hand. He said to her, 'It's all right for the children. They can eat. Only we adults shouldn't till the funeral rites are done.' He came out with Praneshacharya. They feared that the kinsmen next door might eat before they got the news, so they ran from house to house—Praneshacharya to Udupi Lakshmanacharya, Garudacharya to Lakshmidevamma, the half-wit, and to Durgabhatta down the street. The news of death spread like a fire to the other ten houses of the agrahara. Doors and windows were shut, with children inside. By God's grace, no Brahmin had yet eaten. Not a human soul there felt a pang at Naranappa's death, not even women and children. Still in everyone's heart lay an obscure fear, an unclean anxiety. Alive, Naranappa was an enemy; dead, a preventer of meals; as a corpse, a problem, a nuisance. Soon the men moved towards the Acharya's veranda. The wives blew words of warning into then husbands' ears:

'Don't be in a hurry. Wait till Praneshacharya gives you a decision. Don't agree too quickly to perform the rites. You may do the wrong thing. The guru will excommunicate you.'

The Brahmins gathered again, just as they did for the daily reading of the holy legends, crowded against the other. But today an obscure anxiety brooded among them. Fingering the basil-bead rosary round his neck, Praneshacharya said to them, almost as if to himself:

'Naranappa's death rites have to be done: that's problem one. He has no children. Someone should do it: that's problem two.'

Chandri, standing against the pillar in the yard, waited anxiously for the Brahmins' verdict. The Brahmin wives had come in through the backdoor into the middle hall, unable to contain their curiosity, afraid their husbands might do something rash.

Fondling his fat black naked arms, Garudacharya said as usual: 'Yes. Ye…es. Ye…es.'

'No one can eat anything until the body's cremated,' said

Dasacharya, one of the poorer Brahmins, thin, bony as a sick cow.

'True...true...quite true,' said Lakshmanacharya, rubbing his belly, jerking his face forwards and backwards, batting his eyelids rapidly. The only well-fed part of his body was his belly, swollen with malarial bubo. Sunken cheeks, yellow eyes deep in sockets, ribs protruding, a leg twisted—altogether an unbalanced body. The rival Brahmins of Parijatapura mocked him for walking with his buttocks out.

No one had a direct suggestion. Praneshacharya said: 'So the problem before us is—who should perform the rites? The books say, any relative can. Failing that, any Brahmin can offer to do them.'

When relatives were mentioned, everyone looked at Garuda and Lakshmana. Lakshmana closed his eyes, as if to say it's not for him. But Garuda was familiar with law courts, having walked up and down many; he felt it was his turn to speak up. So he raised a pinch of snuff to his nose and cleared his throat:

'It's but right we should go by the ancient law books. Acharya, you are our greatest scholar, your word is Vedic gospel to us. Give us the word, we'll do it. Between Naranappa and me, it's true, there's a bond of kinship going back several generations. But, as you know, his father and I fought over that orchard and went to court. After his father's death, I appealed to the guru at the Dharmasthala monastery. He decreed in my favour. Yet Naranappa defied it, even God's word—what do you say?—so we swore we'd have nothing between us for generations to come, nothing, no exchange of words, no wedding, no rite, no meal, no hospitality. That's what we swore, what do you say....'

Garudacharya's nasal sentences punctuated by his what-do-you says suddenly halted, but were spurred on again by two more pinches of snuff. He gathered courage, looked around, saw Chandri's face and said boldly:

'The guru will also agree to what you say. What do you say? Let's set aside the question of whether I should do the rites. The real question is: is he a Brahmin at all? What do you say? He slept regularly with a low-caste woman....'

There was only one man from the Smarta sect, Durgabhatta, in this colony of Madhva Brahmins. He was always checking and measuring the rival sect's orthodoxy with a questioning eye. He looked sideways at Chandri and cackled:

'Chi Chi Chi, don't be too rash, Acharya. O no, a Brahmin isn't lost because he takes a low-born prostitute. Our ancestors after all came from the North—you can ask Praneshacharya if you wish—history says they cohabited with Dravidian women. Don't think I am being facetious. Think of all the people who go to the brothels of Basrur in South Kanara....'

Garudacharya got angry. This fellow was mischievous. 'Not so fast, not so fast, Durgabhatta! The question here is not simply one of carnal desire. We don't have to advise our great Praneshacharya. He knows all about alliances and misalliances, has studied it all in Kashi, he knows all the scriptures, earned the title "Crest-Jewel of Vedic Learning". What do you say? Our Acharya has won all sorts of arguments with all the super-pandits, yours and ours, won honours at every seat of learning in the South, fifteen lace shawls, and silver platters...our Acharya...what do you say?'

Embarrassed by the way this conversation had turned away from the question at hand towards his own praise, Praneshacharya said: 'Lakshmana, what do you say? Naranappa was married to your wife's sister, after all.'

Lakshmana closed his eyes.

'It's your word, your command. What do we know of the subtleties of dharma? As Garuda says, Naranappa had contacts with a low-caste woman. He stopped in the middle of his sentence, opened his eyes wide, and dug into his nose with his upper cloth. As you know, he even ate what she cooked....'

Padmanabhacharya who lived right opposite Naranappa's house added:

'And he drank too.'

'Besides drinking, he ate animal flesh.' Turning to Durgabhatta, Garudacharya said, 'Maybe even that doesn't matter too much to you people. Shankara, your great founder, in his hunger for full experience, exchanged his body for a dead king's and enjoyed himself with the queen, didn't he?'

Praneshacharya thought that the talk was getting out of hand. He said, 'Garuda. Stop talking for a while, please.'

'Naranappa abandoned his lawful wife after tying the wedding string round her neck. You may condone even that...' Lakshmana had closed his eyes again and started talking. 'He went and got mixed up with some woman. My wife's sister became hysterical and died: he didn't even come to the funeral rites. You may condone even that; but he didn't care to observe the death anniversaries of his own father and mother. I'm not the sort who would hide anything about him just because he was my close relative. He was my wife's uncle's son. We tolerated things and sheltered him in our lap as long as we could. In return, what does he do? He comes to the river in full view of all the Brahmins and takes the holy stone that we've worshipped for generations and throws it in the water and spits after it! Condone everything if you wish—but didn't he, wilfully, before our very eyes, bring Muslims over and eat and drink forbidden things in the wide open front yard? If any of us questioned him in good faith, he would turn on us, cover us with abuse from head to foot. As long as he lived, we just had to walk in fear of him.'

Lakshmana's wife, Anasuya, listening to him from inside the house, felt proud that her husband said all the right things. Her eyes fell on Chandri sitting against the pillar, and she cursed her to her heart's content: may tigers trample her at midnight, may snakes bite her, this whore, this seducing witch! If she had not given him potions, why should he, Anasuya's own maternal uncle's son, push aside his own kinswoman, call her an invalid, squander all his property, and throw all the ancestral gold and jewels on the neck of this evil witch! She looked at the four-strand gold chain round Chandri's neck and the thick gold bracelet on her wrist, and could not bear to think of it. She wept loudly. If only her sister had been alive, that gold chain would have been round her neck—would a blood-relative's corpse lie around like this without even the benefit of a rite? All because of this filthy whore—won't someone brand her face! Anasuya simmered and simmered till she boiled over and cried.

Dasacharya lived entirely on the meals that Brahmins get at death rites and anniversaries. He would walk ten miles for such a meal any day. He complained: 'As you all know, we let him stay in our agarahara, so for two whole years we didn't get calls for any meal or banquet. If we do the rites for him now or anything rash like that, no one will ever invite us for a Brahmin meal. But then we can't keep his dead body uncremated here in the agrahara either, and fast for ever. This is a terrible dilemma. Praneshacharya should tell us precisely what's right and what's wrong. Who in our sect can dispute his word?'

For Durgabhatta, this was an internal issue. He sat unconcerned in his place, ogling Chandri. For the first time his connoisseur eyes had the chance to appraise this precious object which did not normally stir out of the house, this choice object that Naranappa had brought from Kundapura. A real 'sharp' type, exactly as described in Vatsyayana's manual of love—look at her, toes longer than the big toe, just as the *Kamasutra* says. Look at those breasts. In sex, she's the type who sucks the male dry. Her eyes, which should be fickle, are now misty with grief and fear, but she looks good that way. Like Matsyagandhi, the fisherwoman in the Ravi Varma print hung up in Durgabhatta's bedroom, shyly trying to hide her breasts bursting through her poor rag of a sari. The same eyes and nose: no wonder Naranappa threw away the holy stone for her, ate meat, and drank liquor. One wonders at his daring. One remembers Jagannatha, the Brahmin poet, who married the Muslim girl, and his verses about the alien's breasts. If Praneshacharya were not present, if Naranappa weren't lying dead right there, he would have happily quoted the stanza and expanded on it even to these barren Brahmins. 'To the lustful' that is, to Naranappa and his like 'there's no fear, no shame', as the saying goes.

Noticing that the audience was silent, Durgabhatta spoke up: 'We've anyway said whatever needs to be said. What's the use of raking up dead men's faults? Let Praneshacharya speak. He is a guru, for me as for you, regardless of what Garudacharya may say in his passion.'

Praneshacharya was weighing every word, knowing full well that the protection of the entire Brahmin agrahara was now on his shoulders. He spoke haltingly.

'Garuda said: an oath stands between him and Naranappa. Yet the Books of Law have ways of absolving such oaths—you can perform a rite of absolution, give away a cow, make a pilgrimage. But this is an expensive matter, and I've no right to ask anyone to spend his money. And as for the question raised by Lakshmana and Dasa and others that Naranappa didn't behave as a well-born Brahmin, that he's a smear on the good name of the agrahara, it's a deep question—I have no clear answer. For one thing, he may have rejected Brahminhood, but Brahminhood never left him. No one ever excommunicated him officially. He didn't die an outcaste; so he remains a Brahmin in his death. Only another Brahmin has any right to touch his body. If we let someone else do it, we'd be sullying our Brahminhood. Yet I hesitate, I can't tell you dogmatically: go ahead with the rite. I hesitate because you've all seen the way he lived. What shall we do? What do the law books really say, is there any real absolution for such violations?'

Suddenly Chandri did something that stunned the Brahmins. She moved forward to stand in the front courtyard. They couldn't believe their own eyes: Chandri loosened her four-strand gold chain, her thick bracelet, her bangles, and placed them all in a heap before Praneshacharya. She mumbled something about all this jewellery being there for the expenses of the rite, and went back to stand in her place.

The women calculated swiftly: that heap of gold was worth at least two thousand rupees. One after another, the wives scanned their husbands' faces. The Brahmins bowed their heads: they were afraid, fearful that the lust for gold might destroy Brahmin purity. But in the heart of every one of them flashed the question: if some other Brahmin should perform the final rite for Naranappa, he might keep his Brahminhood and yet put all that gold on his wife's neck. The new reason inflamed the jealous hatred between Lakshmana and Garuda even further: 'Suppose this wretch should rake in all that gold giving a poor starving cow as a token gift, insuring both the goods of this world and the other?' Durgabhatta said to himself: 'If these Madhvas get tempted and cremate Naranappa, I'll roam the towns, spread the news, expose these so-called Brahmins.' The eyes of the poorer Brahmins like Dasa grew moist, their mouths watered. Would Garuda and Lakshmana let anyone else do the rites?

Praneshacharya grew anxious. Why did Chandri spoil everything with her good intentions? Every Brahmin present was afraid that someone else might be tempted to agree, and vied with the others in lurid accounts of Naranappa's misdeeds—things done not to them but always to others.

'Who induced Garuda's son to run away from home and join the army? Naranappa, who else? Praneshacharya had taught the boy Vedic scriptures, but what mattered finally was only Naranappa's word. That fellow was hell-bent on corrupting our young people....'

'Look at poor Lakshmana's son-in-law now. Lakshmana picks an orphan, nurses him, brings him up and gives his daughter in marriage to him—then Naranappa comes along and turns the young fellow's head. You hardly see him here once in a month.

'And then those fish in the temple pond. For generations they were dedicated to Lord Ganesha. People believe that anyone who catches the sacred fish will vomit blood and die. But this outcaste scoundrel didn't care two hoots, he got together his Muslim gang, dynamited the tank, and killed off God's own fish. Now even low-caste folk go there and fish. The rascal undermined all good Brahmin influence on the others, he saw to it. And then, he wasn't content with ruining our agrahara, he had to go and spoil the boys of Parijatapura too, make them run after dramas and shows.'

'The casteless scoundrel should have been excommunicated, what do you say?'

'How could that be Garuda? He threatened to become a Muslim. On the eleventh day of the moon, when every Brahmin was fasting, he brought in Muslims to the agrahara and feasted them. He said, "Try and excommunicate me now. I'll become a Muslim, I'll get you all tied to pillars and cram cow's flesh into your mouths and see to it personally that your sacred Brahmanism is ground into the mud." He said that. If he had really become a Muslim no law could have thrown him out of the Brahmin agrahara. We would have had to leave. Even Praneshacharya kept quiet then, his hands were tied too.'

Dasacharya put in his last word. He was upset he had to get up from his meal before he'd a chance to taste one morsel of his rice. He was hungry.

'After his father's death, no Brahmin here got a taste of that jackfruit in his backyard—and it used to taste like honey.'

The women kept staring at the heap of gold and they were

disappointed by their husbands' words. Garuda's wife, Sita, was outraged by the way Lakshmana had shot his mouth off about her son joining the army. What right did he have to talk about her son? Lakshmana's wife, Anasuya, was outraged by Garuda talking about her son-in-law being corrupted—what right did he have? Thinking what an ordeal this whole affair was getting to be, Praneshacharya said, almost in soliloquy:

'What's the way out now? Can we just fold our arms and stare at a dead body laid out in the agrahara? According to ancient custom, until the body is properly removed there can be no worship, no bathing, no prayers, no food, nothing. And, because he was not excommunicated, no one but a Brahmin can touch his body.'

'Not excommunicating him at the right time—that's the cause of all this mess,' said Garuda, who for years had screamed for an excommunication. He got his chance now to say, 'I-told-you-so, you-didn't listen-to-me.'

The Brahmins countered him as one man: 'Yes, yes, if he had actually become a Muslim, we'd have had to leave the polluted agrahara; there'd have been no two ways about it.'

Dasa, who had meanwhile been imagining the hardship of a whole day without food, suddenly came out with an idea. He stood up and said:

'I have heard that Naranappa was very friendly with the Brahmins of Parijatapura. They ate and hobnobbed together. Why don't we ask them? Their orthodoxy is not as strict as ours, anyway.'

Parijatapura's Brahmins were Smartas, not quite out of the upper set, their lines being a little mixed. Once upon a time some lecher got one of their widows pregnant and their agrahara tried to hush it up. The rumour was that the guru at Shringeri heard of it and excommunicated the whole colony. On the whole the Brahmins of Parijatapura were pleasure-lovers, not so crazy about orthodoxy and strict rules; they were experts at running betel nut farms, and rich too. So, Durgabhatta had a soft spot for the whole clan; furthermore, he was a Smarta himself. He had secretly eaten their flat-rice and uppittu and drunk their coffee. He was not brazen enough to eat a whole meal with them, that's all.

Furthermore, he was fascinated by their widows who didn't shave their heads and grew their hair long, who even chewed betel leaf and reddened their mouths. He got into quite a rage at Dasacharya—'Look at this Madhva's gall, though he can't afford a morning meal.' He stood up and said:

'Look, that's a foul thing to say. You may think them low hybrid Brahmins, but they don't think so themselves. If your sect will be polluted by laying hands on your own dead man, wouldn't it pollute them worse? Go ahead, be cheeky and ask them—you'll get an earful. Do you know that Manjayya of Parijatapura has enough money to buy up every man's son here?'

Praneshacharya tried to pacify Durgabhatta's anger. 'You're quite right. It's not truly Brahminical to get someone else to do what you don't do yourself. But friendship is as strong a bond as blood, isn't it? If they and Naranappa were friends, don't you think they should be told of their good friend's death?'

Durgabhatta said, 'Agreed, Acharya. The Brahminism of your entire sect is in your hands. Your burden is great. Who can go against what you decide?' He had spoken all he felt. He didn't speak again.

The question of the gold ornaments came up again. If the Parijatapura people chose to perform the rites, shouldn't the gold go to them? Lakshmana's wife, Anasuya, could not bear the thought of her sister's rightful jewels falling into the hands of some hybrid Brahmin in the next village. Unable to contain herself any more, she blurted out: 'Who does she think she is? If things were straight, they would have been around my sister's neck.' Then she broke into sobs. Lakshmana felt the tightness of his wife's words, but he didn't want his status as a husband to be lowered in public. So he snarled, 'You shut up now. Why are you prating in an assembly of menfolk?' Garuda, angry now, thundered: 'What kind of talk is this? According to the decree of the Dharmasthala guru, this gold belongs to me.' Wearily Praneshacharya consoled them.

'Be patient. What's before us is a dead body waiting to be cremated. About the gold—leave the decision to me. First send someone to Parijatapura with the news. If they decide by themselves to perform the rites, let them.'

Then he stood up and said, 'You may go now. I'll look into

Manu and other texts. I'll see if there's a way out of this dilemma.' Chandri pulled her sari's end over her head respectfully, and looked imploringly at the Acharya.

II

There were cockroaches in the buttermilk shelves, fat rats in the store room. In the middle room, ritually washed saris and clothes hung out on a rope stretched for a clothesline. Fresh pappadams, fries, and marinated red peppers spread out to dry on the veranda mat. Sacred balsam plants in the backyard. These were common to all the houses in the agrahara. The differences were only in the flowering trees in the backyards: Bhimacharya had parijata, Padmanabhacharya had a jasmine bush, Lakshmana had the ember champak, Garuda had red ranja, Dasa had white mandara, and Durgabhatta had the conch-flower and the bilva leaf for Shiva-worship. The Brahmins went to each other's yards each morning to get flowers for worship and to ask after each other's welfare. But the flowers that bloomed in Naranappa's yard were reserved solely for Chandri's hair and for a vase in the bedroom. As if that wasn't provocative enough, right in his front yard grew a bush, a favourite of snakes, with flowers unfit for any god's crown—the night queen bush. In the darkness of night, the bush was thickly clustered with flowers, invading the night like raging lust, pouring forth its nocturnal fragrance. The agrahara writhed in its hold as in the grip of a magic serpent-binding spell. People with delicate nostrils complained of headaches, walked about with their dhotis held to their noses. Some clever fellows even said Naranappa had grown the bush to guard with snakes the gold he had gathered. While the auspicious Brahmin wives, with their dwarfish braids and withered faces, wore mandara and jasmine, Chandri wore her black snake hair coiled in a knot and wore the flowers of the ember champak and the heady fragrant screw pine. All day the smells were gentle and tranquil, the sandal paste on the Brahmins' bodies and the soft fragrance of parijata and other such flowers. But when it grew dark, the night queen reigned over the agrahara.

The jackfruit and mango in the backyard of each house tasted different from all the others. The fruit and flower were distributed, according to the saying: 'Share fruit and eat it, share flowers and wear them'. Only Lakshmana was sneaky, he moved out half the yield of his trees and sold it to the Konkani shopkeepers. His was a niggard's spirit. Whenever his wife's people came visiting, he watched his wife's hands with the eyes of a hawk—never sure when or what she was passing on to her mother's house. In the hot months every house put out kosambari salads and sweet fruit drinks; in the eighth month they invited each other for lamp offerings. Naranappa was the only exception to all these exchanges. A total of ten houses stood on either side of the agrahara street. Naranappa's house, bigger than the others, stood at one end. The Tunga river flowed close to the backyards of the houses on one side of the street, with steps to get down to the water, steps built by some pious soul long ago. In the rainy month the river would rise, roar for three or four days, making as if she was going to rush into the agrahara; offer a carnival of swirls and water noises for the eyes and ears of children, and then subside. By mid-summer she would dry to a mere rustle, a trickle of three strands of water. Then the Brahmins raised green and yellow cucumber or watermelon in the sandbank as vegetables for rainy days. All twelve months of the year colourful cucumbers hung from the ceiling, wrapped in banana fibre. In the rainy season, they used cucumber for everything—curry, mash, or soup made with the seeds; and like pregnant women, the Brahmins longed for the soups of sour mango mash. All twelve months of the year, they had vows to keep; they had calls for ritual meals occasioned by deaths, weddings, young boys' initiations. On big festival days, like the day of the annual temple celebrations or the death anniversary of the Great Commentator, there would be a feast in the monastery thirty miles away. The Brahmins' lives ran smoothly in this annual cycle of appointments.

The name of the agrahara was Durvasapura. There was a legend about it. Right in the middle of the flowing Tunga River stood an island-like hillock, overgrown with a knot of trees. They believed Sage Durvasa still performed his penance on it. In the Second Aeon of the cycle of time, for a short while, the five Pandava brothers had lived ten miles from here, in a place called Kaimara. Once their wife Draupadi had wanted to go for a swim in the water. Bhima, a husband who fulfilled every whim of his wife, had dammed up the Tunga River for her. When Sage Durvasa woke up in the morning and looked for water for his bath and prayers, there wasn't any in his part of the Tunga. He got angry. But Dharmaraja, the eldest, with his divine vision, could see what was happening, and advised his rash brother Bhima to do something about it. Bhima, son of the wind-god, forever obedient to this elder brother's words, broke the dam in three places and let the water flow. That's why even today, from the Kaimara dam on, the river flows in three strands. The Brahmins of Durvasapura often say to their neighbouring agraharas: on the twelfth day of the moon, early in the morning, any truly pious man can hear the conch of Sage Durvasa from his clump of trees. But the Brahmins of the agrahara never made any crude claims that they themselves had ever heard the sound of that conch.

So, the agrahara had become famous in all ten directions—because of its legends, and also because of Praneshacharya, the great ascetic, 'Crest-Jewel of Vedic Learning', who had settled down there, and certainly because of that scoundrel Naranappa. On special occasions like the birth anniversary of Lord Rama, people mobbed the place from the neighbouring agraharas to hear Praneshacharya's ancient holy tales. Though Naranappa was a problem, the Acharya nursed his invalid wife to uphold the great mercy of God, bore up with Naranappa's misdeeds, dispersed little by little the darkness in the Brahmins' heads filled with chants they did not understand. His duties in this world grew lighter and more fragrant like sandalwood rubbed daily on stone.

The agrahara street was hot, so hot you could pop corn on it. The Brahmins walked through it, weak with hunger, their heads covered with their upper cloth; they crossed the three-pronged river and entered the cool forest to reach Parijatapura after an hour's trudging. The green of the betel nut grove lifted the earth's coolness to the heat of the sky. In the airless atmosphere the trees were still. Hot dust burned the Brahmins' feet. Invoking Lord Narayana's name, they entered Manjayya's house in which they had never set foot before. Manjayya, a rich man shrewd in wordly affairs, was writing accounts. He spoke loudly and offered right and proper courtesies.

'Oh oh oh, the entire Brahmin clan seems to have found its way here. Please come in, please be good enough to sit down. Wouldn't you like to relax a bit, maybe wash your feet? Look here, bring some plantains for the guests, will you?'

His wife brought ripe plantains on a platter, and said, 'Please come in.' They thanked her politely, and went in. Garuda made a hissing sound as he sat down and mentioned Naranappa's death.

'O God! What happened to him? He was here eight or nine days ago on some business. Said he was going to Shimoga. Asked me if I wanted anything done. I asked him to find out if the markets had sold any areca nuts. Shiva, Shiva he had said he'd be back by Thursday. What, was he sick? With what?'

Dasacharya said, 'Just four days of fever—he also had a swelling.'

'Shiva, Shiva,' exclaimed Manjayya, as he closed his eyes and fanned himself. Knowing Shivamogga town as he did, he suddenly remembered the one-syllable name of the dreaded epidemic; and not daring to utter it even to himself, merely said, 'Shiva, Shiva'.

In the blink of an eye, all the lower-caste Brahmins of Parijatapura gathered on the bund.

'You know,' began Garuda, shrewd man of the world, 'we agrahara people had a bad fight with Naranappa, we didn't exchange even water and rice. But you here were all his friends, what do you say, now he's dead, his rites have to be done, what do you say?'

The Parijatapura folks were unhappy over their friend's death, but quite happy they were getting a chance to cremate a high-caste Brahmin. They were partly pleased because Naranappa ate in their houses with no show of caste pride.

Shankarayya, priest of Parijatapura, intervened. 'According to Brahmin thinking, "a snake is also a twice-born"; if you happen to see a dead snake, you've to perform the proper rites for it; you shouldn't eat till you've done so. As that's the case, it's absolutely wrong to sit back with folded arms when a Brahmin has passed on to the bosom of God. Don't you think so?'

He said this really to display his knowledge of the texts, to tell those Madhvas 'we here are no less than you', and to bring down their pride.

Durgabhatta was very agitated by this man's words. 'Look at this stupid Brahmin, rashly opening his stupid mouth. He'll bring a bad name to the whole Smarta clan,' he thought, and spoke in his own crooked way.

'Yes yes yes, we understand all that. That's exactly what Praneshacharya also says. But our dilemma is something else: is Naranappa, who drank liquor and ate meat, who threw the holy stone into the river, is he a Brahmin or is he not? Tell me, which of us is willing to lose his Brahminhood here? Yet it's not at all right, I agree, to keep a dead Brahmin's body waiting, uncremated.'

Shankarayya's heart panicked and missed a beat. His clan had already been classed low, and he didn't like them to fall lower by doing something unbrahminical. So he said:

'If that's so, wait, we can't do anything rash. You, of course, have in Praneshacharya a man known all over the South. Let him look into it and tell us what's right in this crisis. He can untangle the delicate strands of right and wrong.'

But Manjayya didn't hesitate to say, 'Don't worry about the expenses. Wasn't he my friend? I'll personally see to it that all the necessary charities etc. are done,' meaning really to jibe at the niggardly Madhva crowd.

III

When the Brahmins left for Parijatapura, Praneshacharya asked Chandri to sit down, came into the dining room where his wife lay, and proceeded to tell her how pure Chandri's heart was, how she'd laid down all her gold, and what new complications arose from that generous act. Then he sat down among his palm leaf texts, riffling them for the right and lawful answer. As far back as he could remember Naranappa had always been a problem. The real challenge was to test which would finally win the agrahara: his own penance and faith in ancient ways, or Naranappa's demoniac ways. He wondered by what evil influence Naranappa had got this way, and prayed that God's grace should bring him redemption. The Acharya fasted two nights in the week for him. His painful concern and compassion for Naranappa had stemmed also from a promise he had made to the dead man's mother. He had consoled the dying woman: 'I'll take care of your son's welfare and bring him to the right path. Don't worry about him.' But Naranappa hadn't walked the path, he had turned a deaf ear to all counsel. By sheer power of example, he'd even stolen Praneshacharya's own wards and Sanskrit pupils—Garuda's son Shyama, Lakshmana's son-in-law Shripati. Naranappa had incited Shyama to run away from home and join the army. The Acharya, wearied by complaints, had gone to see Naranappa one day. He was lolling on a soft mattress, and showed some courtesy by getting up. He didn't take counsel well and talked his head off; sneered at the Acharya and his Brahmin ways.

'Your texts and rites don't work anymore. The Congress Party is coming to power, you'll have to open up the temples to all outcastes,' and so on irreverently.

The Acharya had even said, 'Stop it, it isn't good for you. Don't separate Shripati from his wife.'

A guffaw was the answer. 'O Acharya, who in the world can live with a girl who gives no pleasure except of course some barren Brahmins! You fellows—you Brahmins—you want to tie me down to a hysterical female, just because she is some relative, right? Just keep your dharma to yourself—we've but one life—I belong to the "Hedonist School" which says, borrow, if you must, but drink your ghee.' The Acharya pleaded, 'Do whatever you want to do yourself. Please, please don't corrupt these boys.' He just laughed. 'Your Garuda, he robs shaven widows, he plots evil with black magic men, and he is one of your Brahmins, isn't he? All right, let's see who wins, Acharya. You or me? Let's see how long all this Brahmin business will last. All your Brahmin respectability. I'll roll it up and throw it all ways for a little bit of pleasure with one female. You better leave now—I don't really want to talk and hurt you either', he said finally.

Why had he, the Acharya, objected to excommunicating such a creature? Was it fear or compassion? Or the obstinate thought he could win some day? Anyway, here is Naranappa testing out his Brahminhood in death, as he did in life.

The last time he saw Naranappa was three months ago, one evening on the fourteenth day of the moon, Garuda had brought in a complaint. Naranappa had taken Muslims with him that morning to the Ganapati temple stream, and before everyone's eyes he'd caught and carried away the sacred fish. Those free-swimming man-length fish, they came to the banks and ate rice from the hand—if any man caught them he would cough up blood and die. At least that's what everyone believed. Naranappa had broken the taboo. The Acharya was afraid of the bad example. With this kind of rebellious example, how will fair play and righteousness prevail? Won't the lower castes get out of hand? In this decadent age, common men follow the right paths out of fear—if that were destroyed, where could we find the strength to uphold the world? He had to speak out. So he had walked quickly to Naranappa's place and confronted him on the veranda.

Naranappa was probably drunk; his eyes were bloodshot, his hair was dishevelled. And yet, didn't he, as soon as he saw the Acharya, put a cloth to his mouth?

The Acharya felt a dawning of hope when he saw this gesture of respect and fear. He sometimes felt that Naranappa's nature was a tricky maze he had no way of entering. But here in this gesture, he saw a crack, a chink in the man's demoniac pride, and felt his forces of virtue rush towards him.

He knew that words were useless. He knew, unless his goodness flowed like the Ganges silently into Naranappa, he would not become open. Yet, a desire welled up in the Acharya, a lust, to swoop on Naranappa like a sacred eagle, to shake him up, tear open the inward springs of ambrosia till they really flowed.

He looked at Naranappa cruelly. Any ordinary sinner would have been terror-struck and fallen to the ground under that gaze. Just two repentant drops from this sinner's eyes, and that would be enough: he'd hug him as a brother—he looked at Naranappa with desire.

Naranappa bowed his head. He looked as if the sacred bird of prey had swooped and held him in its talons, as if he'd been turned to a worm that minute, bewildered as when a closed door suddenly opens.

Yet, no; he put aside the cloth that covered his mouth, threw it on the chair, and laughed out aloud: 'Chandri! Where's the bottle? Let's give the Acharya a little of this holy water!'

'Shut up!' Praneshacharya was shaking from head to foot.

He was angered at the way the man slipped from under his influence, and felt he had missed a step on the stairs he was descending.

Aha! The Acharya too can get angry! Lust and anger, I thought, were only for the likes of us. But then anger plays on the nose tips of people who try to hold down lust. That's what they say. Durvasa, Parashara, Bhrigu, Brihaspati, Kashyapa, all the sages were given to anger. Chandri, where's the bottle? Look, Acharya, those are the great sages who set the tradition, right? Quite a lusty lot, those sages. What was the name of the fellow who ravished the fisherwoman smelling of fish, right in the boat, and gave her body a permanent perfume? And now, look at these poor Brahmins, descended from such sages!'

'Naranappa, shut your mouth.'

Naranappa, now angry that Chandri didn't bring the liquor to him, ran upstairs making a big noise, brought the bottle down, and filled his cup. Chandri tried to stop him, but he pushed her aside. Praneshacharya closed his eyes and tried to leave.

'Acharya, stop, stay a while,' said Naranappa. Praneshacharya stayed, mechanically; if he left now he would seem to be afraid. The stench of liquor disgusted him. 'Listen,' said Naranappa in a voice of authority. Taking a draught from his cup, he laughed wickedly.

'Let's see who wins in the end—you or me. I'll destroy Brahminism, I certainly will. My only sorrow is that there's no Brahminism really left to destroy in this place except you. Garuda, Lakshmana, Durgabhatta…ahaha, what Brahmins! If I were still a Brahmin, that fellow Garudacharya would have washed me down with his aposhana water. Or that Lakshmana—he loves money so much he'll lick a copper coin off a heap of shit. He will tie another wilted sister-in-law round my neck, just to get at my property. And I'd have had to cut my hair to a tuft, smear charcoal on my face, sit on your veranda, and listen to your holy-holy yarns.'

Naranappa took another draught and belched. Chandri stood inside watching everything fearfully, folded her hands, and gestured to the Acharya to go away. Praneshacharya turned to go—what's the point of talking with a drunkard?

'Acharya, listen to this. Why this vanity, why should the agrahara listen to your words all the time? Why don't you listen to a thing or two I say? I'll tell you a holy yarn myself.'

'Once, in an agrahara, there lived a very holy Achari—that is, once upon a time. His wife was always ill and he didn't know what it was to have pleasure with a woman—but his lustre, his fame had travelled far and wide to many towns. The other Brahmins in the agrahara were awful sinners—they knew every kind of sin, sins of gluttony, sins of avarice, love of gold. But then, this Achari's terrific virtue covered up all their sins; so they sinned some more. As the Achari's virtue grew, so did the sins of everyone else in the agrahara. One day a funny thing happened. What, Acharya-re are you listening? There's a moral at the end—every action results not in what is expected but in its exact opposite. Listen to the lesson and you can go tell the other Brahmins too.

'Here comes the funny part. There was a young fellow in the agrahara. He never once slept with his one lawfully wedded wife because she wouldn't sleep with him—out of sheer obedience to her mother's orders. But this young man didn't miss an evening of this Achari's recitations of holy legends, every evening he was there. He'd good reason. It's true, that Achari had no direct experience of life, but he was quite a sport with erotic poetry and things like that. One day he got into a description of Kalidasa's heroine, Shakuntala, in some detail. This young man listened. He was already disgusted with his wife, because the stupid girl complained to her mother that he came to her bed only to pinch her at night. But now the young man felt the Achari's description in his own body, felt a whole female grow inside him, a fire burn in his loins—you know what it means, don't you, Acharya-re? He couldn't stand it, he leapt from the Achari's veranda and ran. He couldn't bear to hear any more, he ran straight to plunge his heat in the cold water of the river. Luckily, an outcaste woman was bathing there, in the moonlight. Luckily, too, she wasn't wearing too much, all the limbs and parts he craved to see were right before his eyes. She certainly was the fish-scented fisherwoman type, the type your great sage fell for. He fantasied she was the Shakuntala of the Achari's description and this pure Brahmin youth made love to her right there with the moon for witness.

'Now, you explicate it, Acharya-re, didn't the Achari himself corrupt the Brahminism of the place? Did he or didn't he? That's why our elders always said: read the Vedas, read the Puranas, but don't try to interpret them. Acharya-re, you are the one who's studied in Kashi, you tell me, who ruined Brahminism?'

As Praneshacharya stood silently listening to Naranappa's words, he began to worry: Is this a drunkard's rigmarole? Could it be he himself was responsible for such awful things? With a sigh, he said: 'Only sin has a tongue, virtue has none. God have mercy on you—that's all.'

'You read those lush sexy Puranas, but you preach a life of barrenness. But my words, they say what they mean: if I say sleep with a woman, it means sleep with a woman; if I say eat fish, it means eat fish. Can I give you Brahmins a piece of advice, Acharya-re? Push those sickly wives of yours into the river. Be like the sages of your holy legends—get hold of a fish-scented fisherwoman who can cook you fish soup, and go to sleep in her arms. And if you don't experience God when you wake up, my name isn't Naranappa.' Then he winked at the Acharya, quaffed the liquor in his cup, and let out a loud, long belch.

The Acharya, angered by Naranappa's sneering at his invalid wife, scolded him, called him a low-born scoundrel, and came home. That night, when he sat down for his prayers, he couldn't still the waves of his mind. He said, 'O God', in distress. He gave up telling the luscious Puranic stories in the evenings and started reciting moral tales of penance. The result—his own enthusiasm for reciting the Puranas faded and died. The young listeners who used to look at him with lively eyes and bring joy to his heart, stopped coming. Only women bent on earning merit, uttering the names of God over yawns in the middle of the stories, and old old men, were his audience now.

As he sat reading and contemplating his palm leaves, he heard his wife's moan and remembered he hadn't given her the afternoon's medicine. He brought it in a small cup, and leaning her head against his chest, poured it into her mouth, and said, 'You'd better sleep now.' He came back into the hall, muttering to himself obstinately, 'What do I mean by saying there's no answer to this dilemma in the books?' And started reading through them again.

Translated by A. K. Ramanujan

From the portico he stepped down to the courtyard and stood there. He suppressed a desire to look back. An uneasy feeling came to him of being watched from behind, by his aunt, the priest, the cook, and the cook's children. He felt his aunt's look whipping his back. He could have got rid of this suffering by looking her in the face, simply shattering her entreaty. He was frightened. To look her in the eye and defy her thus seemed to him to be excessive violence. The hand which gripped the casket was damp. Perhaps this saligram of Lord Narasimha had never crossed the threshold of the house before. It must have stunned his aunt's whole being to see this happening now. With all the force of life in her eyes she must be drawing him back in her prayer. He did not know why he had come to a standstill. He looked up and saw before him the Holeyas, dressed in panche, standing like orphans outside the courtyard. Their vacant eyes just looked on. They had no idea about what was to explode. Nor did they care.

Slowly he began to move towards them. The red mass of the sun was sitting on the shoulder of a distant hill. The weak yellow light of retreating evening fell on the haystack. The last bus from Shivamogga appeared on the curved road under the hill, raising dust. The cattle were returning to their sheds, bells jingling on their necks. At this time of the day, Aunt should have been waiting for them near the shed. Kaveri crossed the courtyard, carrying a load of firewood on her head, her steps brisk under the weight, and her sari tucked up. These bonded Holeya men, dressed in white shirts and clothes, must have looked comical to her. She tittered.

Jagannath thought what an absurd situation this was. For his part this saligram was just a pebble. Still, what an intense drama around it! He was turning the whole courtyard into a magnetic field with the Holeyas in front of him and Aunt behind. How removed was his person that had concluded, by pure logical thinking, that there never was a God!

The absurdity of his action flashed in his mind. It was he who had made a saligram of this stone by taking it out to the Holeyas to touch it. He stopped. With great effort he looked round. Aunt and the entire household were standing there. At one corner of the veranda he saw the servants. All were watching him. Aunt's tongue must have dried up or she would have certainly called him back. She was standing there like a mother staring at the dead body of her son being taken away for cremation. None had ever dared to take this thousand-year-old saligram out of the house. Whatever she was thinking had become part of Jagannath's own mind. He felt the presence of her eyes on him and the black stone held tightly in his hand burned like cinder.

Was he doing this for the sake of the Holeyas or for his own sake? Was it to discard Brahminism? Discarding everything, was he now going to tread what Adiga would call the path of a mystic? It bewildered him to realize how at this very moment all his Marx and Russell were going up from him in vapours.

He tried to clear up his thoughts. The Holeyas, who had never hoped for anything, are standing before me like impersonal ghosts. I cannot stop here forever in a state of palpitation. The moment my resolve weakens I will be swept over and put down by Aunt's eyes. But I am going forward with the saligram in my hand and at the same time backing out with misgivings. Why did this action get into my head at all? The Holeyas should touch the family god before they touch the village god Manjunatha. Otherwise this resolve of mine will not be solid and real, the Holeyas will not give up their past and accept a new life. If I am prepared for the violence necessary for this action, I will have learnt the first lesson of the violence of change. I should therefore go ahead, believing in my own thoughts. Otherwise Aunt will triumph. It was bitter but once again he looked round. There was a ghastly desolation about the house. It had rejected him, he felt, and had reduced him to a dry useless thing flung into the courtyard.

This moment of fear and anxiety must have perplexed the Holeyas who had already been feeling guilty in their new clothes. If he did not go to them and offer them the stone in his hand they would be gone. He realized that he was in a situation where something had to be done urgently. He walked quickly towards them. The important question is, he thought, why God has invaded me like this. What I wanted to show as stone has now become a saligram. Why is it so? Why are the bells ringing in me? At every step I have turned this stone into a saligram. Like the priest of some unique ritual act. All the time trying to shout out that this is not a saligram but a piece of hard stone. The eyes of the Holeyas are on me; and are vacant like the eyes of cattle grazing in the field. They are not aware of a past or of any future. But those eyes at my back are compassionate and they tug at me. Shall I dodge now or shall I turn over and come to fulfilment in the minds of the Holeyas?

He went and stood near them. Seeing him so close they stepped back. Jagannath opened the lid of the casket. The entire action was nonsense. If a conch blew now and a pair of cymbals clanged, it would be a fair comment on it all. But the spell of giving to the Holeyas the black naked stone in his palm overwhelmed him without his knowing it. The veins of his throat swelled. He said in a deep trembling note: 'Touch this.'

He looked around. The sun was setting. Aunt and the priest were at the door, terror-stricken. Janardhana Shetty could be seen in a corner of the courtyard. The Vokkaliga workers, with their sickles at their side, had huddled together in another corner. Kaveri was leaning against the parapet, wiping her face. In front of him the Holeyas stood gaping like idiots. His body shook and his hair stood on end. He said again, coaxing them: 'Touch this.'

Words stuck in his throat. This stone is nothing, but I have set my heart on it and I am reaching out to it for you: touch it; touch the vulnerable point of my mind; this is the time of evening prayer; touch; the nandadeepa is burning still. Those standing behind me are pulling me back by the many bonds of obligation. What are you waiting for? What have I brought? Perhaps it is like this: this has become a saligram because I have offered it as stone. If they touch it, then it would be a stone for them. This affliction of mine becomes a saligram. Because I have given it, because you have touched it, and because they have all witnessed this event, let this stone change into a saligram, in this darkening nightfall. And let this saligram change into a stone. You, Pilla, you are not afraid of a wild boar or a tiger; so, touch it. One step further and you are already inside the temple. Centuries will alter. Touch it now. Let you learn. Touch! How easy! Touch!

His hands were sweating profusely. The Holeyas moved back. All had turned him down—these Holeyas and those people behind him. The evening had turned him down. He knew that the Holeyas were afraid. They had seen how they caught thieves at the temple, by taking round a charmed coconut and asking the suspects to touch it. Crimson mantrakshata on a salver and a peeled coconut on it with its tuft turned to the front, sprinkled with kumkum.

The coconut would have the appearance of a human face. Everyone would have to touch it. But there would always be some person who gasped for breath when the salver came near him, his veins standing out. And he would fall unconscious. The Holeyas had undergone all this. The oracle of Bhutharaya must have appeared to them now in this contingency, with a bunch of areca flowers in his hands, with kumkum on his body, quivering all over, and pronouncing their individual punishments.

Jagannath tried to soothe them. He said in his everyday tone of a teacher: 'This is mere stone. Touch it and you will see. If you don't, you will remain foolish forever.'

He did not know what had happened to them, but found the entire group recoiling suddenly. They winced under their wry faces, afraid to stand and afraid to run away. He had desired and languished for this auspicious moment—this moment of the Holeyas touching the image of God. He spoke in a voice choking with great rage: 'Yes, touch it!'

He advanced towards them. They shrank back. Some monstrous cruelty overtook the man in him. The Holeyas looked like disgusting creatures crawling on their bellies.

He bit his underlip and said in a firm low voice: 'Pilla, touch it! Yes, touch it!' Pilla stood blinking. Jagannath felt spent and lost. Whatever he had been teaching them all these days had gone to waste. He rattled dreadfully: 'Touch, touch, you TOUCH IT!' It was like the sound of some infuriated animal and it came tearing through him. He was sheer violence itself; he was conscious of nothing else. The Holeyas found him more menacing than Bhutharaya. The air was rent with his screams: 'Touch! Touch! Touch!' The strain was too much for the Holeyas. Mechanically they came forward, just touched what Jagannath was holding out to them, and immediately withdrew.

Exhausted by the violence and distress within him, Jagannath pitched aside the saligram. A heaving anguish had come to a grotesque end. Aunt could be human even when she treated the Holeyas as untouchables. He had lost his humanity for a moment. The Holeyas had seemed to be meaningless things to him. He hung his head. He did not know when the Holeyas had left. Darkness had fallen when he came to know that he was all by himself. Disgusted with his own person he began to walk about. He asked himself: When they touched it, we lost our humanity—they and me, didn't we? And we died. Where is the flaw of it all, in me or in society? There was no answer. After a long walk he came home, feeling dazed.

Translated by K. V. Tirumalesh

AVASTHE

There he lies dying, not yet fifty years old. One might guess at his state of mind as he reminisces while battling death. In his boyhood, Krishnappa Gowda used to be a swimmer. When the river rose in flood, he would jump in and swim all the way across. Once, he and his friend went swimming like this. Just when he had swum halfway across the river, with his friend about a yard out, Krishnappa's arms tired and he could swim no further.

'My friend, I can't swim any more, I'm drowning, you go ahead,' he shouted quickly and went under. His courageous friend—his name was Hanumanayaka—managed to save him. He had felt sure he was dying, but in that moment his mind was totally calm, unperturbed. Remembering it now in his paralysed state, Krishnappa's big eyes fill with tears.

He was short-tempered. Once, when he was in high school, he went to a watch-repairer's shop to fetch a friend's watch. The watch-repairer, the shop's owner, knew Krishnappa well and resented that a poor boy like him went about with a superior air. Magnifying glass tucked in one eye, looking at him from the corner of the other, he said to Krishnappa, 'Do you expect me to hand the watch over, just on trust?'

'Watch out, mister! You talk like that one more time, and I'll smash this glass case of yours to pieces.'

'You know what a poor man's pride will get him? Only broken teeth!' snapped the watch-repairer, pecking at something with a pair of tweezers. Right away, Krishnappa snatched up the glass case with the repair tools and scattered parts of watches, he threw it to the ground, shattering it to bits, and walked off. He had such a bad temper, it would scare anyone.

When he is angry now, the most that might happen is that his lips quiver, his nostrils dilate, and his eyes well up. It is sad to see this Durvasa lying in bed, unable to move.

Sometimes, he picks up the stick by his side and tries to hit his wife. As for her, she is driven crazy, having to care for a sick husband, slogging at that bank where she is a clerk, looking after a five-year-old daughter who sits in a corner whining and dripping snot. Her hair is always in disarray. 'Dump this empty pride of yours in the kitchen fire,' she once told him, and pinched her daughter's face until the child's lips had blood.

Despite the daily turmoil, it is not that Krishnappa's mind cannot regain its poise. He narrates the story of his earlier life to the simple-minded Nagesh, who is there every day to take down these dictations. It does not concern him much whether the young man is able to grasp the material of his memoirs. Their narration is, for Krishnappa, a means of making sense of his present state.

As a young boy, Krishnappa had to work as a cowherd. Head draped in a coarse blanket, a sickle in one hand and a flute in the other, he would walk through the village, rounding up the cattle, and his charges gathered, he would head to the grazing fields.

He talks about this as though only he can mine its profound meaning. Now that he is dying, does he feel sometimes that something mystical entered his life? Is such a belief necessary in order to transcend the banality of the present? It's hard to say.

Intellectually, Krishnappa is an atheist. Yet, he talks about the god-crazed mystics of the land, such as Kabir, Nanak, Allama, Mira, and Paramahamsa in a way that is admiring, mocking, and sceptical all at once. He jokes about his feeling of oneness with them. It is hard to say what his overall outlook is.

He harks back to those boyhood years.

At the crack of dawn, he would go to the front of each house, untether the cattle, take them to the hillside or to the river or to the grassy meadows, and bring them back with the fall of dusk. He tries to remember the thoughts that came to his mind under the tree, watching the cattle with lazy eyes, playing a fanciful tune on a bamboo flute.

And suddenly, an incident of some significance appears before his eyes. But he prefaces its narration with a laugh: 'Please, young man, do not think that I was having a grand time of it. If the cows happened to see a green field of standing paddy, I was in trouble. Before you knew it, they would have crashed the fences and trampled the crop. All alone, in driving rain, I would helplessly steer the cattle. In the end, there was nothing for it but to give up and sit dumbstruck, thinking of the beating that was sure to come.' His expression bears the fear and the pain he felt. At this point, he remembers Maheshwarayya, who freed him from the drudgery of being a boy cowherd.

No one knows who Maheshwarayya was or where he was from. Let's say he moved from somewhere to this new place.

The first thing he did was set up a tidy house. Although he lived alone, he kept a cook. But he would wash his own clothes. You should have heard him recite Kalidasa's poetry in Sanskrit, or his classical Hindustani style singing. A great pleasure-loving man he was.

His handlebar moustache above lips that were reddened from chewing betel leaf, the glittering diamond studs in his ears, his closed-collar coat, the pure white dhoti that he wore elegantly, the silver-handled cane in his grip, and his serene demeanour, Krishnappa describes these and adds that he was also a great ascetic.

Though Maheshwarayya himself would not have been so open, it is Krishnappa's guess that he had left home upon coming to know of his wife's taking a lover. After letting his wife have a part of the estate, Maheshwarayya, who was a millionaire, put the rest in the bank, retired from everything, and set out wandering from place to place. He read all the time.

The man was a visionary who knew the past, the present, and the future. Let's say he arrived at a house. Upon sitting down, suddenly, he would let out a cry: 'Bho!' Then there would settle an uneasy look on his face. Though he knew a sense of foreboding had come over him, he wouldn't say more, no matter how much his host begged. Later, he would whisper his misgivings in Krishnappa's ear.

People avoided running into him for fear he might blurt out 'Bho!' It was so spontaneous that he couldn't help it. That is why he would sometimes refuse invitations. To Krishnappa, he would say, 'I don't know what disaster awaits that poor man—I won't go to his house.' Sadly, though Maheshwarayya could foretell the future, he rarely saw any good in it. The one time it was different, he saw in Krishnappa's future something good. This is how it went:

The boy Krishnappa, in his dirty shorts and shirt, was sitting under a peepul tree on the riverbank. The paddy had been harvested; he was not worried about the cattle straying into people's fields.

With the murmur of the flowing river and the tinkling of the cowbells, Krishnappa must have felt blissful, perhaps more blissful than usual. Instead of playing the bamboo flute, that day he felt like singing the lines from Kumaravyasa's Bharata.

He had studied only up to the fourth standard, and so it was not something he had read while at school. He had picked it up from listening to the old Brahmin Joisa, who was his teacher. That day, as he got carried away, he sang with great feeling. Not far from where he was sitting, Maheshwarayya, who had been camping out in a nearby town, was washing his coat in the river.

How he happened to be at that very spot that day is a wonder. It seems earlier that day, when he was walking in the market, he was stopped by a retired schoolteacher who had gone somewhat crazy. The man asked Maheshwarayya for his coat. 'Of course you can have it,' Maheshwarayya told him, 'but because I have worn it, I want to wash it before giving it to you.' He bought a bar of soap and came to this riverbank, walking two miles from the town.

Maheshwarayya stood before the singing boy and said, 'Bho!' Embarrassed, Krishnappa stopped. 'Hey, boy! After you are done grazing the cattle, come back here in the evening and wait for me,' Maheshwarayya said, the coat dripping in his hand while he looked distractedly into the distance. He walked away, wringing the coat. Krishnappa now remembers the two flamboyant parrots in the guava tree across from where he was sitting under the peepul. He says that he had seen an unusually coloured bird on that tree before.

In the evening, Krishnappa waited. Maheshwarayya arrived, swinging his walking stick. 'What a dumb boy! All this time, you haven't understood who you are, have you? Come with me,' he said, and they went directly to where Krishnappa lived.

His mother lived with her elder brother in his house, doing chores for him and his wife, chores such as grinding batter for kadubu, cooking the cattle feed, gathering leaves and twigs from the forest for the compost, all the while being nagged by the brother's wife.

the same dexterity of hand which had made the nine triangles meet in sacred unity.

Hoping that, if he spoke English, his mother would not recognize his distress, Narayan said to Dinakar, 'My son Gopal, who I am certain was born to me and who has legitimate status, I do not feel is my son at all.'

Having said this, Narayan changed the topic out of a kind of delicacy, sensing that what he would otherwise go on to say might embarrass his friend. He turned the question into one of having a common personal law for the whole country, and waited for Dinakar's opinion. Having already eaten two masala dosas at Sitamma's urging, Dinakar—after more urging—began to eat a crispy plain dosa. Then Chandrappa's voice was heard calling 'Amma!' Sitamma, who was about to serve a dosa to her son, brought it instead to the backyard on a banana leaf. After serving it to Chandrappa, she came in.

'Chandrappa asked whether Gangu should come here to see the lawyer or go to his office in the city,' she said. 'I told him, "Let her come here at least for a moment, even if she has not taken a bath. Then she could also have hot dosa. Isn't it a holiday for her today, and doesn't she always make gruel for everyone in her house?" Since it would anyhow take time to make gruel, I asked her to come here. She can also take dosas for all of them. Anyway,' she continued to Narayan, 'what is your big hurry? The office is always there, you can reach half an hour later. I don't know why my royal grandson hasn't come for his food yet. The little one is always at the phone and forgets to eat.'

So, speaking in her sprightly manner, she went inside to see if there was enough batter for Gangu's dosas and, seeing that there was enough and more, she lowered the stove's flame and asked Narayan, 'Shall I give you another?' Gratified when he belched in satisfaction, she went to the backyard to speak to Chandrappa. But Chandrappa had already left, having thrown the used leaf plate into the bin outside.

22

Gangu, in another of her beautiful saris with matching glass bangles, and wearing jasmine in her long braided hair, looked fresh from her bath. Sitamma served her dosas in a separate dining room kept for

Narayan's friends who were not orthodox. After finishing the dosas, Gangu threw the leaf outside, and although she had been told it was unnecessary to purify the eating place with cow-dung and water, Gangu nonetheless cleansed the place where she had sat and eaten, and then went upstairs to meet Narayan.

When their conversation was finished, Narayan dressed in a black coat, white pants, and a bow tie under his starched white collar, and with a gown and some files in his hand, came downstairs with Gangu, who was behind him. She touched Dinakar's feet and asked in Hindi, 'Will you come in the evening? Your Prasad said that he wanted to meet you.'

Noting with admiration the Hindi she had learnt in school, Dinakar agreed to come. Narayan said, 'Gangu's house is close by. Just walk on the road opposite to our house for a while, then turn to your right, and soon you will come to a mailbox. From there, turn to your left and go a little distance, until you see the Syndicate Bank. If you stand in front of the bank, you will see a narrow pathway to the left. Hers is the fifth house on the path. It is named "Rishikesh". A fitting house for Prasad,' Narayan said, laughing.

Dinakar suddenly remembered their visit to Sivananda's ashram in Rishikesh. One day Narayan, carrying a howling Gopal, went with Sitamma back across the bridge, and Dinakar and Gangu had unexpectedly enjoyed a rare moment of privacy. And this was the same Gangu who now stood before him expressionlessly.

Then Narayan said, 'Never mind, Gangu, better to send Chandrappa along with Dinakar, let him not lose his way,' and turning to Dinakar, he added, 'Come with me now to the office, I must speak to you. I will send you back later in the car.'

He took Dinakar's arm and led him to the car. Gangu stayed back to share her news with Sitamma.

While driving, Narayan talked to Dinakar as if he had just been saved from a big crisis. Gangu had told him how afraid she had been that morning when she saw Prasad with his head shaved. But after finishing his musical practice, Prasad touched her feet, stood up before her, and said, 'Let Narayan Tantri start coming home. I will also live at home, although I will go away sometimes and stay at other places.' He also told her that he didn't want the attachment even of saffron robes.

'Do you understand, Dinakar? This was the first time he ever spoke my name to Gangu. She could hardly believe it. And Prasad spoke of me with affection and calm. He has shed his hatred of me.

'Gangu told me all this with tears in her eyes. When the son becomes a great ascetic like Adishankara, stands before his mother looking like a bestower of fearlessness, would not his mother feel as if she had been given a new birth? Gangu told me, "You don't have to tie a mangalsutra around my neck for the sake of appearances." She also told me that, feeling it was an auspicious moment, she revealed to Prasad the truth about you. That is why Gangu said that you should go and bless him. That's why she called you home. Gangu is a great woman.'

23

Radha was weaving a garland of jasmine with banana fibre. Shastri, watching her, said, 'Saroja used to get completely absorbed when she wove jasmine flowers. When she sang, she looked like a devi.' Then, pacing around the veranda, he added, 'I wish Mahadevi could see her daughter again.' Radha stopped weaving the jasmine and silently prayed, 'Bhagavan, let the moment that I have been waiting for be now.'

It was morning. The young sun rode over the clouds, and its early rays shot through now and then. The air was pleasant, and the tidied veranda clean and cool.

Shastri walked about the veranda twice more and said, 'Radha?' He stood silently for a while, clasping his hands behind his back. 'Is he my son? And even if he is my son, would he accept me as his father? He looks like one who may be searching for his father in God. I can only pray that he should succeed. Whether he is my son or not, he seems to be one who can give me a new life. I wish, by God's grace, that the howling within me would stop.'

Shastri's blossoming continued as Radha, weeping, revealed the secret that she had been hiding within her.

24

Being a rich landlord, Shastri had placed his daughter in Mangalore College for study. Mangala was an intelligent girl, and he desired that she should have a good education. Mahadevi, anxious to guard her daughter's virtue, had wanted her to stay with a relation. But Shastri had abruptly dismissed her worry. There wasn't anyone he cared to send his daughter to, therefore he put her in a hostel. As a result of this freedom, she became friendly with a boy who was a very good debater. She herself was a bold girl, good at debates, and in her zeal for debating she developed a passion for politics as well. The boy, born in a poor family of the Malnad Halepyka caste, was intelligent enough to have got a scholarship to study engineering. He was handsome, sported a beard, and dressed attractively in kurta and pyjama.

He had caught the attention of everyone by changing his name from Thimmaiah to Charvak. It was like an addiction for him to attract people's attention by doing something or the other. He would always use new, striking words to denounce landlords and casteism. Radha had no understanding of such things. She only knew that Mangala had told her that Charvak had gone even further than a communist. Mangala was very impressed by Charvak's arguments, which also happened to give support to her dissatisfaction with her father. When she came home, even though urged by her mother, she wouldn't bow down to God. And she would argue that all Brahmins were like leeches. Both Mahadevi and Radha took care not to repeat her ideas to her father.

The change in Mangala's thinking made her feel close to Radha. She even insisted on eating in Radha's house. Radha wasn't happy to encourage this, but she couldn't refuse her food. Mangala had also confided in Radha about Charvak. 'We don't believe in marriage. We will work secretly to bring about a unity among all people and start a revolution,' she had said. In the beginning, when Mangala talked like this, Radha didn't believe her.

But finally she became convinced that this mad girl was truly serious. She was not like other Mangalore girls. She had no interest in ornaments or clothes, and would make fun of people who were fashionable. She had even made Radha feel that it was shameful to wear gold bangles.

Mangala always dressed in a white sari and white blouse, and she wouldn't put on either earrings or a necklace.

One day, they were arguing and Mangala said, 'Why do you have anything to do with my murderous father who, everyone says, killed his pregnant wife? People like you should be liberated.' She had said this very harshly. Radha thought Mangala very sharp-tongued, just like her father, and kept quiet. In the house of her benefactor, everyone was dear to Radha.

Both Mangala and Charvak gave up college and ran away. God knows where they stayed and what they did for six months, or what they achieved in their revolutionary endeavour. Finally, Charvak came to Shivamogga and took up the job of mechanic in a garage. Mangala wrote a letter to Radha saying that what he earned was not enough even for food. 'Don't let my father know where we are. He might kill my husband because he's a Shudra. If it isn't a hardship for you and you would like to, send me some money.

Long live the revolution!'

Radha began to send at least one thousand rupees every month.

But after a few months, Radha noticed a discordant note in Mangala's letters. She regarded this as the ordinary occasional disharmony between husband and wife. But Mangala didn't see this as a question of 'husband-and-wife quarrel lasts until they eat and lie down together.' Instead, she had seen the quarrels as a complication to be found in the lives of all revolutionary activists. Although such explanations were beyond Radha's understanding, she was pleased by Mangala's readiness to confide such things in her.

'Charvak doesn't come home on time, he has begun to drink, and he quarrels with me, saying that by tagging onto a woman like me and taking to family life, he has lost the opportunity to be part of the revolution. But he doesn't seem to realize the true nature of revolution. Only a woman who has become a householder can truly understand the meaning of revolution.' Radha, who had abundant instinctive cunning in such matters, had replied, 'Become pregnant and win over your husband. Everything will be all right.' Mangala listened to this advice without giving up her revolutionary fervour.

'And now your daughter is seven months pregnant,' Radha told Shastri. 'If you allow me, I will bring her here. Let her deliver in her own mother's house. I will anyhow be there to help.' She said this apprehensively, although adopting a manner of lightness. 'Just because your son-in-law is not a Brahmin, you don't have to keep your daughter at a distance. And the child to be born is innocent. What caste can it have? Am I not also a Shudra?' she teased him.

Shastri said, very gravely, 'Bring her.' Praying to Bhagavati that, by Radha's grace, his mind should retain its calm, and hoping that the curse on him was at an end, Shastri added, 'I will get a garage in Udupi for that wretched boy. If my daughter is far away from him and there is no one to control him, he will become a drunkard.'

Impatient to tell all this to Mahadevi, and excitedly planning how to arrange the house so that his grandchild could be born there, Shastri suddenly thought, as he neared home, 'If Dinakar isn't my son, the gold in that trunk is mine alone, and therefore should belong to my daughter's child.'

Then, as he entered the house, he found himself praying, 'O Bhagavati, let me not think such unworthy thoughts.'

Later, whenever his mind was troubled by these old conflicts, he would remember that on this day he had entered the house praying that such thoughts should never again come to him.

25

Dinakar, having gone up the Sabarimala hill for Ayyappa darshan and come down again, was not surprised to realize that the whole experience had been like a picnic for him. After coming down the hill he bathed in the river and told himself, 'That is not to be won if you seek it wilfully.' The river water was cold, and in brisk high spirits he rubbed his body before putting on the new red-bordered Kerala dhoti and white khadi shirt which he had bought before climbing the hill. As he was putting on these clothes, he thought of the winter evening in Mangalore which had shaken him.

Prasad had been sitting in the lotus posture, fingering the strings of the tambour resting on his arm. When Dinakar, who did not know who his own father or mother were, saw him for the first time, he was filled with a desire to know whether Prasad was his son. Yet the image that slowly, gradually, prevailed was of Prasad's long eyes half closed, as if half asleep, in inward-looking contemplation.

The veranda he sat in was open to the skies, and in its soft evening shadow Prasad appeared like the young son of a sage, his lean, strong muscled body straight-backed, seated in meditation.

Dinakar stood a small distance away, filling his eyes with him. Prasad must have shaved off his long hair and beard only that morning—the shaved portions looked pale, and it was clear that for a long time they had been hidden from the sun. The rest of his body, which was constantly exposed to the sun and wind, was even toned, the dark Krishna colour which had intoxicated the gopis.

A white cloth was wound around his waist, another white cloth carelessly flung over his shoulder. Dinakar observed that Prasad's nose was long and straight, slightly curved at the tip, that his chin was firm, and his forehead broad. Unquestionably, his ears were not Narayan's. But they were certainly not Dinakar's either. They were like Gangu's, the lobes small and delicate. If he wore earrings, the earrings would be perfectly displayed. His whole face had a beauty that would be irresistible to women.

Thinking this, Dinakar recalled his own erotic life and felt shame at his motive in examining Prasad's face so closely.

Then, moved by Prasad's music, he thought, 'But why should I be ashamed? Adishankara must have looked like Prasad when he wrote the commentary to Brahma Sutra. And, although only a boy sanyasi, hadn't Adishankara described the goddess, head to toe, even better than anyone who possessed sexual experience?'

Chandrappa, in undershirt and shorts, put aside his hoe and, disregarding the mud on his hands, listened in open-mouthed wonder to Prasad's singing. Dinakar had come and stood in the shaded front garden which was full of parijata, champak, jasmine, and hibiscus flowers. It was Chandrappa's labour that had made the whole place so fragrant.

Gangu saw Dinakar looking lovingly at her son. She brought hot milk in a silver cup and placed it on the edge of the pyol, saying in greeting, 'Have you come?' She invited Dinakar onto the veranda. With her pallu draped over her head and sandal paste on her forehead, she looked like an auspiciously married woman.

Dinakar didn't know how long he sat on the veranda. Shadows lengthened and it became time for lighting the lamps. Prasad was still sitting, singing to himself, motionless. His alap came in waves, returning again and again to the note from which it had emerged. Look, it is simple. Look, now it gathers into complexity. In the enchantment of its rising and falling, it seemed as if Prasad had touched what he wanted to touch.

Dinakar felt that the unseen for which he was searching would be like what Prasad had found already. Stillness in motion. Still, even while moving. Because the motion is without resistance, there is stillness. But the sensation can only be fleeting for people like himself. 'What does it matter if he is my son? Or if he is not?' Dinakar thought. Prasad had touched what he himself had not yet touched. What was only a flash for him, Prasad must have gazed at steadily. His entire peaceful being spoke of it—he showed how a person can live in bhava without giving it much regard.

And so Dinakar looked at Prasad as if he were a guru.

It was a sacred moment. Dinakar felt, 'Whether I am his father, whether I am not, I should touch his feet.' Just then, Prasad—like one who lives in the world yet remains untouched by it—opened his eyes, which seemed to have been dwelling in a dream. Without wondering whether this man before him was his father or not, as if curiosity and anxiety had no hold on him at all, he looked at Dinakar, bringing him totally, with complete attention, into his gaze. Dinakar became captive to Prasad's unshakeable calm, and for that moment at least he was fully open, free of any desire or expectation.

Prasad touched the tamboura to his eyes and suddenly stood up. At that moment, Dinakar experienced the welling up of love for a child and he thought, 'How sweet-natured and tall and beautiful this boy is.'

Prasad's eyes, which he had found so attractive, closed slowly. Then, standing with folded hands, Prasad went on to prostrate before him, as if to a god. Dinakar, feeling as if he had turned over, stood in awe, and could not find the words for a blessing. Gently he touched

Prasad's head, and Prasad came to his feet. Then, holding Prasad's face between his hands, Dinakar bent and smelt the crown of his head.

Gangu, watching from a distance, began to cry. She lit the lamp and said, as if to herself, 'From now, my son is a sanyasi. He cannot touch anyone's feet after this. He has himself become the holy feet.'

Then she wiped her eyes with the end of her sari. Despite her sorrow in giving up all motherly hopes for her son, she did not neglect to treat Dinakar courteously, and saying, 'Go, and come again,' walked with him up to the gate.

Translated by Judith Kroll

POETRY

LOVE AND DUTY (1989)

My father had told me
about the epiphany
Gandhi felt from the unanticipated response
he got while resting
at the foot of a hill.

A girl, very young,
carrying a child in her arms
with care and affection,
her bare feet kicking the folds of her skirt playfully,
is climbing up the hill panting, the sun is hot.
She is graceful.
She is wearing a patched-up skirt.
She has tied flowers on the plaited hair falling over her bare neck.

Watching this sight in the tree shade,
Gandhi, overwhelmed by pity, walked down
and asked:
'Isn't it very heavy for you?'

Continuing to walk,
moving the child from one arm over to the other,
with affection, care and delight, the girl said:
'He's my little brother.'

MITHUNA (1992)

The Flawless One himself, I hear, is imperfect, my love
He gently, lovingly falls under the spell of his beloved
unsatiated, He draws her close again, not feeling fatigue
I hear they don't perspire, choke and split in two like us
They unite and make love as two sides of the same thing

A wave riding upon another wave, such
is the pleasure when they make love
A probe with their eyes planted in each other
I hear they don't shut their eyes like us
Ignited they eject a spring, like lords
After making love, they don't collapse feeling low

Radha, I hear, is all grown up, a firm breasted virgin
a little thief who like you who feels bashful
He is like a baby to the breasts, a rush of air to the thighs
A husband, also a paramour, both are God to her
They don't collapse splitting in half

She is said to be fair, and He dark
When they make love, it is impossible, it seems, to tell who is
dark or fair they unite only to flow, they flow only to unite
like the water at a confluence, a true union, it seems
Giving over wholly, they don't remain separate.

GANDHI'S CHAPPALS (1992)

As the chappals that
Mohandas Karamchand Gandhi,
a spinner by occupation, had made and walked in
began to wear off,
the mighty British empire also wore off.

The chappals that the miser wore on his last day,
yet to wear out,
are still there.

GANDHI AND HENRY VIII (2009)

Don't mothers stop eating when they are unhappy?
Don't they stop talking?
Though seeming to have stopped all activity,
don't they—while dusting, cleaning,
fasting, doing anything else—
watch over the people of the house and nurture them?

If for Gandhi who shared the same moral impulse,
the country felt like a village,
the village a house,
and history the turmoil, anger, rage, and the occasional
commotion seen inside a family,

The British king called Henry VIII
felt he was the country
and that the country could survive only through a son born
of his seed,
and sought a womb fit to bear this royal scion.
Marrying in succession,
the wombs unable to bear him a son seeming to be traitors,
killing successively the ones he had married in succession
and carrying on his rule was for Henry VIII
the divine resolve fulfilling through him,
the history of obtaining the ninth Henry.

THE DALAI LAMA AND HISTORY (1992)

The Dalai Lama's compassionate Tibetan Buddhist followers
apparently believe that truth alone triumphs in history,
the Realized Ones;
Whatever triumphs in history alone becomes the truth,
so it seems believe the Chinese, the cunning worldly ones.

While going over the terrible recent plight of his country's
people with concern, focus and a gentle smile in Delhi one day,
the Dalai Lama saw a black ant on his ochre robe.
The soft-spoken holy man paused,
lifted the ant with his fingertips with great care,
placed it on the table to let it scurry away
and resumed his words, smiling all the while.

Even if the Chinese seem to have triumphed at the moment,
thus the Dalai Lama waits—
in time's vast momentariness,
in its eternalness—
for truth to triumph.

Poems translated by Chandan Gowda

SHORT STORIES

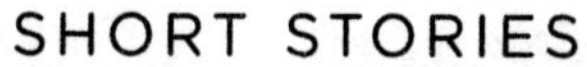

GHATASHRADDHA

It was still dark as I got up and stood rubbing my eyes. Sheshagiri Udupa was standing there in the yard with a bundle in his hand, ready to leave. He saw me and said: 'I'll look up your parents while I am in Kudumallige.' At the mention of my parents, the thought that if I were at home now I'd be sleeping at this time, draped warm in my mother's sari, crossed my mind. I felt homesick at the thought that Mother would wake me up, wash my face, and give me coffee.

Just as he was about to step over the fence, Sheshagiri Udupa stopped and called out to his daughter, 'Yamuna!' Yamunakka came and stood by the door, covering her head with the end of her red sari. Sheshagiri Udupa said as he crossed the stile, 'I'll leave now, okay? Keep an eye on the boys. Don't let them swim too long in the stream. It may be more than three months by the time I finish the yaga* at Gokarna and then go to Udyavara. See that the children do their daily recitation. I've told the rest to Upadhyaru.'

Sheshagiri Udupa was older than my father. I was scared of him. But then, I always took liberties with Yamunakka. She was much younger than Mother. The moment Udupa turned his back, I started pestering her—I wanted to go home. 'Listen, keep quiet. Wash your face and go and pluck some tulasi leaves,' said Yamunakka as she went in. Just then Vishwanath Shastri and Ganesha came there. They laughed at me as I stood crying, watching the figure of Sheshagiri Udupa disappear in the darkness. I went with them to the well to wash my face. 'What are you doing, sissy?' enquired Shastri. Ganesha let the pitcher down the well and said as it was filling up, 'Say, Shastri. I believe this fool sat up crying the night before his upanayana because someone told him that they'd cut open his thighs and stuff it with toads.' I went to the kitchen crying. 'Come, we'll draw water for you,' they cried out to me.

---

*Funeral rites for the living.

Yamunakka was churning buttermilk. She looked sad. After I had called her a couple of times, she looked at me and tried to console me, 'Let them be. Don't go with them. I'll wash your face.'

After I had my face washed, I picked up a basket and headed eastward, alone. I plucked the tumbe flowers along the way. As I was small and very short, Shastri always teased me: 'We'll have a ladder fixed to the tumbe plant, okay?' Shastri was older than me—actually, he looked like a much older boy. He was an orphan. And was studying the Vedas with Udupa, just like me. One of his eyes was very small and the other large. Ganesha teased him as one-eyed Shukrachari. They formed a pair. I was always alone. I walked along to Gopala Joisa's house. As there was a bilva tree in his yard, I asked Gopala Joisa's sister Godavaramma for a pole. Godavaramma, too, like Yamunakka, was a widow. But Yamunakka is much younger than her. Yamunakka is pink and round, and looks much nicer than even Mother. I believe Yamunakka's husband died of a snake bite, just a few days after their wedding. And after Sheshagiri Udupa's wife died, she came back to stay with her father, to take care of him. Ganesha had told me all this. He was distantly related to Udupa.

Seeing me jumping, pole in hand, trying to pluck the bilva leaves, Godavaramma took the pole, saying, 'Come, I'll pluck them for you.' And later when I was plucking the tulasi leaves in the yard, she asked: 'Has Udupa left for Gokarna?'

I said 'Yes.'

'How's Yamuna?'

'She's fine.'

'She's not been coming to the temple for some time now—I heard she's not well.'

'I don't know.'

'What do you mean, you don't know? Won't she be resting in bed? Didn't Udupa say anything?'

'The other day she said she was feeling dizzy and lay down. Udupa gave her some medicine. That's all.'

'Is that all!' she laughed.

And as she went in, Godavaramma called out to Gopala Joisa:

'Did you hear that! I believe Yamuna has no fever. Just a lump, without any fever. Poor thing!' And she laughed.

On my way back, I picked up some dry twigs for agni karya from the asvata tree at the end of the lane. When I returned, I found Yamunakka waiting for me. 'How long you take! Look, Upadhyaru has been waiting for you.' And she hurriedly drew a couple of pitchers of cold water from the well, poured them on me, and said, 'Quick. Go sit for japa.' I squeezed the water from the waistcloth, dried my long hair with it, tied it into a knot, and ran inside with the same wet cloth around me. I took a clean cloth from Yamunakka, wrapped it around my waist, covered my shoulders with another and set off with a panchapatre in my hand. 'Hey, have you worn your loin cloth?' Yamunakka called out. I had forgotten. Yamunakka laughed, tucked a loincloth round my silver waistband and said: 'Now, go.'

The pockmarked Upadhyaru scolded me, 'Why so late?' Udupa never scolded me. 'You still haven't learnt your japa mantra!' and then he made me go through the japa. Shastri who was sitting nearby doing his japa was delighted to see me being scolded. He looked at Ganesha with his one eye and smiled. After the japa was over, I did the agni karya. Once that was done, Upadhyaru left for the temple puja. On his way, he said, 'After you've had your meal, come over and grind me some sandal paste.'

Inside, the leaves had been laid out in a row. We ran in and sat down. Yamunakka served us rice gruel and coconut oil. She also gave us some baby mango pickle. On days when coconuts were plenty, we'd have rice cooked in coconut milk.

We noisily ate our meal and got up. Shastri and Ganesha went out. I stayed back in the kitchen.

'Today you'll have lunch at the Sahukar's house. He had come yesterday to call you over,' said Yamunakka. I was thrilled—it meant a payasa meal after the puja at the temple. I'll also get a dakshina. Before my thread ceremony I'd only get a paisa. But now, I get a full anna. I'm glad that I've had my upanayana. But then, it also means I can't climb trees. Can't play with dogs. Can't wear shorts. Can't talk while eating—I miss all that. Yet, the tinkle of the anna as it falls into the panchapatre kept beside the leaf makes me happy. Yamunakka kept a money box with a slot in it. I would save the dakshina collected in it. 'Give it to your mother when you go home,' Yamunakka had said. 'Miser!' Shastri would taunt me.

'Why did you come so late, Nani? You got a scolding from Upadhyaru for nothing,' said Yamunakka. I said that I had been to Godavaramma's house for bilva leaves, and told her what she had asked me. Yamunakka was aghast. 'What else did she ask? Tell me! Tell me!' she persisted. 'Some fever, some lump, they talked amongst themselves, and laughed.' Yamunakka covered her face with the end of her sari and wept.

'If anyone else asks, tell them I have fever, okay?' she said. Since I found Yamunakka lying down whenever she was free, and since she had also stopped going to the temple, I thought it must be true that she was not keeping well. It was noon by now and I sat down for my japa. After the puja in the temple, all of us, except for Yamunakka, had a grand meal at the Sahukar's house. When the meal was over, Upadhyaru called us over and said, 'I can't come over today. You study by yourselves. Hey Shastri, see that this boy studies properly,' and put me under Shastri's charge. Every afternoon, after the meal, Udupa made us memorize Sri Sukta, Purusha Sukta, and other such mantras, while he sat at the spinning wheel making sacred thread. Yamunakka would sit in a corner stringing the flowers into a garland for the temple. When Udupa was at home, this routine was never missed. I was thrilled that I was free today.

Shastri called me over and said: 'Now let us see you recite the Purusha Sukta.' He had had more lessons than me. Yamunakka always scolded him, saying he had grown up like a young buffalo. I stood in front of him, tongue-tied. 'Let it be. At least recite your pravara and gotra properly.' Ganesha was laughing.

I began: 'I, angirasa, ambarisha yaunashua trayarshreya pravaranvita, angirasa, gotra, ashvalayana sutra rikshakadyayi narayana sharman…' Shastri interrupted: 'Here, say it properly. Standing up and touching your ears.'

I once again started from the beginning and ended: 'Aham bho abhivadaye.'

'Now prostrate before me.' I prostrated. 'Listen, if you do as I say, no more lessons for you.' I was overjoyed. The moment he said go, I ran to Yamunakka.

Yamunakka had served herself some food on the plantain leaf and sat in front of it holding her head in her hands. She had poured some mango curry on the rice. But it didn't look like she'd even had a morsel. When I sat in front of her, she pretended to eat a few mouthfuls and then went and threw the rest into the garbage. 'Why, Yamunakka?' I asked. I knew she was fond of mango curry.

'Don't know why. Just don't feel like it,' she said and sighed. I placed the coin that was my dakshina on her palm. She said as she put it into my money box, 'Go tell Shastri to go to Shivapura and get a seer of dry chillies and some coriander from the shop.' I went to the Sahukar's house in search of Shastri. The servant boy said he was upstairs. I went upstairs. A carpet had been spread out. Sahukar's son, Ranganna, a couple of boys from the agrahara, and Shastri were sitting in a circle. They had some paper cards in their hands which they were holding close to their chest. Ganesha sat watching them. I stood watching. They kept throwing the cards in the middle, saying words like ace, king, queen, jack, and looking at each other's faces. I asked Ganesha what it was. 'Cards!' he whispered. I told Shastri what Yamunakka had asked me to tell him. 'A bear in the middle of a Shiva puja,' he grunted angrily and passed what he had in his hands on to Ganesha and got up. 'If you tell anyone, I'll knock your teeth out! Do you understand?' he threatened as he came out with me.

He told me to go with him to Shivapura. I said I'll have to ask Yamunakka. 'Don't be a sissy all your life,' he growled. Since I wanted to go to Shivapura, I went along. At the end of the agrahara is a tank. Once you cross that, there is the big forest with a little temple and a path. We took the path. After we had walked some distance, he left the path, turned into the bushes, and asked me to follow him. There was a huge tree there. It had a hollow at about a man's height. I stood watching anxiously as Shastri put his hand into it. He took something from inside, held it in his closed fist and asked, 'Guess what's in it?' When I said I don't know, he opened it. There was a pack of bidis. He put his hand inside once again and this time pulled out a matchbox. 'Sit,' he said. I sat down. 'Do you know what pleasure there is in letting out smoke through one's nose,' he said as he let out a whiff of smoke. 'You too smoke one,' he insisted. I said no. I sat watching him, with my mouth wide open, frightened.

'Don't ever tell Yamunakka about this, okay? One mustn't gossip,' he said. I agreed. 'Even if you tell, I am not afraid, do you understand? Don't I know about Yamunakka. Let her try scolding me one more time—I'll spill everything. The cat drinks milk with its eyes closed and thinks no one has seen it.'

I didn't understand what Shastri was talking about. But I was afraid. I thought I shouldn't have come without telling Yamunakka. As we were climbing down the Shivapura hill, having bought the things from Gopala Kamti's shop, Shastri said, 'On our way back, let's take a different path. Along the bank of the stream.'

I was too scared to say no. One look at one-eyed Shastri, and the thought of how he would bully me as he stood squeezing his pimples, was enough to frighten me. On the way, he said, 'I'll show you something interesting. You'll understand everything once you see it. Why should I become a bad guy by speaking the truth?'

After we had walked for a long while, we came across an old agrahara in ruins. It was on the bank of the stream. It was known as Hodala. I had come here once long ago with Yamunakka to collect firewood. The houses had all collapsed and only some walls and their foundations still remained. An ancient Jain monastery and a temple without a deity were now occupied by bats. Yamunakka had said 'People used to live here once. Now it is all in ruins.' I was afraid that there may be ghosts there. 'Ayyo, you coward,' laughed Shastri as he took me behind the walls of a ruin, carefully stepping over the bushes. He bid me to watch through the crack in a wall and himself went over behind a window and waited.

Sometime later I saw a man approach at a distance. I got scared and said to Shastri, 'Let's go!'

Shastri shot back angrily: 'Do you want to grow up or not? Or do you want to remain a wimp all your life? You are Shukamuni's reincarnation!' I sat watching, frightened. I was a bit relieved when I realized that the man wearing a dhoti and shirt with well-combed hair was someone I saw every day. He was the master at the school next to Udupa's house. He is from Tumkur, stays at Shivapura, and comes everyday on his bicycle. During Rama Navami he had played the harmonium at the temple. He was lean, tall, and looked a townsman.

I said, 'Let's go.'

Shastri replied, 'Wait for some time.'

Peeping through the crack in the wall, I noticed a snake. 'A snake!' I said, frightened.

'Keep quiet!' growled Shastri. After a while, another man, with a big moustache, arrived there. I didn't know who he was. The two of them stood talking.

Having seen the snake, I began to get nervous and wanted to leave. Shastri too must have gotten bored. 'You are a wimp. Come, let's go,' said Shastri as he led me stealthily back to the dirt track. From there we headed home. It was evening by the time we reached. Yamunakka was sitting looking very sad. I only told her about having gone to the shop. I was too scared to tell her about having visited the ruined agrahara or about the snake that I had seen there. We bathed and sat down for evening prayers. And then we ate. Yamunakka had some parched rice mixed with curd.

At night, Shastri, Ganesha, and I spread our mattresses in the chavadi*. Yamunakka was sleeping in the middle room. I was scared, having seen the snake in the evening. That night, even Udupa was not sleeping with us in the chavadi like he did every night. When I said I wanted to go and sleep in middle room, Shastri taunted, calling me sissy and a coward. So I continued to lie there. I couldn't get to sleep. I thought of my parents. And thinking that I was in some strange house with some strange people, I began to cry. Shastri, who was sleeping next to me, gently put his hand over me and slid near. I was disgusted by the smell of bidi that came from his mouth. He untied the knot of my dhoti and slipped his hand down to my groin. I got up and went to the middle room and lay down by Yamunakka's side. Yamunakka was awake. 'I'm scared,' I said.

'Come sleep here,' she said and draped her sari over me.

As I was beginning to fall asleep, I thought I heard footsteps

---

*A raised platform in front of a house, attached to the front wall, on either side of the main entrance, used as a sit-out.

around the house. I woke up in a fright. I started to tremble at the thought that it must be a ghost. Yamunakka put her arms around me. There was the sound of somebody coming to the door. Then a knock. I clung to Yamunakka. A voice called out softly, 'Open the door.' It could only be a brahma rakshasa—in this darkness, coming in the inauspicious direction and knocking on the door. I was convinced of it, and broke into a cold sweat. Yamunakka got up. I clung to her hand, begging her not to go. She got up and went. I followed her. 'Don't come. Might be a ghost. I'll place a broom at the door so it can't enter,' said she and went, leaving me alone in the room. I stood crying, waiting for her to return. Yamunakka went to the rear door but did not open it. If she had, I would have heard a creaking noise. I only heard her say 'Go away, don't come here.' When Yamunakka returned, I was even more frightened—she had just spoken with a brahma rakshasa. She pulled me along and forcibly made me lie down. I fell asleep after a long while.

I got up before sunrise, but was scared to go to the well alone, so I asked Yamunakka to come with me. I was afraid that if Shastri got to know of it, he would make my life miserable, teasing and taunting me. Later, when I picked up the basket and set out to collect tulasi and flowers, Shastri said, 'I am coming with you.' I didn't have the courage to say no. What with a brahma rakshasa roaming around the house and also having seen a snake, I was afraid to go alone.

On the way, Shastri inquired: 'What did the brahma rakshasa tell Yamunakka last night?'

I said I didn't know.

'Yamunakka got up and went. Didn't she say anything?'

'She said—Go away, don't come. Then she placed a broom near the door and came back.'

'Do you know who that brahma rakshasa is? You are still a child. They say the cat drinks milk with its eyes closed. Someday you'll understand. Yamunakka doesn't like me, right? But she secretly gives you unde and kodubale, doesn't she?'

I didn't know what to say and kept quiet. When we went to Godavaramma's house for bilva leaves, she asked:

'How's Yamuna?'

'It's true that Yamunakka has fever,' I said.

'No fever. No nothing. Last night a brahma rakshasa was going around the house and then came and knocked on the rear door,' said Shastri with his single eye glinting. Godavaramma, with great relish, sought out all the details.

After we had plucked the bilva leaves, Shastri said to me: 'Hey, you idler, let's go to Subramanya temple and pluck some sampige flowers.' We crossed a field and went there and gathered the flowers. Shastri asked: 'Will you touch the deity, Lord Subramanya when you are in an unclean state. Do you have the guts?'

'They say if you pollute Lord Subramanya, you'll be haunted by snakes. I don't want to get into trouble,' I said.

'That's why we call you things—a wimp, a sissy, a fink, an idler. What a coward you are! If someone tells you a brahma rakshasa is running around the house, you believe it. No? Now watch me. I'll touch it,' said he and walked right into the sanctum and touched the deity. I was overcome by fear and revulsion. He said, 'You touch it too', and dragged me along and made me touch the deity. 'A-ha, I have the Garuda mole on my palm. That's why I touched it so boldly. Now a snake will certainly bite you!' he laughed and began to dance around me. I began to weep.

'Listen, if you do as I say, nothing will happen. I'll see that the snake doesn't come near you. The only thing is you shouldn't tell Yamunakka what I tell you. If you do, I'll tell everyone that you touched the deity when in pollution.' I came back home, wiping my tears. When Yamunakka asked what had happened, I kept my mouth shut out of fear. Yamunakka called Shastri and scolded him: 'What you eat, does it go straight to your head?'

I avoided Shastri all day. I was afraid that a snake might pop out of any corner. I went around with the Gayatri mantra on my lips all the time. At night I slept by Yamunakka's side. The brahma rakshasa didn't come that night.

From that day onwards I kept away from Shastri. Whenever he caught me alone, he'd give me a dirty look and threaten me: 'If you say anything to Yamunakka, you'll die of snake bite.' I never spoke. I started to follow Yamunakka wherever she went. Shastri, Ganesha, and the Sahukar's son Ranganna were always huddled together, whispering to each other.

One day Yamunakka said: 'Come, let's get some firewood,' and took me along the path that led to the ruined agrahara. Halfway there I got scared. I sat down and started to cry. 'There is a snake there,' I insisted. She threatened me, pleaded with me. I didn't relent. She came back home with me, grumbling.

Another day, in the morning, I went to Godavaramma's house to get bilva leaves. Godavaramma saw me and beckoning me, put her hand on my shoulder and led me in. She took me to the kitchen and offered me coffee. I said no. 'Nothing will happen if you have it once in a while.' I was tempted by the sight of coffee. I wanted it. And as I sat drinking it, Godavaramma said:

'Not bad. You are a very disciplined boy. Not like those others. Where do they listen to you these days? There's a saying—japa has slipped away and the agni karya has climbed up into the attic. Now look at that Sahukar's son Ranganna. He is a street bull. He has grown up like a buffalo and is sprouting a beard.'

And as I got up to go, she asked: 'Why isn't Yamuna coming to the temple these days? Doesn't she get up at all?'

I said no.

'Who cooks for you poor things? Udupa is not at home. That brahma rakshasa, does it come around the house still?'

'Not since that day.'

'What, does Yamuna vomit and things like that? They say if there is a lump, one vomits a lot. I had asked her to take some medicines the other day. Does she take anything?' she continued. I didn't know what to say. I got up and left.

When I got home, I told Yamunakka everything. Yamunakka sank down, aghast. Her eyes were brimming with tears. She asked me not to go there anymore. I agreed. That afternoon, Ganesha's father, Thippa Shastri, came from Horani. When Yamunakka tried to talk to him, he didn't talk. He didn't touch the sweet drink that she offered him. He told Ganesha to pack up his clothes and things and took him along. Yamunakka cried for a long time.

That night, when I went to the backyard to wash my hands

after my meal, I heard footsteps along the path leading to the house. 'Yamunakka!' I shrieked. Yamunakka and Shastri came out running. We saw someone running away in the dark.

'What is to be done about this brahma rakshasa?' said Shastri with a sneer, looking at Yamunakka.

'You shut up!' snapped Yamunakka.

I cried all night, wondering why my father too, like Ganesha's, couldn't come and take me home with him. Yamunakka clung to me and wept, saying: 'Don't ever leave me.'

Yamunakka stayed in the house all the time. When Godavaramma came one day and knocked on the door—it was evening—she made me tell Godavaramma that she was not there. At noon when Upadhyaru got up to go after finishing our lessons, Yamunakka brought him some sweet drink. He said 'I don't want it,' and left. She always stood in some corner or other, lost in thought and crying.

One afternoon Upadhyaru finished our lessons and left. Shastri went away to meet Ranganna. Yamunakka and I were the only ones at home. Puttarangi, the Konkani woman, came to the rear door and sat down to talk with Yamunakka. She said, 'What, Yamunamma! These days you look very nice. You've put on weight and look very healthy.' The moment these words were out of her mouth, Yamunakka got up and went in and never came out. Puttarangi waited for a long time, then went away saying, 'Did Amma get angry at something?'

That night Yamunakka made me lie down by her side, and kept crying for a long time. Later, she untied the knot of her sari at the waist, slid it down, placed my ear on her lower belly and asked, 'Nani, do you hear anything?' I felt immense pleasure at the touch of her warm, soft belly against my cheek. I was reminded of my mother. And when Yamunakka started to cry, I too cried with her. She pressed my face against her breasts and caressing my back said, 'Nani, you don't ever leave me and go, okay.' I slept happily that night.

The day after, Upadhyaru didn't come—neither to make us recite the japas nor for the Veda lessons. He finished the puja in the temple and went away from there. And thereafter he never came to the house. I was pleased, as I didn't have to bathe three times nor do the sandhyavandana.

One day, Shastri, who set out to get the tulasi and bilva leaves, didn't return. He stayed in the Sahukar's house. If ever he saw me, he'd mock me from a distance.

Yamunakka never let me go out of the house those days. I got very angry. I sat at the window all day, looking out. One-eyed Shastri chatted and played with Ranga. The primary school children kicked up a ruckus playing tree monkey or with tops. Not a worm strayed near our house. Yamunakka and I spent a week like this. I'd cry wondering why my father didn't come and take me home. I'd get angry at the sight of Yamunakka. And when she saw me get angry, tears would well up in her eyes and she'd cry, 'Don't leave me.' One day when Yamunakka tried to caress me, I kicked her. But then I said I was sorry. That night, when everyone in the agrahara was asleep, she woke me up and took me along to the temple. There she lit a lamp in front of the deity, sat with her eyes closed for a long time, prostrated before it, and returned home.

One afternoon I was sitting alone by the window. I was very angry with Yamunakka. Why didn't Father come and take me? On the street, the girls were playing hopscotch. Shastri came on to the street with Ranganna and saw me. He came near the window and waved to me to come out. I shook my head to say no. 'Come, let's run around.' I was tempted to go out.

'I'll ask Yamunakka,' I said.

'Yamunakka is not at home,' he said. I went in, looked around, and was surprised to find that Yamunakka was not there. I went out with him.

Three other boys of the agrahara—the ones who were playing cards that day—came along with Shastri and Ranganna. As we were walking along the bank of the tank, I realized that they were taking me to the ruined agrahara and was frightened. 'I'm not coming,' I insisted.

'Let him go. He's a wimp,' Ranganna said to Shastri. But Shastri wouldn't listen. He dragged me along.

'We've written to your father. To come and take you away. But before that I want you to see some fun,' said Shastri very sweetly, holding my hand. I was afraid that they'd start teasing me as a sissy again, and so I went along. All along the way, I was haunted by the thought of having touched Lord Subramanya while in pollution, seeing the snake and the brahma rakshasa running around the house. Added to that was the fear that these five would start mocking me at any moment.

We walked for a long time by the pathway in the forest and came near the Jain monastery that was in one corner of the ruined agrahara. We could hear the stream from there. Shastri whispered, 'From here, follow me quietly.' He led the way and we followed stealthily and came to the broken wall that Shastri and I had hidden behind the other day. Shastri and I sat at the crack in the wall and peeped. The other four were taller and stood peeping from above the wall. I remembered the snake and my heart began to pound. Shastri said, 'See what's there.' At a little distance from us, Yamunakka was sitting on a flat cobblestone with her back to us. She sat stooped with her head resting on both her hands. I was baffled—what is she doing here? Alone? Isn't she afraid? Doesn't she know there are snakes here? After some time, seeing Yamunakka get up, the ones who were watching from above the wall ducked down. Yamunakka walked in our direction as if she were looking for someone. I wanted to call out 'Yamunakka, we are all here. Peeping. There's a snake here.' But before I could open my mouth, Shastri's hand closed on it. Ranganna glared at me with his finger at his nose.

I kept quiet.

Yamunakka started in our direction then stopped and stared at the broken wall. Shastri held his breath and his hand tightened over my mouth. Yamunakka wiped her eyes with the end of her sari, groped around like a blind woman, and then went and sat on the stone like before.

I was getting bored sitting. Sahukar's son Ranganna and the others got tired of standing and sat down. They whispered in Shastri's ears, to let them know the moment he saw anything. Ranganna lit a cigarette. He gave one to Shastri. Shastri said to me, 'In a short while the brahma rakshasa will come here. You can see him for yourself.' I was frightened. After a long time, it was evening.

I thought of my parents. I've gotten myself trapped in someone else's plot. I was worried whether I'd ever go home or not. I told Shastri, 'Let's go back.'

'If you want to go back, go. But, on the way the snake will come chasing you. I have the Garuda spot in my hand. You know it, don't you?' he scolded me and then laughed. I kept quiet.

After a while we saw someone approach from a distance. He was lean and tall and was wearing a dhoti and shirt and had cropped hair. When he came closer, I realized that he was the same man we had seen the last time we were here. He had come from Tumkur and came daily to our school on his bicycle. I didn't know the name of this wheat-complexioned townsman.

Shastri snapped his fingers and announced, 'The brahma rakshasa has arrived.' All those who were sitting stood up and peeped over the wall.

I was surprised when he sat by Yamunakka's side, with his back to us. 'Look, look. Look properly, Shukamuni,' said Shastri poking me. The man said something to Yamunakka. Her whole body shook. He held her hand. She pulled it free and slid away from him. Shastri whistled, lit a cigarette, and looked at me with his eyebrows raised.

As I sat peeping through the crack, I noticed a snake slowly creeping. 'Snake,' I said. Everyone looked at it. 'Must be a rat snake, keep quiet,' they said. I was about to shout. Ranganna slapped me on the face and shut me up. When I started to cry, Shastri said, 'Don't cry. There's more fun coming. Just watch.' I kept quiet.

I sat rubbing my cheek. The snake was silently crawling to where Yamunakka was sitting. She never looked back. The snake crawled along, glistening, smelling here and there. 'Rat snake. Don't worry,' said Shastri. And then, 'Don't look at the snake. It'll wind its way to its hole. Just watch their fun.' The snake turned left, away from Yamunakka. Then it turned right and again started to slither in her direction. One of the boys said, 'This widow has polluted the deity. That's why this snake.' The rest nodded their heads in agreement. I trembled at the thought of having touched Lord Subramanya while in pollution. I looked around me. Ranganna said, 'If it's God who has sent this snake, then surely it'll bite her. As punishment for her sin.'

The snake coiled around and stopped. Opened its hood and looked around. I was scared that it might see me. 'Cobra! Cobra!' everyone muttered. I got up. Shastri pulled me down. The snake began to crawl again, towards the cobblestone.

The man continued talking to Yamunakka. But Yamunakka sat with her hands covering her face. He moved closer and put his hand on her shoulder. Yamunakka pulled herself away and stood up.

Those that were watching over the wall sat down. I was glad that Yamunakka might now see the snake. But then, she didn't see it at all. She once again sat by his side. I felt like crying. The snake crept along near the cobblestone on which she was sitting. I closed my eyes and prayed, 'Subramanya! Subramanya!' The snake was feeling the edge of the cobblestone with its head. I shook all over. Shastri grasped my hand and said 'The right punishment for the wrong she's done.'

The snake found a gap along the stone and went inside it. My hair stood on end at the thought that the snake might bite her in the leg. Perhaps the snake didn't find enough place in the gap between the stones, because it came out. It glistened in the evening sun that emerged from behind the clouds.

The man was still saying something to Yamunakka and once again put his hands on her shoulder. I thought Yamunakka will now pull away from him and stand up and then she'll see the snake and heaved a sigh. But Yamunakka didn't get up like I thought she would. She pressed against him and cried, then embraced him. She rested her head on his lap.

I pulled away my hand and leapt. Before Ranganna and Shastri could catch me, I went round the broken wall and ran towards her shouting, 'Ayyo, Yamunakka! There's a snake there!'

Yamunakka leapt to her feet. In a panic she ran ten steps and stood stunned. Those behind the broken wall jumped down and ran. The man with Yamunakka, the moment he saw them, pulled up his dhoti and ran away in another direction. I picked up a stone as I was running and ran towards the cobblestone. With all the strength in me I threw it at the snake, broke into a sweat, ran towards Yamunakka and embraced her. The stone must have hit the snake. It opened its hood wide, hissed, and stung at the cobblestone. I was scared to death as I stood there, my head pressed against Yamunakka's belly and my arms grasping her tightly. I picked up another stone and threw it in the direction of the snake. It slid down from the cobblestone. Swaying its long thin body, hissing, it headed towards us. We ran. I ran ahead, dragging Yamunakka along by her hand. I stopped only when Yamunakka said she could run no more, and sank down and sat. I was sweating all over and felt dizzy. I sat down by Yamunakka and opened my eyes only when I had recovered my breath. The snake put its head into a hole in the anthill in front of us. Slowly, it drew its long body inside and finally only the sharp tip of its tail could be seen. Then even that disappeared. I sat watching it without batting an eye. In the desolate ruins of that agrahara only the three of us remained—Yamunakka, I, and the snake that slithered into the blackness of its hole, wounded but not killed, hissing in seething anger.

I lifted Yamunakka to her feet and took her home, getting in through the rear door. My legs were trembling. But since I was feeling quite heroic, I didn't cry when I reached home. I latched and bolted all the doors and came to the middle room. There, Yamunakka was rolling on the floor. She kept moaning and crying like someone about to die. I stood silently. As I had closed all the doors, the middle room was quite dark. I couldn't see Yamunakka. I could only hear the sound of her rolling around and crying. For a long time I stood in the corner.

Yamunakka stopped rolling around and called out to me to come to her. In the darkness, I groped my way to where she lay. She put both her arms around and embraced me. It was then that I realized that she was stark naked. She took my face in her hands and placed it on her belly crying, 'Ayyo, the burning, the burning!' My face that was pressed against her soft warm belly was drenched in sweat. I couldn't breathe. 'Ayyo, let me go! Let me go!' I cried, broke free, and stood up. Yamunakka became silent. She lay stretched out, motionless. I sat quietly for some time. I wished I too were at home, like Ganesha. If Yamunakka were to die, then I could go home. Then the fear that she might already have died gripped me. 'Yamunakka, Yamunakka,' I called out. There was no reply. I got scared. 'Yamunakka, I'm hungry,' I cried. I heard Yamunakka get up and put on her sari. She went to the kitchen, mixed some parched rice in curd, and gave it to me. 'What about you?' I asked.

'You eat,' she said and sat in the dark. Eating the rice in the dark,

I started to cry. 'Don't cry,' said Yamunakka, tenderly.

Outside, someone was banging on the door. Some four or five voices were shouting, 'Open the door! Open the door!' Yamunakka didn't get up. She didn't utter a word. Then Ranganna called out, asking her to send me out. Yamunakka said to me, 'If you want, you go.'

'I won't go,' I said. I sat holding Yamunakka's hand. Once again, the banging on the door started, this time as if to break it down. Then there was silence. After some time, a voice called out: 'Don't touch the deity and pollute it. Don't come to the temple. Udupa will be back tomorrow or the day after. After he comes, we'll decide.' Then everything was engulfed in silence. I must have sat in the darkness for a long time. I don't know when I fell asleep.

I woke up with a start to find myself sleeping on a mattress. I was covered. When I felt around me, Yamunakka was not there. I was afraid. I called out to Yamunakka. I went over to the front yard and looked she was not there. I went over near the well and started to cry. Where did Yamunakka go after putting me to bed? I got angry with her. At a distance I could see the chavadi* of a house; some people were sitting around a lantern and talking. I didn't know what time it was. Was it just after sunset? Or later? Before sunrise? I looked at the sky. There were stars. And as it had been many days since I had last said my japa, I didn't even know the day, the date, or the day's star. I was afraid it was new moon. I remembered the brahma rakshasa. Where did this Yamunakka go? She has abandoned me—I cried and cried and stood leaning against the wall of the well. I stood up with a start when I heard: 'Amma!'

Someone called out loudly, 'Amma, Amma!'

'Who is it?'

'It's me Katira, Ayya. No gruel for me, today?' said a voice from near the fence.

'Aye, Katira, come here.'

'I am not to come there, Ayya.'

I went near him and said, 'Amma is not at home. Come with me.'

---

*A chavadi is traditionally a meeting place in the village, often in the front yard, where discussions take place and taxes are collected.

I thought Yamunakka has again gone to that ruined agrahara—all the others would also be there—and felt sad.

Katira walked a few steps ahead of me. As I was scared by the silent darkness of the forest, I narrated to Katira all the happenings of the evening in a loud voice. I don't think he understood anything of it. He walked ahead silently, without acknowledging anything. We came to the tank. There, some of his Holeya* kinsmen were catching fish, holding torches. He took a torch from them and said, 'Ayya, there is a short cut here, come,' and took me through a path covered with dense bushes. After we went some distance I began to get scared.

Katira started to sing to himself. And as he was far ahead of me I couldn't see the path clearly. I had to bend down and push the bushes apart and walk. Katira said hoosh, hoosh as he parted the bushes. When he did, there was the rustle of all kinds of creatures running about in the bushes. 'Let's go back, Katira,' I said and started to cry.

'We're almost there,' said Katira. We stood in a small open area.

'Katira, hold my hand,' I said.

'How can that be, Ayya? Am I not an Holeya?' he said, and walked even further away and stood holding the torch. I was frightened by the sight of the dark, tall, lean naked body covered only by a loincloth that stood glistening in the torch light. His shock of unshorn hair brought to my mind the image of the deity Panjurli. 'Katira, Katira, aren't you Katira?' I asked. I ran up to him and tried to touch him. He put down the torch and ran away. I picked up the torch and started to cry. He came up from behind and said, 'You lead the way.'

As I stood in the middle of the little island of light thrown by the torch, I imagined the dark immensity of the forest to be inhabited by all sorts of creatures and shadowy demons that stealthily groped towards me. Wherever I put my foot down, I imagined that it landed on a snake. I walked on, reciting the Mrthyunjaya mantra. Suddenly, I felt fearless. Why should I be afraid? After all, once the darkness is gone and light breaks through, I will see that I am only surrounded by bushes and trees. It is my responsibility to save Yamunakka. I'm not a little boy anymore. I've gone through my upanayana, been taught the gayatri,

*Holeya is a Dalit community from Karnataka.

and am grown up. I felt bold. Katira followed me, singing to himself.

When we came to the anthill, Yamunakka was there, all by herself. She was reclining against the anthill. Her hand was inside the hole into which the snake had disappeared earlier in the evening. I was not frightened by that sight. What to do now if Yamunakka is dead? I thought. The next moment I was shaking all over. 'Katira, wake up Yamunakka!' I cried. Katira didn't move from where he stood. I remembered the wounded snake that had entered the hole. I also remembered Mother telling me: a snake bears a grudge for twelve years, and panicked. Swinging the torch, I looked around my feet, picked up a long pole and poked it at Yamunakka. She rose to her feet and said, 'Go away! Go away!'

I said, 'I won't go! Come with me!' She quietly came with us. Katira, without uttering a word, took us home, and went away humming some song.

Once we reached home, Yamunakka sat in the dark without speaking. Then she said, 'Why didn't you let me die?' I was silent.

'I'm feeling sleepy. Come let's lie down,' I said after a while.

'I've got to go somewhere.' I got angry and started to cry. 'You come with me,' she said.

I said, 'I won't. Send me home.'

'It's not so far. Come with me,' she persisted.

'Ayyo, I can't. My feet are aching.'

She held me close, and then applied coconut oil and massaged my feet. Then she said, 'You sleep,' and set out to go by herself. I was too scared to stay alone so I went along with her.

In the moonless night the agrahara looked desolate. Not a single soul was to be seen. Just the two of us. A jackal howled in a nearby cane field. A shiver ran through my body. Yamunakka held me close to her. 'If it's to that ruined agrahara, then I am not coming,' I cried.

'It's not there. I swear, it's not there.'

'Then where?' 'It's someone's house. But you shouldn't tell anyone that we had been there. Tomorrow when my father asks you, say you don't know anything and keep quiet.'

I agreed.

After we walked a long while along the cart track, we took a fork which led us over a hillock. Climbing down the hillock and walking for some distance by the side of the fields we finally came to a house. The light was still burning in the house. The school master who rode the bicycle was there. I was shocked at the thought that he would once again put his arms around Yamunakka's shoulder. He glared at Yamunakka and said, 'Why so late? How long must I wait? Didn't I tell you to reach here as soon as it was dark?' Yamunakka didn't say a word. He called out, 'Hey Parbu' and took Yamunakka inside. I sat outside.

It didn't look like a Brahmin house and I felt disgusted. This is the first time I'd ever been to a house like this. After my bath I wouldn't even talk with the Shudra boys. I hated myself for being there. There was a chicken coop in the yard. In front of the house was a large copper pot for bathing. Parbu stood on the veranda, spat into the yard, and went in. I, sitting there, with my hair tied in a knot, an angavastra around my waist, an angavastra over my shoulders, wondered: where am I? What am I doing here? And felt sad. It's all because of Yamunakka, let my father come, I'll tell him everything and show her! I was angry. Someone stood in the yard and called out to Parbu. Then he came near the veranda and said, 'Oh! What's Bhattaru doing here!' I recognized Parbu when he came from inside with a lantern in his hand. He was the one I had seen from behind the broken wall the first time we had been there. The big man with a big moustache. He wasn't wearing anything except for a pair of shorts. He had something tied around his neck. Parbu tilted the large earthen pot on the veranda and poured some sour-smelling thing and gave it to the man standing in the yard.

A woman brought some foul-smelling stuff on leaf from inside and gave it to him. It must be that foul smelling fish that I've seen come in carts from the Kanara coast to Kudumallige town. Mackerel, they called it. I was overcome with revulsion. He sat in the yard eating and drinking. He staggered all over the yard, singing. Then it occurred to me that what Parbu had poured for him was liquor. I sat, mortified by the thought that this drunk might pounce on me. He came to me, said, 'Bhatta-re, hey, Bhatta-re, Pooje-Bhatta-re' and giggled, he he he. I stood up. And ran inside.

There they had laid out Yamunakka on the floor, naked. Only the place one urinates from had been covered. Her belly was smeared with cow dung and on it they had placed an earthen lamp. And as I stood watching, Parbu gently covered the lamp with a bowl and said, 'Let it be. Let it draw.' Around Yamunakka were Parbu, a woman, and 'him'. I was frightened by the sight of Yamunakka lying naked, with her hands splayed on the mat. I took the angavastra off my shoulder and covered her breasts. Parbu pushed me away.

I started crying, 'Yamunakka come. Let's go home. I feel sleepy…I am scared…come.' Yamunakka didn't open her eyes. 'He' dragged me away. That woman, with her mouth full of betel juice, said something to Parbu in Konkani, then went out, spat, and came back. She had no kumkum on her forehead. She had a head full of unkempt hair.

Parbu and 'he' went out. I followed them. 'I'll look after everything. You leave now,' said Parbu. 'He' took some money from his pocket and gave it to Parbu saying, 'I'll go right away to Kudumallige on my cycle. From there I'll catch a bus,' and then he said some things in a whisper. When I heard him mention the word Kudumallige I was reminded of home and wanted to go there. As 'he' climbed on to his bicycle, he said to Parbu, 'Don't let anyone know.'

'I'm coming with you,' I shouted. 'He' went away as if he didn't even hear me.

The man who was drinking in the yard started to laugh and sing again. I could hear Yamunakka groaning. 'Aha, Bhatta-re!' the drunk sang out aloud. Parbu scolded him and told me to stop crying. I called out to Yamunakka as I heard her groaning, 'Yamunakka, I want to go home.' Parbu scolded me.

I heard another voice in the yard. I was relieved when I recognized Katira's. 'Aye, Katira,' I called out. Parbu threatened me and lifted his hand as if to hit me. I sat quietly. After some time, Katira started to sing and talk to himself aloud. 'Aye, Katira,' I called out again.

Katira came near and said, 'Give me some more.'

'Aye Katira. It's me,' I said.

'Who are you!' said he and staggered and stumbled away. I was annoyed that Katira did this to me. No matter how many times I tried to tell him who I was, he didn't recognize me at all.

Yamunakka cried, 'Ayyo, ayyo, ayyo…ayyo amma….'

I shouted 'Yamunakka, Yamunakka, I am here, let's go.'

Parbu came out and said, 'Sleep now. You can go in the morning,' then he placed a tumbler saying, 'Drink.' I said no. 'It's not liquor. It's milk.' he said laughing. I didn't relent. I sat there crying.

When I woke up it was morning. How early I did not know. Where was I? How did I get here? I was confused. I tried to recollect what had happened. Sometime long ago Mother saw me off in a bullock cart from Kudumallige to Udupa's house, to learn the Vedas—that's all I remembered. I had left in that cart, how did I land here? All over the yard, chicken were running around. There was the sour smell of liquor. As I sat in the chavadi, rubbing my eyes, I saw a boy of my age in front of me. He had cropped hair and was wearing a dirty pair of shorts and shirt. He looked at me—a Brahmin boy with his hair in a knot and wearing an angavastra—and mocked me, saying, 'Bhatta, Bhatta, burnt a fowl; gave his neighbours a smell so foul.' I sat flustered.

The woman I had seen the previous night told him something in Konkani. The boy got down to the yard and started chasing a chicken. It ran here and there, through nooks and corners, beating its wings, saying cock, cock, and eluded him. Finally, he caught it and held it upside down by its feet. It struggled for a while. Then it hung its head down and continued 'cock, cock'. He took it inside. After a while I heard the sound of the fowl beating its wings furiously and cackling, as if it were fighting for its life. Then there was silence. I trembled. 'Yamunakka, Yamunakka,' I cried. 'I want to go home,' I kept repeating these words over and over again.

Yamunakka came out, slowly, groping and leaning against the wall. Her face was blanched. I ran and embraced her. She started to cry. Parbu said to her, 'Stay for a while. Go when you feel better.' Yamunakka held my hand and said, 'Come, let's go.'

I felt very happy and was excited at the thought that we were going back home. Yamunakka walked slowly, groaning and in evident pain. I saw blood stains on her faded red sari and got frightened. 'Yamunakka, the back of your sari, it's all blood,' I said. Yamunakka sank down right there. I too sat down and held her close to me. She slowly opened her eyes. 'Get up Yamunakka, let's go home.'

'I can't. You go,' she heaved a long sigh.

'Get up, Yamunakka, get up,' I kept pulling her hand, persisting.

'I'm thirsty. I can't. You go,' she said.

'I won't go if you don't come.'

'How far are we from home, Nani?'

At a distance, I saw Shastri and Ranganna walking in our direction along with the Brahmins of the agrahara. 'Yamunakka—they're all coming, Yamunakka. Let's get away soon, Yamunakka. I'll take you home, Yamunakka,' I said. I felt like crying. Yamunakka didn't get up.

She let out a long sigh and said: 'Let them come, child. I can't get up and walk. Let all of them come and see. I...here itself....'

I shook Yamunakka and said, 'I want to go!' Yamunakka held me tight and ran her hand on my back, caressing me. They surrounded us. Shastri pulled me away. I beat him and bit his hand. 'Yamunakka, Yamunakka,' I cried. Yamunakka sat with a distant look in her eyes, not noticing anyone. Tears overflowed from her eyes and ran down her cheeks.

I was very happy when Father came and took me home. The moment we reached home, they changed my sacred thread and performed the purification rites. When Mother asked me, I told her everything that had happened. 'Dirty widow! Why did she have to get pregnant?' she said. Didn't Mother get pregnant? Why shouldn't Yamunakka get pregnant? Why all this ruckus, I wondered. A few days later the news reached us that Udupa had performed the funeral rites for Yamunakka while she was alive, and thrown her out of caste. Father and Mother said what a good man Udupa was and berated Yamunakka, calling her an immoral slut.

Sometime later, we got a letter inviting us to Udupa's wedding. I was revolted at the thought of Udupa, who was older than Father, getting married to a little girl, and spat in disgust, 'Thoo!'

Father asked, 'Why, I say?'

'After that immoral slut had been sent away, doesn't Udupa have to live? Doesn't he need someone to cook for him? In all, these are evil times!' said Mother.

Translated by Manu Shetty

MOUNI

Bhavikere Kuppanna Bhatta and Sebinakere Appanna Bhatta are like the cobra and the mongoose. Theirs is an old enmity, its origin lost to memory. Their houses stand on two hillocks half a mile apart. A fence in the valley separates their estates. Both of them are tenants of Narasimha, the deity of the Sri Matha. Years ago both of them had come here to work on the areca plantations, with just a copper tumbler each and not a coin between them. Now both have accounts in Gopala Kamti's grocery shop six miles away.

Kuppanna Bhatta is the older of the two. His face looks like a sour dried mango, his fifty-odd years etched on it. There was a time, in fact till just two years ago, when he was known for his sharp tongue—one lash from it was enough to split anything. His short, hairy frame has been shrinking with each passing day, but the way he carries himself has not changed at all. The same shining bald head, the same pudgy nose, that curved jaw heightening the resemblance to a mango. But the small eyes, fiery once, are now milky, and look as if they are covered with a layer of ash. The banana stains on his dhoti and the dhotra thrown over his shoulder, like his debts, have stayed with him through the years. He still keeps a wad of tobacco tucked into one cheek. Earlier, when angry, he would wait with drawn lips until his adversary stopped speaking, stride to a corner of the courtyard, spit out the tobacco, and return to utter something which was like a tight slap. The other man would be left speechless. And Kuppanna Bhatta would mix another little pellet of tobacco with lime in the palm of his hand and, transferring it into his mouth, lapse into a long silence. Nowadays, his face is like a locked door. If anyone tries to pick a quarrel with him, the closed expression on his face seems to say, 'You and I have nothing to do with each other.'

Appanna Bhatta, on the other hand, has always been popular. He is a man who gets along with everyone. Words slide off his tongue as smoothly as a strand of hair drawn through freshly-churned butter.

Even the Brahmins of Buklapura, the agrahara two miles away, are his friends. More so because Kuppanna Bhatta has antagonized them. Appanna Bhatta keeps a good house and his estate is pleasing to the eye. There are chrysanthemums at his doorstep, a canopy of coconut fronds shades his courtyard. Coloured mats are spread out for visitors and no one leaves his house without being offered a cup of coffee. A far cry from Kuppanna Bhatta's courtyard. Cow dung here, children's shit there, garbage and flies everywhere, and leeches which latch on to the soft flesh between the toes. Appanna Bhatta often says, 'Even the hut of Koraga the sweeper is better kept than this.'

Kuppanna Bhatta's arrears with Gopala Kamti have mounted from year to year. He must owe Kamti more than a thousand rupees. Everyone knows that a messenger from Gopala Kamti goes to Kuppanna Bhatta every few days to demand payment. Appanna Bhatta is very different. At the end of each year he clears his account to the last rupee. He is equally prompt in paying his dues to the matha from which both Kuppanna Bhatta and he have leased their areca estates. Not a single nut does he withhold. Not only that, the agent of the matha who comes to collect the dues is shown the utmost respect, and served a special meal with payasam.

As for Kuppanna Bhatta, he owes the matha some five thousand rupees.

Every year he is short of ten or twelve maunds of areca nut.

The matha authorities have warned him to either pay up or surrender his tenancy. The agent is also worried about Kuppanna Bhatta's neglect of the plantation. He has often said that the only way to save the areca palms is to hand the land over to Appanna Bhatta.

Before the Swamiji of the Sri Matha went to Kashi, Appanna Bhatta had invited him over to his house. Humbly, he had made an offering of fifty silver rupee coins on a silver plate and prostrated himself at the holy feet.

Even his own brother-in-law believed that Kuppanna Bhatta was to blame for his unpopularity. Little wonder then that the Brahmins of Buklapura nodded when Appanna Bhatta said, 'I can understand his resenting my shadow. But what wrong have you people done to him? Could he not have performed the upanayana of his oldest son here and invited you all to the feast? Did he have to go all the way to Agumbe by bus and spend twice as much money in the temple there?' Then he continued in a soft voice, winking, 'One should not stretch one's feet beyond one's bed, our elders have said. But, believe my words, this man has got some concealed wealth. Otherwise, how could he have afforded such a lavish show?'

Why does he sit so listlessly, wondered Kuppanna Bhatta's wife, Gowramma, who is confined by asthma to a corner of the hall. Even after the evening birds have fallen silent, the cows have come home and been milked, and his daughter Bhagirathi has lit the lamp in the puja room, he has to be reminded three or four times to sit down to his evening prayers. In the past he had never allowed the children to light the kerosene lantern for fear that they would break the glass. Now the older son wipes the glass, lights the wick, and places the lantern on the jagali.

Gowramma remembers...two years ago, her brother Subrahmanya had come to visit her. Hardly anyone comes to their house now. But never mind. At least one of her brothers is now a prosperous farmer, earning enough to live a decent life. That makes her happy. But why wasn't her husband able to do this? Appanna Bhatta too had come here in search of his fortune. He had done well and was now even able to invite the Swamiji of the matha to his house! After the meal was over, Swamiji had sent a boy to fetch Kuppanna Bhatta. But how much should her husband tolerate? How could he step into his adversary's house, over a threshold he had not crossed for thirty years? How would it have been possible for him to stand there and be humiliated by Swamiji in front of Appanna Bhatta? So he had done something he had never done before in his life. He had taken refuge in the kitchen and said to Bhagirathi, 'Tell the boy I am not at home.' Naturally, Appanna Bhatta added his own twist to the story when he narrated this to Swamiji.

It is all one's fate. Otherwise, why would he be tied down to someone like her, an invalid, racked by asthma twenty days out of thirty? Across the fence, Appanna Bhatta's palms are laden with bunches of areca nut. Here, in her husband's plot, the nuts fall off the diseased trees. No labourer stays with him. They all go to the other estate. He has antagonized everyone. There is not a single two-legged creature in the entire region he has not quarrelled with. But he has never taken advantage of people. He does not know what deceit is and has never told a lie to save his skin. But what a temper! It is all in his stars. Just as it is in mine to suffer before I die. Fate. That's all.

What was I thinking about? Ah, Subrahmanya's visit. He had not been patronizing. In fact he had shown great deference. 'Bhavayya,' he had said, 'you have no friends here. I hear the matha people too are asking you to hand over the land. Bhagirathi has come of age. How long can you keep a girl who has shot up like a banana plant in the house? When you approached those Tirthahalli people, Appanna Bhatta came in the way. He is always sharpening his knife.... I have no right to advise an elder. But frankly, this plantation does not seem to suit your horoscope. Give it up and come away with me. You know that I have some five hundred areca palms in Halasoor. You can take care of as many as you wish to. I shall look after the rest.'

No matter how humble and hesitant Subrahmanya had been when he had said all this, Kuppanna Bhatta, like Parasurama, had flown into a towering rage. 'Wait till I am dead. After that you can look after your sister and her children. Until then, mind your business,' he had said harshly, dismissing Subrahmanya. That was two years ago. Where was all that anger now? Since the bill collector saab from Kamti's shop and that rude man from the matha had begun to pester him, he had shrunk to half his size.

Then one day, he who had never asked for anything, came to his wife and said, 'Will you give me your ornaments? I will return them to you in six months.' The note of supplication in his voice drove a dagger through her heart. All she thought of was, let my husband and my taali, the symbol of my marriage, be safe. She opened her box, and took out the jewels which had come to her at her wedding and which she had saved for Bhagirathi's marriage—earrings, a four-strand necklace, a chain, a gold belt, an ornament for the hair. She gave them to him, taking care not to let him see the tears in her eyes. She made only one plea to God: 'Protect my husband, and let Bhagirathi get married into a good home.' She kept telling herself, 'What do I need these ornaments for? His self-respect is more important.' But who would look at a girl who had no gold? She had kept the ornaments for only one reason. Her own disease-racked frame had no use for them. Tormented by the change in her husband's manner she waited anxiously for Subrahmanya to visit them again. She could confide in him and lighten her grief.

Bhagirathi was in the kitchen trying to coax some flames from the damp firewood. Her mother could hear her coughing from the smoke in her lungs. A few minutes later, Bhagirathi came out, wiping the tears streaming down her cheeks, her hair tousled. 'Amma, there is nothing to make hooli with,' she said. Gowramma told her, 'Then make cucumber-seed saaru.'

Why couldn't her husband go to Halasoor? How long could he carry on here? Appanna Bhatta has been pursuing him like a Yamadootha. If he can build a bund to prevent his plantation from flooding, can't he build a fence to keep other people's cattle from straying in? Or at least chase them away? Why did he have them sent to the pound four miles away? Her husband had waited and waited for the cattle to come home, and when they didn't, he trudged all the way to the pound, paid the fine, and had them released. Appanna Bhatta surely has his eye on their plantation.

Ganapa, who was five, and whose belly was swollen from disease, went weeping to his mother. 'Give this child some of the water you have washed the rice in,' she told Bhagirathi.

No one in the neighbourhood cares whether we are alive or dead. Not once has anybody given my daughter a string of flowers or asked her how she was. Suddenly, the memory of the jewellery brought forth all the tears she had held back when she had given it to her husband. A fit of coughing followed. Wheezing, gasping for every breath, she stared at the darkness in the house around her, too weak to move from her corner.

Kuppanna Bhatta had decided that if his wife demurred even a little he would not touch the jewels. But she had not said a word. She had just opened the box and given him the small bundle wrapped in silk and he was overwhelmed. 'This is my last chance to get rid of my debts,' he had thought as he pledged them in the bank for two thousand and five hundred rupees. He vowed to redeem the jewels in six months and restore them to his wife. Then Kuppanna Bhatta sought out the smaller cultivators, those who had only a hundred or two hundred areca palms, and advanced them twenty-five rupees a maund, with the promise that he would pay another twenty-five after the sale. Even Appanna Bhatta had never gone beyond forty-seven or forty-eight rupees a maund, and had never paid more than fifteen in advance. So the smaller growers agreed to go along with Kuppanna Bhatta, who was then able to transport a hundred maunds to the wholesale mandi at Shimoga. 'When the price goes up a little, I will come and conclude the sale. Let me know how the market is,' he told the traders.

All this infuriated Appanna Bhatta. His regular clients had been snatched away from him. He told the whole town that here was clear proof that his rival had come into money. Kuppanna Bhatta had failed to pay the rent, but had enough for speculating on the market.

Meanwhile Kuppanna Bhatta made a careful calculation of his liabilities. He scrutinized all the figures he had noted in the margins of the panchanga. He owed five thousand rupees to the matha, one thousand to Gopala Kamti, and three hundred for the medicines for his wife's treatment. There was the interest on the sum borrowed from the bank. And the money he needed for Bhagirathi's marriage. The first thing he had to do was to get the jewels back. He could pledge them again the following year.

Areca nut should sell at sixty this year. That would give him a clear thousand by way of profit. He would pay two hundred rupees to Kamti, fifty to the doctor, two hundred and fifty to the matha agent. He would get the gold back with the remaining amount and use it as his reserve capital. A few more such careful transactions and he would be a free man. He took the cowries from his bag, laid them out and looked for the omens.

A fly flew up from the manure-pit and sat on his nose. Mango-gnats and mosquitoes hovered around his face. As it was summer, the courtyard was dry. Every whiff of breeze brought with it the smells of the cowshed. A withered jackfruit tree stood in one corner. The child with the malarial belly was defecating a few feet away, a black cur near his feet. A grey dog dozed on the ash-heap.

Kuppanna Bhatta rose, scratching the spot on his foot where a mosquito had bitten him. He went out and came back with a twig of tube cactus which he tied to a beam in the roof to attract mango-gnats. Just then Bhagirathi came out with a pot of water and asked Ganapa, 'Have you finished?' The black cur and the grey mongrel rushed to the spot vacated by Ganapa and Kuppanna Bhatta, disturbed by their barking, shouted, 'Hacha, hacha,' to chase them off. From a corner of the room came the sound of wood being sawed. It was Gowramma's wheezing. 'Give her some medicine, Bhagirathi,' Kuppanna Bhatta told his daughter and began pacing up and down the jagali.

The tiles will have to be re-laid before the monsoon. Or the damp walls will crawl with hairy caterpillars. There are a hundred holes in the floor where the water has dripped from the roof. It is difficult to find a dry spot for the children to sleep. And there is mildew everywhere—on the mat, in the rice container, even under the box which contains the family deities. It does not grow on people's buttocks, yet. That's all.

The flies covered the octopus-like branches of the cactus, making its green turn black in no time. Kuppanna Bhatta stood there, looking out in front of him. There was nothing in the landscape to hold his attention. Paddy fields in front of the house and then the jungle. A hill in the distance. A cart-track cut across the jungle from left to right. Someone seemed to be walking along it.

'Who is it?' shouted Kuppanna Bhatta.

'It is me, Manja,' said the man who was carrying a large load of dried branches, without slackening his pace.

'Wait a moment. When will you come to our place to split the firewood?'

'After I have finished the work for Sebinakere ayya,' replied Manja, moving away.

Feeling utterly helpless, Kuppanna Bhatta picked up a knife and went into the garden to bring in some banana leaves. By the time he returned, the three older boys had come back from school, which was four miles away. Bhagirathi was waiting for the cattle. The sound of wood being sawn continued to be heard from Gowramma's corner.

The medicine had had no effect. Ganapa sat in the corner, stuffing his mouth with dry avalakki and pieces of jaggery. Areca nut that season went up to fifty-one, fifty-two, and, in a month, to fifty-five rupees a maund. Kuppanna Bhatta waited for it to touch sixty. 'Your money has gone down the drain,' Appanna Bhatta mocked those who had sold their stock to his adversary. They in turn gave Kuppanna Bhatta a hard time. Every day, ten to twelve people came to his doorstep and demanded immediate payment. Making excuses and holding them off exhausted Kuppanna Bhatta. With abject humility, he pleaded with them to wait for a month more. But they would not listen. So he was compelled to go to Shivamogga and raise a loan of two thousand and five hundred rupees at 15 per cent interest on his stock. He paid his suppliers ten rupees per maund and promised to pay the remaining fifteen in a month's time.

Seeing all these transactions being made by his rival, Appanna Bhatta instigated Gopala Kamti and the agent of the matha to demand a settlement of their dues. 'This is the right time for it,' he whispered to them.

Gopala Kamti's bill collector turned up one day at Kuppanna Bhatta's house and planted himself on the jagali. No amount of pleading could move even a hair on his moustache. He shouted at the top of his voice that he would not stir until he had been paid at least five hundred rupees.

If Kuppanna Bhatta had been the sort of person to weep he would have cried. As the bill collector's voice rose, Gowramma's breathing became more agonized. Like a man in the grip of a nightmare, Kuppanna Bhatta seemed incapable of any movement. Whenever someone passed by the estate, the bill collector's voice became louder. At last, Kuppanna Bhatta went in, opened his box and brought out four one-hundred rupee notes. The bill collector took them, mounted his bicycle, and, still muttering, rode off. On the way back, he met Appanna Bhatta, reported to him what had happened and was treated to a tumbler of coffee. Hardly had the bill collector left when the doctor's compounder presented himself. His peace was purchased with a hundred rupees. There were still a thousand rupees left. The loan would have to be repaid now from out of the profit. It was all right,

Kuppanna Bhatta reassured himself.

But early next morning, the agent of the matha turned up. Kuppanna Bhatta laid out a seat for him and asked him if he would have some coffee. The agent refused. 'I have come to you even though there is a swelling on my leg. Anybody else would have treated you roughly. You do not show your face at the matha on your own. Even when Swamiji sent for you from Appanna Bhatta's house, you did not come. He who deceives the Sri Matha Narasimha, will not prosper, Bhatta-re. You had better settle your debts,' continued the agent, as he sat there fanning himself. He had come to know that Gopala Kamti had received four hundred rupees.

The more Kuppanna Bhatta pleaded, the angrier the agent became. 'I will bring a search warrant and a notice of attachment tomorrow,' he said, preparing to leave.

Kuppanna Bhatta resigned himself to the inevitable. He counted out eight hundred rupees and handed them over to the agent. 'You must pay the remaining amount by the next date or else you will have to give up the plantation,' he warned before he left. And he hurried off to Appanna Bhatta's house for his afternoon meal.

The next day some of those who had sold areca nut to Kuppanna Bhatta besieged him. 'We are in financial difficulties, Bhatta-re. The rainy season is coming. We need to buy things for the house,' they said. The whole world seemed to know that Kuppanna Bhatta had some money!

The price of areca nut did not rise beyond fifty-five. In fact it tumbled to fifty. In dismay Kuppanna Bhatta hastened to Shivamogga by bus and sold off the stock. He paid back the short-term loan to the last rupee, including the interest. He also paid his suppliers in full. Only the jewels remained in the bank.

Just before the rains set in, Subrahmanya turned up in his bullock cart and implored Kuppanna Bhatta to go with him. 'Come with me, Bhavayya,' he urged. 'I will find a groom for Bhagirathi. Gowramma's health has deteriorated and Ganapa is as thin as a stick.'

Turning to Gowramma, he said, 'Akka, my wife is pregnant. If you and Bhagirathi come and stay with us for a few months, you will do me a favour. There is no one to take care of her. Bhagirathi will be a great help. I will look for a boy for her. Don't listen to your husband. Come with me to Halasoor.... Why did you give him all your gold, Akka? He is a selfish, stubborn man. He cares only about his pride, his self-respect. His wife and family mean nothing to him. Why has he not done well like the other areca growers, tell me? I just don't understand any of this.'

Gowramma replied, 'How can I leave him in this condition....'

'I am asking you to come only for a few months, Akka. Till the confinement,' Subrahmanya persisted.

Kuppanna Bhatta did not say yes, nor did he say no. 'It's her wish,' he told Subrahmanya and left it at that. He refused to go with them. 'There is no one to look after the plantation,' he said.

Gowramma was torn between anxiety for her husband and the pull of the home of her birth. But Bhagirathi's marriage had to be thought of. And without the gold to give as dowry, finding a husband for her had become more difficult.

Kuppanna Bhatta spent the whole of the monsoon alone, cooking his own kanji. Without his wife and her wheezing, the house seemed to be swallowed up by silence. As the rain poured down, Kuppanna Bhatta spent many nights awake, his eyes wide open. And he came to a decision. He would get the gold back from the bank. He did not want to be obliged to anyone.

Where Kuppanna Bhatta had expected a hundred maunds of nuts from his own plantation, the yield that year was only fifty. Swamiji was away in Kashi at that time. Kuppanna Bhatta wrote a letter, and with great humility, asked for leniency just this once. He undertook to hand back the land the following year.

He waited for fifteen days. There was no reply. If he waited any longer, Kamti's bill collector and the agent would descend on him and carry away the crop. The ornaments in the bank would remain unredeemed.

The areca nut had to be moved to the market before the debt collectors could lay their hands on it. If he allowed the ornaments to remain in the bank, the interest would mount and he would not see them again in this lifetime. He went to the town to inquire whether there was any lorry bound for Shimoga. There was only one, it belonged to Gopala Kamti's relation. He struck a deal, thinking, whatever has to happen will happen. The very next day, Kamti's bill collector presented himself outside Kuppanna Bhatta's house. His heart sank. Whatever he tried to say was drowned out by the bill collector's ranting. The man insisted that Kamti had ordered him to come back with not a coin less than six hundred rupees, plus fifty rupees more by way of interest.

The argument was conducted at such a pitch that one of Appanna Bhatta's servants heard it and carried the news to his master. Appanna Bhatta yoked his bullocks to the cart and promptly proceeded to the matha.

By afternoon, Kamti's man, who had gone back to report to his master, returned with some gunny bags and scales. 'Sell us fifteen maunds of areca nut at forty-five rupees a maund, then we will have to pay you twenty-five rupees,' he said, taking the money from his pocket.

The selling price in Shivamogga was fifty rupees. Besides, Kamti's weighing scales were adjusted, so he bought at one weight and sold at another. 'Not possible,' said Kuppanna Bhatta gruffly.

The bill collector saab made bold to step into the house. For Kuppanna Bhatta, a Muslim crossing the threshold was the limit. He sprang towards the room in which the areca nut was stored and shouted, 'You will see me dead before you touch this door.'

The man was taken aback at the outburst. Wiping his face with a towel, he sat down, the scales in front of him. 'What can you do when grown men behave like children?' he muttered. Kuppanna Bhatta made no reply. He shook with emotion. His lips trembled. But he continued to sit outside the door, his arm stretched across it. The bill collector just stared at him.

Fifteen to twenty minutes had passed, when the sound of the bells of a bullock cart were heard. Kuppanna Bhatta recognized it as the cart from the matha. For a moment, his body went limp and he shut his eyes. But he quickly steadied himself. The agent of the matha walked straight in, accompanied by the shanbhog—the village accountant—the matha storekeeper, and a servant with another set of weighing scales. 'What is going on here?' asked the agent loudly.

Kamti's bill collector told him.

'He is our tenant. God's dues will be paid first, the annual rent as well as arrears. The grocer's claim can only come later. Go tell your master that,' the agent said to the bill collector. But the saab was not so easily cowed. He said Kuppanna Bhatta had promised that Kamti's debt would be cleared first. This was not true. He also described how he had foiled Kuppanna Bhatta's plan to move the areca nuts secretly to Shimoga.

'So this is what you have fallen to, Kuppanna Bhatta? You think you can swallow and digest what belongs to Narasimha?' asked the agent contemptuously.

With a meekness he had never shown in all his life, Kuppanna Bhatta told him about the petition he had addressed to Swamiji at Kashi. He took his janiwara between his thumb and forefinger and vowed that if he was given a reprieve this time, he would clear the dues the following year.

'Clear the dues, he says! With what face can you say it? You have money to speculate on the market, but you have no money to pay what you owe to God. You were arrogant enough to defy Swamiji and not come when he sent for you. You are eating his food, God's food! You don't bother to take care of the plantation. Look at the way you have kept this place. Thath! Anyone would think that it belonged to an outcast! Anyway, this is Swamiji's order.' He took a piece of paper from his pocket and read it out. It said that the estate should be taken away from Kuppanna Bhatta and entrusted to Appanna Bhatta for cultivation.

The shanbhog put on his reading glasses and added up Kuppanna Bhatta's dues—unpaid rent, loan, and interest—and pronounced, 'Six thousand.' The agent told the storekeeper, 'Weigh the areca nuts kept in the room.'

The storekeeper had recently been employed by the matha, after having lost all his money through trading in buffaloes. He was a dark, hefty man, built like Bhima. As soon as he heard the agent's words, he scrambled up to impress him. 'Move. Move...' he bellowed.

'Hoi, fifteen maunds of it should go to Kamti.' The bill collector was persistent.

'Will you clear out of the way, or should we set you right?' the agent threatened the bill collector, looking as if he was ready to swallow him up. The bill collector hurriedly climbed onto his bicycle and left unceremoniously, wondering what excuse to give when his master scolded him.

Once again the storekeeper shouted, 'Move out of the way,' to Kuppanna Bhatta, who sat there, barring the door.

'Before you touch one areca nut in this room, you will have to go over my dead body,' said Kuppanna Bhatta, loudly and firmly.

The shanbhog and the storekeeper were speechless. 'What did you say?' the agent challenged.

'That you will see me dead before you get to the areca nuts,' Kuppanna Bhatta replied, his whole body burning with the fire of his resolve.

'You, born a Brahmin and you are descending to this, Bhatta-re!' said the agent. The shanbhog put in his bit of advice. But Kuppanna Bhatta was unmoved. 'Very well, you will see what you are in for,' the agent said, as he made ready to leave with his entourage. On the way he went to Appanna Bhatta's house, instructed him to keep an eye on Kuppanna Bhatta in case he tried to move the areca nuts at night, and went off without having any coffee.

∽

Kuppanna Bhatta sat for a long time where he was, until his legs went dead under him. Late in the afternoon, he got up and stretched his limbs to get the blood flowing in them again. He latched the front door, bathed, and boiled some kanji for himself. When the cows came back a couple of hours later, he tied them up in the shed, gave them bran-water and milked them. He lit the lantern and sat down in the courtyard. He did not feel like cooking, so he warmed some milk, drank it, and lay down right there. But sleep eluded him. After a long time he opened the door and went out. From the clearing in front of the house, he looked up at the sky. Through the still silence of the trees, he could see the silver of pre-dawn spread across the sky. He calculated the hour, then went back into the house, bolting the door behind him. His eyelids drooped with weariness.

It was only when the cowherd called his name that he woke up. After the cows were led away, he drew water from the well and poured it over his head. He put a vessel of water on to boil.

Soon he heard someone pounding on the door. 'Bhatta-re, it is me, the ameen. Open the door.'

Kuppanna Bhatta made no reply to the bailiff. He went and sat at the threshold of the room where the areca nuts were stored. After a while, there was the sound of a bicycle bell. Then came the voice of Kamti, 'Open the door, Bhatta-re. I shall pay you forty-seven per maund. You can clear my account.' Kuppanna Bhatta did not move.

Kamti's bill collector shouted, 'Will you open the door or not?'

An altercation between the ameen and Kamti ensued. The ameen hurried away, threatening to summon the agent of the matha.

Again Kamti said, 'Bhatta-re, open the door. I will pay you fifty rupees. Settle my account. When there was no answer even to this, he began abusing him.

'If I had known what kind of a shameless man you are, I would never have let you set foot in my shop!' he said.

Then he said to his bill collector in a loud voice, 'Budan, go to this man's brother-in-law in Halasoor and demand a settlement of our accounts. Do not move from there until you are paid the money. He cannot be as shameless as this man is.'

Just then the agent arrived. He and Kamti began to quarrel. They sounded like the raucous crows that gather around the rice balls offered to them during a shraddha.

The agent used his ultimate weapon. He told the town crier, 'Go and announce to the whole of Buklapura that Kuppanna Bhatta's movable property is going to be publicly sold.'

The man began his job right there. Kamti's protests were drowned in that noise. Gradually, the drumbeats moved farther away.

'I will go to court,' threatened Kamti. 'Why don't you?' replied the agent.

The sound of the town crier's drum faded into the forest. Silence descended on Kuppanna Bhatta's house. Outside, the noonday sun blazed.

'You have to take the next step now,' the agent told the ameen.

'Do whatever is necessary. The storekeeper will help you. If Kuppanna Bhatta gives any trouble, send for me. I shall be at Appanna Bhatta's place,' he added, before he left.

'Bhatta-re, for the last time, will you open your door, or do you want us to break it?' The storekeeper called out.

There was no answer. He picked up a crowbar and rammed the door with it. The bolt rattled.

'Open the door now at least.'

There was still no response. One more blow and the door flew open. Like a Yamadootha, the ameen stood in front of Kuppanna Bhatta who looked as if he was deep in meditation. The ameen signalled to him to get up but Kuppanna Bhatta remained sitting, his eyes closed.

The storekeeper picked up Kuppanna Bhatta's shrunken body as if it were a handful of sticks and put him down outside, in the hot sun. One by one, he piled up the areca nut sacks in another corner of the courtyard. He was in high spirits. 'Are the vessels and other things to be sold too?'

The ameen pulled out a piece of paper from his pocket and read out the order, 'Everything movable and immovable is to be sold.'

The storekeeper darted into the kitchen. He brought the milk vessel into the courtyard and poured the milk on the ground. Then he brought all the goods out. A copper handi, a set of rice vessels, kadais, a set of bronze thalis, a silver jug, a copper teertha vessel (the same one that Kuppanna Bhatta had brought with him from the plains), a sankha and a brass thali used for the puja, a number of tubs for storing water at feasts, a cradle, a collection of ladles, a torn mat and a framed silver picture of Krishna, a silk dhoti, a pair of brooms—everything except the holy box containing the family deity, the saligram. Kuppanna Bhatta sat amidst his worldly possessions, his hand to his forehead, his eyes lowered.

'Aren't the cattle part of movable property?' the storekeeper asked. 'Of course,' said the ameen.

The town crier had finished his job and come back. 'Go, bring home the cattle grazing on the slopes of the hillock,' the ameen told him.

Then he went inside and fetched a gunny bag for the assortment of vessels. As he shook the gunny bag, four or five baby mice, newborn and still pink, fell out of it. They writhed and wriggled in the hot sun. 'Eesh,' the ameen exclaimed in disgust. 'Thath!' said the storekeeper, as a crow hopped in stealthily and, lunging suddenly, carried off one of the baby mice.

A number of people from Buklapura stood behind the trees around the house. They had ropes and sickles in their hands and pretended to be there in the course of their work. No one dared to step into the courtyard. Not one person made a bid for the goods. 'Why should we commit the sin of coveting another's belongings?' some thought. 'Cheh! Poor man,' cried several others, feeling sorry for him. One by one, they moved away from there. Only a few, who could not conquer their curiosity, stayed back to see what would happen. The agent had the areca nut sacks loaded on to the cart. The ameen made a detailed list of all the articles they had seized. Everything except the brooms, the silver picture, and a couple of broken vessels was placed on the cart. Without looking at him, the agent admonished Kuppanna Bhatta. 'No one who misappropriates that which belongs to Narasimha can survive, let alone prosper. Understand, Bhatta-re? From today, neither the land nor the house is yours. The tenancy has been made over to Appanna Bhatta.'

As he heaved himself up into the cart, he fired a last salvo, 'Anyway, why should you worry? You have already sent your hoarded wealth with your wife to her parents' place!'

~

There was an old ajji in Buklapura whose name was Sitakka. No one knew how old she was. She seemed to have been living there from the beginning of time. She addressed everyone in the singular, showing no respect for anyone. Married and widowed when she was still a child, she lived all by herself in a dilapidated little hut. Sitakka had no one to call her own, not even someone to offer a ball of rice at her shraddha when she died. Every day, she begged for a handful of rice to make some kanji for herself, her only meal of the day.

Sitakka had a sharp tongue, and everyone in the agrahara was terrified of her. If the shadow of a lower-caste person fell across her path, if children accidentally touched her while they were playing, if she found anyone retreating into their homes when they saw her (because she was a widow and hence a bad omen), out would pour a stream of imprecations. It was almost as if she could not sleep if she did not spend a couple of hours a day raving and ranting at someone. Perhaps she thought that unless she picked a quarrel and invoked their forefathers for several generations and cursed these evil times, people would take her for granted. Afraid of her abuse, people gave her rice even before she asked for it! After her meal, she spent her time sitting either on the stone steps leading to the river or on the platform outside the temple, twisting cotton into wicks.

At the sound of the town crier's drum that day, Sitakka's ears perked up. Quickly, she took the mandatory three dips in the river, gulped her kanji down, and went to find out what had happened. The agrahara seemed to have been emptied of all men. None of the women would tell her anything. Finally she got the information from a farm labourer. Sitakka marched into Kuppanna Bhatta's courtyard. There she saw a couple of misshapen vessels and a few brooms strewn around. Kuppanna Bhatta sat among them, his bald head exposed to the fierce sun.

Sitakka's harsh outburst shattered the oppressive silence. 'Which son of a whore has ruined your home? May his house crumble. Let his cattle be seized by tigers. But what is the matter with you? Why are you sitting like this? Have you too begun to believe that a poor man who loses his temper loses his teeth? Where is your arrogance now? Your insolence? You never cared to talk to me, to ask whether I was dead or alive.' Kuppanna Bhatta made no reply. Sitakka was puzzled.

'Let the fire swallow your enemy…' Sitakka began again but stopped when she noticed someone standing under a nearby tree. 'Who is that lurking there like a ghost?' she asked, crossing over to him. It was a young man called Narasimha Bhatta from Buklapura. But she did not recognize him. 'Who are you? Come here, will you,' she said. The man came forward timidly.

Together the two of them took hold of Kuppanna Bhatta by the arms, picked him up, and seated him in the shade of the jagali. Quietly, the young man sneaked away.

Cursing Appanna Bhatta, the agent, Kuppanna Bhatta, the other Brahmins of Buklapura, and anyone else she could think of, Sitakka picked up the pots and pans scattered around and placed them on the jagali. She saw the lock on the door of the storeroom and heartily cursed the hand that had put it there. 'May a snake bite it,' she muttered. Then she hastened to her own home, but before that, she stood in front of Appanna Bhatta's house and showered curses on his heartlessness. She got together some avalakki, asked someone for some curds to mix it with, crushed a green chili into it, added a pinch of salt, and took it back to Kuppanna Bhatta. She wrapped it in a banana leaf, which she pushed in front of him and ordered, 'Eat this. Don't starve yourself like an idiot.' Then she went home, had a bath, and lay down on the bare floor.

After the sun had set, Appanna Bhatta called one of his labourers and told him, 'Go and see what Kuppanna Bhatta is doing—whether he is there or has slunk away to his wife's place. Take care that you're not seen.' The servant did as he was told. In the light of the moon, he saw the still, motionless figure on the jagali, and was frightened. He rushed back to report what he had seen.

'See what a schemer he is!' Appanna Bhatta said to his wife. 'This is another one of his tricks. Do you know what a drama he put on for the benefit of the agent? I tell you, if he does not creep to his wife's home by the first light of the day, my name is not Appanna Bhatta.'

The next day dawned. The man who brought in the firewood announced, 'He is still on the jagali.' Curious to see what was happening, Appanna Bhatta took the key the agent had given him and set off. As he neared Kuppanna Bhatta's house, his heart started thudding. For a while he lingered behind a large tree, pretending to cut down something.

Kuppanna Bhatta was sitting on the jagali, like a stone, his dark body leaning against the wall, his dhotra thrown over his head. Appanna Bhatta's heart missed a beat. As he went nearer, he thought to himself, 'If Kuppanna Bhatta picks a quarrel, I will give him a fitting reply. I will ask him about the wealth that he has already dispatched to his in-laws' place.' He felt reassured and stepped into the courtyard. A grey dog lay in front of Kuppanna Bhatta, gazing intently at him. A plantain leaf with a small heap of dried-up avalakki on it lay untouched. Before he realized it, Appanna Bhatta had called out, 'Bhatta-re!' There was no reply. With a shaking finger, he jabbed at the figure who continued to sit with his eyes closed.

All the blood had drained out of Kuppanna Bhatta's aged face, leaving it wan and pale. Appanna Bhatta shook him by the shoulder.

Kuppanna Bhatta opened his eyes.

'You need not have been so rough with the agent,' Appanna Bhatta stated. There was no reaction, but Kuppanna Bhatta's eyes were open. Appanna Bhatta felt emboldened.

'What do you lack, Bhatta-re? You have carried your hatred of me this long. But I don't hold it against you. After all, you are older than me. As an elder, you should wish me well. That's what I want. You should not leave with hard feelings against me. So I have come to speak to you. I shall send you to your brother-in-law's house in my own cart. Come and eat a meal in my house before you go. Let us forget this enmity of thirty years.'

Appanna Bhatta had not meant to go so far. One word had led to another without his realizing it. Kuppanna Bhatta's continued silence had made him raise his own voice. But it appeared as though his words did not penetrate the other man's eardrums. Not a muscle on Kuppanna Bhatta's face moved. His stillness hit Appanna Bhatta with the force of a blow. And Appanna Bhatta was speechless. After a while, he recovered. As he paced up and down the courtyard, he continued, more softly this time, 'I have not done anything to ruin you, Bhatta-re. For thirty years I have endured your resentment. But did I ever try to compete with you? It is true that I informed the agent that Narasimha's share of the produce was being diverted to Gopala Kamti's account. If I am not telling the truth, let my tongue split into two. Call the elders of Buklapura and let them adjudicate. If they find that I am in the wrong, I shall fall at your feet.'

Appanna Bhatta's voice became shrill. 'Last year you took away all those growers who used to supply areca nut to me. When you had money to trade, was it right to default on your payments of rent? Wouldn't anyone get angry at that? Aren't there some rules in such matters? Like you, I am a man with a family. Like you, I have a daughter to marry off. I also have my troubles. For the past year, I have been suffering from some ailment of the stomach. I am in constant pain. Last month, my buffalo, which used to give a bucketful of milk, suddenly died. It is all our fate, Bhatta-re. Come on. Get up and come with me. Have a meal at my place. I will get the bullock cart ready and you can start for your brother-in-law's place in the cool hours of the evening.'

The grey mongrel looked at one face, then at the other, and then at the avalakki on the plantain leaf. Kuppanna Bhatta's eyes stared vacantly past Appanna Bhatta and into the forest beyond. Appanna Bhatta felt his throat go dry in the oppressive silence. He kept repeating, 'Bhatta-re, Bhatta-re…' as if he were reciting the names of his ancestors during a shraddha. The dog rose, stretched its limbs, and lay down again. Mango-gnats hovered around. The sun blazed. Kuppanna Bhatta sat on his haunches, resting his head on his palm and his elbow on his knees, a towel over his head. Appanna Bhatta looked at him again, as if seeing him for the first time. There was a churning feeling in his stomach. The avalakki on the banana leaf was dry, though it had once been soaked in curds. Flies sat on it. And flies sat on Kuppanna Bhatta's nose. Every few seconds, he blinked.

'Bhatta-re, I don't want your property. Stay on in your house. I will let you cultivate this land as long as you live. Just pay me the rent every year. I am not a butcher. Like you I came from the coast with an empty copper vessel in my hand. All I want is that I should not drop dead on a jungle path as my father did. There was no one even to pour a few drops of water down his throat as he was dying. When I found him, lying there in the sun, the crows were pecking at him. I pray that kind of death does not come to me, that's all, Bhatta-re. Here, take your keys. Keep them,' Appanna Bhatta cried. Overcome with emotion, he blew his nose.

The man who sat there on his haunches, as if waiting for his last breath, did not react. This still, shrouded figure seemed to burn into Appanna Bhatta's mind, and his tongue, never lacking in fluency, grew silent too. Appanna Bhatta put his towel over his head and he too squatted on the jagali, opposite the silent one.

Translated by H.Y. Sharada Prasad

STALLION OF THE SUN

I am writing this about Simpleton Venkata—Venkatakrishna Joysa is his real name—whom I had not seen in fourteen years. He turned up before me in the marketplace that day. He didn't recognize me because I had left the town a long time ago. But how could I ever forget my boyhood friend, this Venkata with kumkum dabbed between his eyebrows, the front half of his head shaved in a crescent shape, his broad, gap-toothed smile? With a burlap bag tucked under his arm, he stood gazing at the vegetable stall like a boy in front of a toy shop. His eyes, which were scanning the mounds of tondekaayi and alasande peas and the banana bunches that hung from the ceiling, shifted the next moment to the cross-eyed Konkani shopkeeper who was watching him with the same indifference with which he watched the cattle that wandered about in the street. I stood there eyeing him as though I had found a stream of cool water on a sweltering day. He too looked at me briefly, but it was a blank look. We were the only two in that marketplace who were not carrying umbrellas. While all others were playing it safe, he, the professional astrologer that he was, was probably flaunting his ability to forecast the weather, confident that although it was the month of July, there wasn't going to be any rain that day. As for myself, I had left the place long ago to live in the city and had been to foreign countries, and so, seeing me in my city attire, no one was likely to be surprised that I didn't carry an umbrella. Venkata, on the other hand, for all appearances unprepared for any downpour, stood there smiling to himself in his secret knowledge, as it were, of the atmospheric phenomena, and looked at the vegetables that had come to the market from the neighbouring districts disinterestedly as if none of it was really edible. Would the thrill I felt suddenly on seeing Simpleton Venkata fade away because of my disappointment at him not recognizing me? I wonder. Memories tend to dry up if they are not nurtured.

Though older than me by at least five or six years, Venkata had been my closest friend when we were growing up. With him around, one felt completely at ease. An incident suddenly comes to mind: I must have been eight or nine years old then. I used to be quite afraid of water. Once he made me go with him to the river without telling my mother. Not heeding my screams and protests, clasping me tight to him, he jumped from a boulder into the stream. Frightened at first, gasping for breath and swallowing water but still in his firm clasp, I felt myself gradually able to come up and go down into the water, to open my eyes in it. Being tickled by the tiny fish, and elated that I was learning to swim at last, I slowly began to feel comfortable in the water. First the neck, then the mouth, then the nose, then the head—I plunged deeper and deeper only to be buoyed up again by the water. Then, coming out of the cool water to lie down in the warm sand and dry out under the sun.... The river in our village is probably all dried up now. As if poised to jump into the water, I stood on tiptoe before Venkata, though he didn't recognize me, and said, 'Hello there!'

'Can you believe the price of cucumbers these days, sir?'

I didn't budge. Staring into his eyes, I stood as if I was about to charge at him.

'Sir, what do you think I have under my arm? A fighting cock?' he said, showing his toothless gums.

'Sure, Budan Saab. But how is it that your cock's comb is drooping like a Brahmin's empty sack of alms?'

'No. This is the cock that got beaten up by my cock in the fight.' He held up his shopping bag to me as if he were holding the cock by its legs.

'What misfortune has brought thee, O Prince, toothless and dishevelled, clutching this cock under thine arm, thus wandering to this strange land on this day of the full moon?'

Recognizing my theatrical speech in the manner of the Yakshagana plays we used to frequent together, a baffled Venkata took a few steps backward, and his buttock scraped the horn of an old cow that was chewing on a banana peel.

'Is it Ananthu?' he said, rubbing his buttock. Then turning back to the cow which was looking for more banana peels in the roadside gutter, he said: 'Pray, tell me, blessed goddess, why did you make me fear that this Ananthu might be an amildar or some such big officer? Or, are you, my ever-haunting sorcerer playing one of your tricks on me?' The cow had picked up a banana peel from the gutter and was now blissfully chewing it, contorting its mouth.

'How much tondekaayi shall I give you?' the cross-eyed Konkani shopkeeper asked me. I took the bag from Venkata and had it filled up with tonde, cucumber, alasande peas, potatoes and onions, and said to Venkata, 'Come on, let's go to your house.'

'Yes, yes. Come home. I will give you such an oil massage that you will see the moonlight. Hot bath water will anyway be ready.' With the purposeful stride of one who is heading home after having bought the provisions needed for a festival, Venkata walked briskly past the people in the street.

'Let me buy some Bhringamalaka oil then,' I said. We went up the steps to Prabhu's shop which smelled of tobacco leaves.

'Visiting your hometown after a long time, aren't you, Mr Murthy? Your brothers still buy on credit from us, just like in your father's time. Come in, come in. Shall I get you something to drink?' said Prabhu who sat there with a pencil tucked behind his ear and showed me a stool to sit on amidst the cannisters.

'I come here for a visit now and then. But I very rarely come to the marketplace. Is everything well with you?' I said. The sweet smell of the jaggery Prabhu was weighing had blended with the pungency of the tobacco leaves.

'How can things be well? No rains. Customers who buy on credit don't pay me back. Last year my eldest son fell ill and died within three days. Not a paisa of profit can be made in this trade; but you go on doing it because that is what your father taught you to do. My sons were not fortunate like you to go to England to study. They just settled down in the family business, trading in tobacco leaves and horse gram. See that one? He is the second son. Over there is the fourth. The other two have opened a cloth shop. I married all my three daughters to lawyers. My eldest son's children are in high school now. How many children have you got now? Where do you live?' He talked, placing the blocks of jaggery on the scale and all the time trying to keep the flies off. The same conversation, at the same place—it was all familiar.

'We live in Mysore. I have two children, a boy and a girl. Have you got Bhringamalaka oil?'

'Oh! Is this for our Venkata Joysa's famous oil-massage and bath? After all, isn't he the one who did the massage and bath for K. T. Bhashyam when they were in jail together during the freedom movement? So many cabinet ministers are known to him, all old-timers. There is hardly an important person in all of Karnataka who has not had himself massaged by Venkata Joysa. Yet, God only knows why he has not received his pension for the last two years. By the way, Joysre, why don't you have our Murthy put in a word for you? At least that way, if you get your pension, we may get back some of the money you owe us. On the whole, like me, Joysa here is down on his luck. He has a son in name only. What a scoundrel he has turned out to be! Doesn't study, doesn't pass his exams. As if that isn't enough, hangs out in coffee shops. Say what you may, our times were far better. Everything is topsy-turvy nowadays.'

Grinning broadly, Venkata put the bag down by his bow-legs, took some snuff out from his pocket and tucked a pinch into his nostrils. Taking the grimy bottle that the shop-boy had brought to him, he said,

'It's B. V. Pandit's brand oil, isn't it? Only that has the cooling effect.'

'Of course, Joysre, fresh stuff. I'm the only stale thing here,' said Prabhu taking the money from me. 'This is the day's first cash transaction. See the sorry state we are in?'

Venkata reached for Prabhu's hand across the cans and, holding it in his hands, contemplated.

'The moment I saw you, Mr Prabhu, I knew. You have too much heat in your system. You need an oil bath. I'll come tomorrow and give you a massage, alright?'

As his hand lay limp in Venkata's, like a bunch of greens, Prabhu let out a sigh wearily and said,

'Is there a single head in this place that this Joysa hasn't massaged, Mr Murthy?' God only knows how such a man got such a son! The other day, I believe the boy recently waylaid the college principal himself at night and beat him up and robbed his money.'

Venkata gestured as if to draw a line across his forehead and raised the eyebrows as if to show the line of fate there. Joining him, Prabhu, too, made a similar gesture. He said, wiping jaggery off his hand, 'Does it mean the jail for him, Joysre?'

Lowering his eyebrows and picking up his bag, Venkata got ready to leave, excited: 'What's written on his forehead has to happen, no?' I got him out on bail. I gave the police inspector a fine oil massage and bath and one to the Principal. Now I've got to give a massage to the judge....' Venkata's laughter made me uneasy. But Prabhu didn't seem to mind. Same old Venkata, he has become the laughing stock of the town. Shameless man.

We walked toward Kerekoppa village. The trail though hadn't changed even after fourteen years. I blamed Venkata with all my heart. He has been always like this, an imbecile. How, once, during the Quit India Movement, this genius got us into trouble! We were in high school then. One day, he woke us up in the middle of the night and said, 'Come, let's go and steal the mail box.' It was pitch dark on that night of the new moon. In the dark, we carried the mail box to the riverbank and buried it in the sand. Next day there was a commotion all over the town. Pretending innocence, we marched, as usual, in the protest parade with everyone else, shouted slogans, hailed the national leaders, 'Kamaladevi! Kasturibai! We too are in the struggle for freedom!', picketed in front of the toddy shop, laid ourselves down on the school-ground—all under the leadership of Venkata. But how could he keep quiet? On the street, someone from out of town stopped him, it seems, to ask where he could get a good cup of coffee. The do-gooder that he was, Venkata took him to Sheenappayya's coffee shop. What the fool didn't know was that the man was a secret agent of the CID. 'What you boys are doing is hardly anything. Do you know what all the students in Shivamogga are doing?' the sneaky CID agent egged him on as he sipped his steaming coffee. Venkata blurted out, 'We are no less than those Shivamogga students, you know.'

'Come on. You boys here don't have the guts to take on the government,' teased the CID agent. Venkata then bragged to the stranger about our adventure last night. The result: the police double-marched us along with Venkata to the riverbank.

Sure enough, the whole town gathered on the riverbank. The police handed us spades and yelled, 'You bastards, start digging now!' After digging endlessly in that hot sun, we at last pulled the mail box out of the sand, and, in front of everyone, were made to carry it back to the post office ourselves. The police were not finished with us yet. Next, they took us in their truck and dumped us in the Sakre Bayalu forest. We dragged ourselves back eating wild berries or whatever else we could find on the way and trudged back to the town the following day.

Since we couldnt help laughing, despite our attempt to recall all these incidents in anger, Venkata put down the bag and danced and clapped in laughter. 'You are an immortal scoundrel, you know,' I told him. He had failed in his classes year after year and ended up as my classmate. By then, he already had a wife—a veritable shrew. Sometimes, on his way to school, he had to bring her along to attend this or that auspicious ceremony at someone's house. Then, when they got to the marketplace, he would walk fast in the street leaving her several paces behind as though she were unknown to him. She, all the while, would be hopping to catch up with him, calling out, 'Listen, listen.' That's how we all came to know, when we were in the Lower Secondary School, that he even had a wife.

Once, when our math teacher started beating him with a cane, calling him, 'You, overgrown buffalo,' Venkata tried to shield himself with a book, pleading, 'Please sir, I'm a married man! Don't hit me!' This made the teacher laugh so much that he took off his turban and started wiping the sweat off his face with his chalk-smeared hand. The grotesque sight of the teacher's dark face, now smeared with chalk powder, set us all laughing. Then Venkata picked up the duster and started wiping the teacher's face with it. This made us laugh more. When the teacher turned to hit him again, he had crawled under the desk and was pleading with joined hands, 'Please don't! If I get welts on my body, my wife will come to know.' The teacher, who had chronic back pain and couldn't bend down, kicked him on the buttocks, shouting, 'Get up, you bum!'

Even now, this Venkata was making me laugh as though to prove that it was impossible for anyone to be angry with him. Still, thinking how he had allowed that son of his to grow up to be so irresponsible,

I began to scold him harshly, 'You are an escapist, an imbecile, a spineless ninny!'

'What does anyone gain by such obstinacy, tell me? Come, I'll massage away all your rage.' Like a boy who has something to show you, he quickened his pace.

'Wait,' I said. I really wanted to tell him: I have treated you with indifference, maharaya. I didn't try to see you on my previous visits. Today I have run into you by chance and so you are exposing me like this. This is a game, I know, which will end sooner or later. Perhaps this buffoonery, too, of yours is a matter of habit with you. I feel I am drying up. I don't fancy anything. A vague anxiety troubles me. Lately, ideas for writing don't come to me at all. I mouth grandiloquent words, and the pliant heads before me nod appreciatively. When this drama is over, I feel only emptiness. Why don't I discern things anymore? Do you see things or do you only pretend to see? This self-effacement of yours is a pose, isn't it? Or, have I perhaps become an empty vessel by trying to write about lofty matters rather than about you whom I have known intimately from childhood?

'I smell kedige flowers,' Venkata said and, flaring his nostrils, he sniffed the air like the mythical demons do on smelling the presence of humans. All this while, I had said nothing of my thoughts to him. He put the bag down and disappeared into the thickets of kedige, saying, 'My daughter, Ganga, is very fond of wearing kedige flowers in her braids.' Was the kedige in season then? I didn't know. 'Damn these kediges. Where the devil are they hiding?' Venkata said, emerging empty-handed after sometime. 'Come, let's go.'

On the way we ran into someone who stopped to talk to us. He had red stone studs in his ears and carried a cloth-bundle on his head. Spitting out the betel juice, he said, 'Ha! Joysa! I just came past your house. Your wife stopped me and began to scold you severely. She said you left home this morning to go to the market and hadn't returned. She began calling you all sorts of names....'

Venkata helped the man lift the load off his head and asked, 'When you talked to her, was she in the backyard or at the front-door? Pray, tell me, O Learned Sage Narada, in what quarter of our abode did my consort receive thee? Please, will you enlighten me?'

The man was amused by this theatricality. He spat out the rest of the betel juice, wiped his mouth with the edge of his dhoti and revealing his few reddened teeth, asked, 'Why do you ask? It was in the backyard.'

'Then it means she will have made the palya dish out of the chogate-soppu that grows in our backyard. My blessed wife is a culinary wizard who can turn even cattle feed into a savoury dish. We are grateful to the Learned One for the good tidings.'

'But, maharaya, her tongue is something else,' the man said preparing to leave; but he stopped, turned round, and said, 'By the way, Joysa, why is your son Subba so mean and ill-tempered? I try to make small talk with him and he tells me to mind my own business. I was about to tell the grumpy boy to go to hell, but not being one to meddle in others' affairs, I just came away. People like me, who feel we belong here, try to show concern for one another. But it's not just your son, everyone who goes to college ends up that way.'

Balancing the bundle on his head and swinging his hands, the celestial messenger departed.

'How right you are!' said Venkata to him and, joining me, started scampering as if nothing had happened, swan-footed that he was.

What a chap! I marvelled. I was now convinced that Venkata had made a mess of all his worldly affairs. Yet, look at the way he goes about untroubled! Is he a madcap, or a perfect phony, or a scruffy-looking mystic? I wondered.

'How many children have you got now?' I asked.

'Four. Our first-born is our illustrious male progeny. The daughters are all still unmarried. And so, my wife, besides being the fierce Goddess Chamundi that she already has been, has now turned into the fire-spitting Kali. In any case, I am a devotee of Kali, and so even her wrath is a blessing to me. Thus, have I managed to remain blissful in this earthly existence.'

His theatrical speech was beginning to irritate me. Why should men like Venkata, who father children, live a life of humiliation at the hands of every passer-by? I said to myself. When Marx talked about the idiocy of the village life, no doubt he had men like Venkata in mind. Venkata appeared to me to typify all those who live in a state of supreme inertia. Lately, in my conversations with my friends, I often expressed my anxieties about whether any change was possible in our country. Now, I tried, as seriously as it was possible to do with Venkata, to expound my theories. But would he listen to anyone?

'Do you know it hasn't rained at all?

'It will be a miracle if the mango blossoms appear this season. Last year there wasn't a single pickling mango.

'You see that tree over there? Sometimes hundreds of parrots come and settle on it.

'"The hill over there is called Peacock Hill. There is a cave there.

'Once my children are all married and settled, I'll go and live in that cave.

'Do you know that the view from that cave is simply breathtaking? I'll just authorize my wife to receive my pension, and then I'll go and live there.'

And so he chattered on and heard me in between his responses:

'What is politics but a change in the way we live?

'But change towards what? Towards the haves, or the have-nots? Why is passion essential for such a change?

'At the basis of all politics, of all science, for that matter, is passion for changing the nature of things and of people into sharing your hopes and aspirations. It is at the basis of religious rituals too. That is also politics, politics of the eternal.

'Don't you wish your wife and children would also pursue what you have realized to be the right path? To wish for the status quo is also politics. Do you know why? Change is in the nature of things. Some try to prevent change for their own selfish ends, but cannot do so for long.

'All things expand all things explode. Nothing remains the same. That is why we should constantly strive for an order that we think is right.'

I said such things as I walked.

'You are whatever you are born with,' said Venkata and put the bag down, turned his face up to the sky and brought his palms together as if to pray.

'I bow deeply to heroes like you. But you people must not mind an imbecile like this Venkata. Besides, when you heroes get your heads all heated, you need people like me to give you a cooling massage,' he said and began tapping with his fingers on the imaginary head before him.

'Go to hell!' I said in mock disgust. Thinking that I was really angry, Venkata said:

'But tell me, Ananthu. I can't even change the woman I married. Can I change the world? I am alive now. What is the guarantee I will be here the next moment?'

We came to a spot where we had to cross a ford over a narrow makeshift bridge made of three areca trunks tied together.

'After you. But be careful!' Venkata waited for me to cross first. I walked over the bridge gingerly and then waited for him on the other side of the ford. Satisfied that I had at last engaged him in my discourse, I said:

'We may die the next moment or we may not. In any case, there will be others who live....' I insisted that he let me carry the bag now. We were walking along the paddy field.

'Do you know, Ananthu, that the grove we were in just before crossing the bridge is inhabited by a Panjurli spirit? The Panjurli is known for its short temper. Once, long ago, I was walking in the grove singing to myself. It was getting dark. Behind me, I heard the rustle of dry leaves. I turned around to see what it was. A tiger! I passed out. When I came to, I saw that I had peed my dhoti.'

'Why are you telling me this?'

'Oh, no particular reason. Look, Ananthu, I am a big coward. I don't know what to say when you talk like this, as though you were possessed by a Panjurli spirit. I tell my wife, "This is the way I am. What can I do?" She may have a sharp tongue, but she is a good person. If I say I have a stomach ache or something, she will bring this or that herb even if she has to walk a mile for it and brew a decoction for me. I got scared when I saw a tiger. Do you know why? Because I don't know how to bring around a tiger and calm it down with an oil massage. If I knew, I would grab it by its whiskers and starting with its forehead, I would gently massage....'

Venkata clutched his belly and started laughing. I too started laughing, remembering our schooldays when he used to get beatings.

But the suspicion that all his unsaid thoughts were contained in his laughter and that I was being exposed by it made me uneasy.

'You idiot! Is it possible for anyone to live without any ego? Even the gentlest of beings needs to have an ego,' I said.

I began to feel that without destroying the likes of this Venkata there would be no progress, no electricity, no river dams, no penicillin, no pride, no honour, no joy of sex, no winning of a woman, no climax, no flying, no joy of life, no memory, no ecstasy, no bliss.

Absorbed in such thoughts, I looked at Venkata as he stood on the edge of the paddy field, barefoot and bubbling with joy. I was confused. Was he laughing at me in pity? I wasn't sure.

'You say that your grown-up daughters are still unmarried. What if they go astray?' I asked. I was trying to hurt this Venkata who could look upon me with pity.

'Maharaaya, I would be so grateful to you if you could find husbands for them. Where do I have the money for their dowry? They are precious gems, those girls. Why would they go astray? Still, if they do, it is their fate. Who am I to avert it?'

Faced with his guileless manner, I was at a loss for words. What should I say to him? That he should go and make money somehow? Revolutionize society? Smiling, but without his playful flare, Venkata said:

'Look, after all, I'm a priest by profession. Worshipping is in my nature—worship whatever I see. If I come upon some heads, I worship. I worship the Panjurli ghosts and sundry spirits, I worship the school inspector, the police sub-inspector, the amildar, now you, and K. T. Bhashyam in the old days. That is how I worship the Mother Goddess as well. What do you get by butting heads with your adversary? Only a swollen head. Mother Goddess has looked after me so far. My wife, Rukku, makes cups out of banana leaves. I carry them on my head to the market and sell them. Soon, I'll be getting my pension back. The other day I gave our MLA a superb oil massage. I was telling him how in jail I used to make K. T. Bhashyam see the moonlight with my massage.... See how these trees and plants embody God within them? Likewise, we too should embody God within ourselves. But probably, there is still some rancour left in me. Or else, my son

Subba wouldn't be so hot-headed.'

Venkata snatched the bag from my hand so that I could walk more freely, and he began to point out all his favourite birds. 'Look at those birds. They don't even wish to be seen by us. They want neither your social change nor my oil massage. Pchk, they drop their excrement on the heads of even the fiercest spirits and then fly away. To live, they have to be neither imbeciles nor dare-devils. Don't you think so, Ananthu?'

I walked briskly, for I was getting hungry. Behind my back, Venkata mimicked my gait, the way he used to mimic me when we were in school. Do I still walk the way I used to when I was a boy? I felt awkward.

Here and there, villagers sat idly, looking anxious because the rains had not come. 'Joysre, when are the rains going to come?' someone would ask idly to which Venkata would reply with mock seriousness, 'Just wait one more week.'

'There aren't even the banana leaves for you to make those cups. Are all your astrology and magic spells just mumbo-jumbo then?' asked a young man in trousers, trying to taunt him.

'Lately, we have been making cups from the muttuga leaves from the forest. The family has to get by somehow, right?' replied Venkata and walked on calmly.

'Lo, Chikka. It seems a cow belonging to your master had been missing. He came to me to have a charm made. Did the cow come home?' he asked a cowherd.

'Yes, it did, Joysre,' said the boy who was playing with some pebbles, without looking up.

This must be Venkata's daily routine, I thought to myself. It was the life of a simpleton, open for everyone to see, neither flourishing nor withering; he laughs and makes others laugh, dreams of living by himself in the cave on Peacock Hill; when something comes charging at him, he steps aside and makes way for it; gets abuses from his wife; he has no secret, hides nothing. The king cobra which has the jewel in its hood also has venom in its fangs. No such venom in this Venkata. With no fury, no envy in him, he is a feckless good-for-nothing. I shouldn't give in to him thinking that he is a spent-force.

Venkata pointed out a tree to me—a huge, massive tree. 'There is something unusual about this tree. Do you see how one of its limbs shaped like a hand is pointing to the ground? They say that is because a treasure is buried under the ground,' he said. I laughed. 'Some greedy folks have even tried to dig up the treasure. It belongs to a spirit called jettiga that inhabits the tree. So, how can anyone else get it?' I was amazed by his intimate knowledge of his surroundings. He, this boyhood friend of mine, could expound on the legends concerning every square foot of this place. Not just that, shaped by the myriad ghosts and spirits of the land, a philosophy of his own had evolved.

∽

This is how I got to know about it: all the while as he led me expertly through the maze of those trails in the woods, he was narrating the legends that would somehow link those hidden paths we were treading to the mythological past. Once Mother Sita…and so he would begin an episode in the Ramayana when Rama and Sita lived a life of hardship in the forest, and then he would show me a gummy leaf which, he said, Sita used for the wick of her oil lamp. The orchid on the tree in front of us was the flower Rama had plucked for Sita to wear in her hair. The rock over there was the rock which Lakshmana pierced with his arrow to release a fountain of water. Pointing to a hollow formed in the rock, Venkata challenged me, 'Let me see you scoop up the water from that hollow with your palms.' I tried, but as I scooped, more water kept filling up the hollow. He asked me to drink the water. I did. The water tasted cool and sweet. 'This is the water with which Shri Rama bathed this linga idol here,' he told me, pointing to a protrusion on the rock and poured on it the water he scooped up from the hollow. Then, with his eyes closed and kneeling down like the bull at Shiva's temple, he muttered words to the following effect:

'Some people look upon the Supreme God as their Mother, some as their Father. Those for whom God is their Mother have their eyes always on her breasts, full and overflowing with milk. They drink from it and don't want to let it go. They want no one else's breast. Those for whom God is their Father, they look into the Lord's eyes and become intoxicated. They want to see everything, they want to drink up the whole world through their eyes and yet their thirst for "seeing" remains unquenched. The infant drinking at the breast sometimes falls asleep suckling; wakes up, and suckles again. I am the drinking type; you are the seeing type. Why did the sage Shankara, who set out to comprehend the universe through seeing, suddenly desire to taste it like a suckling baby? I wonder. You don't have to comprehend something in order to soak it up. The earthworm soaks it up; the tree soaks it up. They live and they flourish…maybe, if the Mother Goddess herself separates you from her breast and puts you down because you have drunk enough, you may perchance open your eyes and see, but it is all at the whim of the Mother Goddess. Sometimes she may even pull you away from one breast and set you to the other. It is a frightening moment, though! Passing from one breast to the other, from life to death, some fortunate souls may even glimpse her eyes, if they don't scream with fright. All that moustache-twirling heroism is not for me. It is as the fool that the likes of me serve this world. Now, you would like to drink at the breast, too. It is only natural. You too fall asleep while drinking. You too kick the mother while drinking. Besides, before you ride off on your heroic mission of making the world bend toward you as you wish, don't you sometimes need cool nourishment from the Mother Goddess' milk, from my oil massage-bath?'

Having spoken like the learned sage in the bhagavata drama, Venkata was entranced by his own eloquence. He stood there and inhaled a pinch of snuff. 'After giving up bidi smoking, I took to this snuff,' he said. 'Wait till my wife sees you with me, her abusive mouth will become sealed instantly.' Gloating over the prospect, he scampered on. Because of his knock-knees, he walked with his feet spread wide.

~

In front of us was a house—an un-whitewashed, un-swept, dilapidated house with a country-style tile roof. 'This is Sheshanna's house. He's very ill. Let's go in and take a look at him,' Venkata said, and, leaving the handbag by the front door, led me inside to a dark veranda. 'This is Ananthu, Achar's son. He is a professor in Mysore. You know him, don't you?' he said. Adjusting my eyes to the darkness and still musing over Venkata's words, I thought to myself: Look at this Venkata, he is a philosopher as well. If I try to answer him, I'll have to use words and phrases in English, or else, equivalent expressions unfamiliar to him. Somewhat like this:

The frivolous insensitivity to suffering, the stoic resignation of a coward...unauthentic being, escapism, complacency born out of superstition, innocence of the village idiocy...and so on....

If he reads what I have written about him, he will read it only as himself. Simpleton that he is, he is untouched by irony. For the one who has no desire of his own, the constant whirling of the world, the flux, and the changes have no meaning. Before such a non-political being, all my knowledge is futile. He is the direct antithesis of Kissinger. Even for Gandhi, with aspiration came involvement. Wait a minute! This Venkata, who came to me as a story, is developing into an essay! I am being confronted by a consciousness which to me in the beginning was only a subject for writing!

'This is Sheshanna. His son works in Bombay, where, it seems, they make atom bombs. A raging bull, just like you. My son also wants to become like him. He has married a white woman. She visited here. In a sari, and with kumkum on her forehead, she looked like the Mother Goddess, Kali. She asked her father-in-law to go and live with them. But how can this man go? He cannot live without his potato and onion curry. Besides, he likes to lord it over the family. Why would a son who is educated put up with it?' Venkata chattered on as he chopped the areca nut into fine pieces.

Sheshanna started coughing. He coughed as though he was going to run out of breath. Venkata sat him up and made him lean against himself, and, patting his back, held a bowl to his mouth. I thought it was the end of Sheshanna. With his head thrown back and coughing incessantly, he was gasping for breath. Propping his head up, Venkata coaxed him to spit. Sheshanna must have spat blood. Venkata laid him down on the bed and went to the backyard to empty the bowl. 'I'll make you some coffee,' he said when he came back and went into the kitchen. Sheshanna was panting heavily with his mouth wide open, his eyes fluttering. I sat crouched in the dim light that came through a glass tile in the roof, counting the gourds that hung from the ceiling beams. On a rickety cot in the corner, covered in a thin blanket, Sheshanna lay like a corpse. He must have been in the advanced stage of tuberculosis. Most probably Venkata himself was nursing him. That was how Venkata had always been, helpful to others. On our way back from school, if you looked in his schoolbag, you would find medicine bottles for all sorts of people, vials in which to bring snuff for the women who had become secret snuff users, ribbons for young girls, double-edged lice-removing combs, silk threads for the Anantha-worship, decoration tinsel for the Gouri festival, sugar candies from the Mussalman's sweetshop for the sundry children—anything and everything, except school books. Along with his own umbrella, he would be carrying two more tattered ones for repair. His clothes showing patches, a basil leaf in his tuft of hair, he sauntered along the market street as though he owned the place. He would sometimes bring us sour plums.

Venkata brought hot coffee from inside and helped Sheshanna drink it. 'God knows when my eyes will close,' he said and slurped his coffee as Venkata blew on it and held the cup to his lips.

'Nonsense!' Venkata said. 'Why would you die so soon? Suppose the Lord of Death, Yama, were to come to your doorstep riding on his water-buffalo, you are the kind who is quite likely to ask him to wait until you have finished eating your delicious potato and onion curry. And if by chance he tasted it, then instead of taking you away with him he would let you stay right here on earth, so there would be a place on earth where he could go when he is in the mood for a good, tasty curry. However, it would be unlike the God of Death to go back from his rounds empty-handed. So, not wanting to waste a trip, he would ask you to show him someone else to take your place to go with him. You would then send him to this buffoon Venkata who, though younger than you, having played out his buffoonery, is ready to go. Then, if the Lord of Death gets scared away by my wife's sharp tongue, I live. If not, I go."

Sheshanna's face perked up a little. Venkata laid his head on the pillow and got up to leave. 'I'll send you rice-gruel mixed with lentil water; my daughter will bring it to you,' he said and motioned to me to get up.

'Your friend might know my son, Dr Subramanya Shastri. He studied in London and is now an engineer in Bombay, where they make atom bombs. They say he gets three thousand rupees monthly. He lives in a nice bungalow,' said Sheshanna, trying to sit up. Venkata made him lie down and told him to go to sleep. Taking leave of him, I came out of the house.

∽

Unlatching the fence-stile, Venkata let me in first. 'Come and see whom I have brought with me,' he called out to his wife, flaunting me as his shield against her. Rukku, who came out fuming, on seeing me cooled down like a burning log being doused. Wiping her wet hands with the edge of her sari, she now beamed at me. 'Ananthu here insisted on bringing these for you. He wouldn't listen to me,' Venkata said, handing her the bag filled with vegetables. The wrinkles on her face etched by a thousand hardships now eased in a smile of gratitude. A broad stripe of kumkum across her forehead, a champak flower tucked in her greying hair, eyes reddened by the kitchen smoke, Rukku looked short, mere skin and bones. Next, Shakuntala, Gouri, and Ganga appeared. The older girls, who had come of age, wore patched clothes, and had their black hair braided neatly. Glass bangles, plain ear studs, fresh fragrant champak in their hair—that was all their adornment. Seeing me, they beamed bashfully. One girl brought warm water for me to wash my feet with, the other brought a small towel. The youngest daughter, I noticed, held a garland of jasmine flowers which she had been stringing. Outside, while washing my feet, I looked around: there were flowers which I hadn't seen in years. Many kinds of jasmines, roses, chrysanthemums, shoe-flowers, tumbe, parijata, champak, shell-flower, the peacock's pride—it was a lush and water-soaked garden. The water in the well hadn't dried up even though the rains hadn't come.

The house, too, was very orderly. The mud floor had been polished to a shiny dark colour. On it were rangoli patterns made of white flour. Whitewashed walls, gourds hanging from the ceiling beams. An almanac hung by a nail in the wall. Venkata removed his shirt and hung it on another nail. In a corner was a neat pile of rolled-up mattresses. On the door-frame hung a lattice-work made from bits of glass bangles and a garland in cotton, probably from the last Gouri festival. The copper pitcher I was given for washing my feet was brightly polished. Shakuntala brought me a brass cup filled with a cool drink made out of a mixture of rice-water, milk, jaggery, and cardamom seeds. 'I too have two children—still very young, a boy and a girl,' I said. 'Is all well at home?' Rukku enquired. She and Venkata started arguing excitedly as they paced back and forth to the kitchen. He wanted to give me his oil massage and hot bath straight away. She argued that I should bathe and eat first and get my massage and hot bath at night. She won in the end. Venkata followed me to the bathroom.

'Thanks to your being here, I wasn't greeted with the usual ceremonial sixteen-course reception,' he said.

I laughed and started pouring hot water on myself. In the room there was a granite tub for the hot bath after the oil massage. Next to it were cauldrons for hot water, a pot filled with cooling matti leaves, and soap-nut powder in tins. Looking at Venkata's paraphernalia, I became somewhat apprehensive about the evening.

'But why do you make your wife angry?' I asked.

'Why would I make her angry? It just happens. It's the weapon that the Mother Goddess has granted her in order to protect me. You see, somehow this simpleton has to be kept within bounds, the house has to be kept tidy, the children should not be untended, the firewood in the house has to be kept dry. I shouldn't be spending time chattering with anyone I meet. So, she has to scare off all those who take this gullible fool for a ride,' spoke Venkata as he pushed firewood in the kiln.

'Where is your son? I don't see him,' I asked.

'He is hooked on card-playing with his cronies. None of these weapons of mine work on him. If he sees me, he becomes inflamed.'

The futility of your philosophy is confronting you in the person of your son, I wanted to tell him, but didn't. Rather, I looked at him in an accusing way as I poured water on myself. He went on talking as if none of it made any sense:

'He gnashes his teeth that his father doesn't command any respect. But will my nature change? The principal of his college didn't allow him to take the examinations because he hadn't attended classes regularly. Do you know what he did? He waylaid the principal at night and beat him. They say he even robbed him of his money. He pesters me to give him money to start a flour mill in the town. I am down and out. Where am I supposed to come up with the money he wants?'

You poor wretch! You don't understand evil at all, do you? You are like the lotus that blossoms only in stagnant water! I don't think I can stand you even for two days. Stoic that you are, the changing times are not for you. You will go on living like this, scratching when it itches, wallowing in complacency, forever playing the fool. I held myself back from speaking out these thoughts and, feeling both affection and disgust for Venkata, I finished washing myself. After me, Venkata bathed ritualistically, chanting prayer to all the holy rivers and letting the bath water flow out onto a bed of kesuvu leaves. Seeing me eye the kesuvu leaves, he said, 'I'll ask her to make the patrode dish from these leaves for the evening.'

For lunch, Shakuntala had placed a plank for me to sit on and, in front of it, the end part of a flame-dried banana leaf, having drawn a rangoli decoration around it on the floor. Served on the leaf were a variety of mouth-watering pickles made from cured citrus, pappads made from jackfruit, different kinds of fries—I was too shy to ask what they were called—and rice payasa in the corner.

'Nothing special, everything was done in a hurry,' said Rukku and, playing the hostess, eagerly served me dish after dish. There were two kinds of tambulis to go with the rice. There was, just as Venkata had predicted, palya made out of chogate leaves; diluted buttermilk garnished with fresh ginger and coriander, the saru made of water drained from boiling rice and mixed with sour buttermilk and then garnished with spices—I had forgotten its name and hadn't had it since childhood. Venkata sat resting on his hand, with his eyes closed, and ate everything with great relish. The meal was so tasty and light and yet quite filling.

Shakuntala and Gouri, competing with each other, had prepared a bed for me. Just as I was laying myself down for a nap, I heard Rukku calling out, 'Hey, Subba, Subba, come and eat.' Half out of anxiety, half in helpless anger, in the voice of the mother, she appealed to her husband, 'For God's sake, ask Subba to come and eat.'

I too came out with Venkata and looked, but saw only the back of a person in shirt and pants, with shoulder-length hair in the style of the hippies. He was walking away briskly without looking back. Only, his gait was just like his father's. But he was taller than his father and lankier. Venkata, shirtless and just in his dhoti, ran after him. Subba stopped, turned round and swinging his hands menacingly, shouted something at his father. His body contorted like an Ashtavakra, Venkata cringed and pleaded with him. Subba bent down suddenly, looked, and picked up a stone. Venkata began to back off, shielding his face with his hands, still pleading. Subba then walked away briskly. I felt uneasy looking at Rukku who stood there helplessly in anguish for her son. Venkata came back, his face downcast. He saw me.

'Subba is all agitated. He was about to pounce on me like a tiger!' he said quivering in mock fear.

'Can't you stop your clowning at least now? Can't you slap the boy and bring him back? What kind of a father are you?' said Rukku and went inside wiping her eyes. Venkata followed her into the house saying,

'You go and eat. Set food aside for Subba. When he feels hungry he will come home. Where else will he go?' said Venkata and followed his wife. I went and lay down. The little girl, Ganga, was playing with cowrie-shells by herself. Rukku was saying to her husband all that I wanted to say to him myself, only more harshly:

'Just because you don't mind rotting here in this place, would your son, who is of this generation, also like to rot here! A worthless nobody in the eyes of the people! How can the son respect such a father, tell me? You just settle down wherever you go, grinning he-he-he stupidly at people. What should the children look up to you for? Why should people like you have a family at all? God knows how many years it has been since your pension stopped coming. I kill myself trying to manage everything—making banana leaf cups, keeping the house in order, attending to the children. I must prepare special food freshly, three times a day, for that stingy Sheshanna. I send him soft-cooked rice and he says, "Couldn't she have sent some mango pickle? Your mother is mighty close-fisted." As if it is not enough that I break my back here for my own household, I get criticism from this man.

None of us, not even the children, have stepped out of this wretched place even for a day. A village fair, or a cinema, or a visit to another town—what have we seen, tell me? That poor boy, Subba. I make his favourite payasa of rice and black gram, but he roams in the hot sun on an empty stomach like a mad dog. He has gotten so bad as to raise his hand against his own father. I know, someone who doesn't like us has put a spell on him. You are so simple-minded that you don't understand evil things at all….'

As I dozed off listening to the litany of the scolding raining down on him, I lost track of time.

When I opened my eyes, I noticed that Venkata was pacing about me with the bottle of Bhringamalaka oil in his hand, restlessly. I sat up, asking, 'What's all this, maharaaya?' With a mouth full of betel juice, he smiled and said, 'Let's go.' I got up and followed him to the bathroom. It was getting dark. He made me undress completely and tie a piece of cloth over my groin. A roaring fire was heating up the water. There were other cauldrons filled with cold water. He shut the bathroom door and made me sit on the wooden board. He was wearing a towel around his waist and had tucked it between his legs above the knees as if he was about to wade into a pond. He had wrapped another towel around his head. Dipping the sacred grass in the oil and touching my forehead and the top of my head with it, he muttered the ritual chants. Putting a little oil on his palm, he smelled it. He spat out the betel-mixed saliva and, beginning with the feet, he applied oil all over my body. Then he sat me on a stool and placed my feet in a bowl of castor oil. 'The coolness of the oil will gradually climb up until it is absorbed by your brain,' he explained. In his cupped palms he scooped up the Bhringamalaka oil and poured it on my head. Invoking the Mother Goddess, he rapped on my head with both hands as though he were beating a drum. 'I am now talking to your head. Doesn't it sound like a mrudanga?' he asked, varying the rhythm and the beat.

'Hm,' I said, out of politeness. All that worship-like attention was making me uncomfortable. From the way he was beating the drum on my head, I suspected that he could even be dancing at my back.

'From your head this rhythm will flow all the way down to your navel,' he said. 'The sound will raise the six coils of your Kundalini. Though I don't know much about such things, I know that it works,' he said breathing fast. I was now certain that he was dancing. I thought of a ghatam player performing in a music concert.

The ritual that followed the drum-playing consisted of many rhythmic actions which were accompanied by a running commentary by Venkata in his soft, quivering, gasping voice. My backside was getting roasted because of the fire. He circumambulated my head as if he were worshipping it. In various rhythmic combinations, his agile fingers worked all around my head—tickling, pinching, plucking, pressing, patting, pulling, pushing, and scratching. 'Now your head will talk to me on its own,' he said wiping the sweat off his face with a towel and getting ready for the second stage of the ritual oil massages and the raising of the Kundalini. As I wondered whether the fingers in his hand were twenty or a hundred, the voice of his running commentary was assuming the tone of an incantation, rhythmically rising and falling according to the need, thus:

'Here we go, Ananthu, Ananthu, entering the forest, entering the forest.... In the forest there is a tree, a tree.... On the tree, a parrot, a parrot, a green parrot, a green parrot in the green leaves. In the hooked beak of the green parrot...a red fruit, a red, red fruit in the hooked beak of the green parrot....

'Down there, a cool bower...a cool, cool, cool bower...the fragrant bower, fragrant with the yellow kedige.... Watch, watch...watch how it's bursting. Watch the rough, long, thorny-edged, green leaf...inside the green leaf, soft yellow...smooth yellow, fragrant yellow, powdery yellow, slippery yellow, slinky yellow.... Walk on, walk softly, softly walk.... Watch. Here is basari, here jack fruit tree...this is nandi...this is muttuga...this is mango. This is ranja...this is banyan...look at the roots that grow downwards from its branches to reach the ground... look at the nail at the tip of the root...the roots are the matted hair of a rishi....

The blue sky above...scattered blue, lurking blue, teasing blue, irritating blue...the vast open space below...walk on....

Look at the little sapling...on the sapling, a leaf...on the leaf something springing...leaping...like this one day, long, long, ago, on your way to school, how it sprang! You dropped the books and stood watching...transfixed…watching the sun's stallion…watching its crooked legs, watching its humped back…here, there, here and there, there, here….

The little horse, tiny horse. You stood watching how the sun rode on its back….

You watched how the sun rode on the tiny green horse…. He, the mighty sun, this tiny horse, green-coloured, tiny horse, leaping lightly. On its humped back sat the mighty sun, sitting lightly, sitting invisibly on it, shimmering in a corner.

Look where the sun shimmers, shimmers in its green feelers… shimmers in the pupil of its eye…shimmers from the cloud's edge, tumbles, slips, breaks into pieces…makes shadows, colours…sets, rises, burns….

See the wide open space, vast space… Above, the burning sun. Carrying him lightly on its back and hopping, all along in the open field, is the sun's stallion…see its saddleless swagger…its crooked legs… its stiff tail…its feelers groping for the world…. It is hopping from leaf to leaf…see the whole of it…see the parts of it…the eyes green…a heap of green…frothing green…. Listen…listen to the stallion of the sun:

What horse am I? What man are you? I am you, you are me.

Brother Ananthu…hopping Ananthu…the one carrying the sun on his back…. Now let go, let go, let go the fury, gone…let go the frowning, let go the ego…. Gone. Greed for the gold, bragging of the birth, all gone…be gone, evil spell…wicked spell…father's spell… mother's spell…priest's spell…shaman's spell…prostitute's spell… paramour's spell…spell of death…spell of vulva… spell of the street… spell of books… all spells, be gone.

All that remains is the stallion of the sun…. You are the stallion… you are the Sun….

In this manner, as the changing tempo of his speech kept up with the changing rhythm, a thousand fingers kept dancing on my head. My eyes started burning because of the dripping oil. Venkata noticed it and wiped it off with the towel which was wrapped around his head.

Eagerly, he asked: 'Ananthu, are you beginning to see the moonlight yet?'

I said, 'Hm,' not wishing to disappoint him. He was drenched in perspiration. Sitting still, naked before him, I became self-conscious.

'This time, you only got a glimpse. Wait till I give you my next oil massage; you will see the real moonlight,' he said inhaling the snuff.

I was wrong. This simpleton Venkata, too, is a scheming politician. What a manipulator! He was trying to alter my very 'being'. He made me sit in the tub filled with hot water and told me to rub myself under the armpits and between the legs. He poured the cool matti essence on my head and vigorously rubbed my head with soap-nut powder. Scooping up water in a pitcher, he poured it on me with force. The steam and the boiling water had baked my body into a ripe red mango. I was too weak to dry myself. He dried me himself. Giving me a cool drink made of jaggery, he smeared my forehead with some soot from the bottom of the cauldron. Then bringing me inside the house, he made me lie down on the bed and covered me with all the blankets that were in the house and said, 'You have to sweat it out.' In a while I was all soaked as if I had taken the bath once again. He dried me again and laid me on the grass mat. He brought me steaming coffee. After drinking it I felt drowsy. In the kitchen Rukku was crying and making patrode.

When I woke up, I heard Venkata pleading with his wife, 'Please make some rice-gruel for Sheshanna. I'll quickly go over and feed it to him.'

'They say his son sends him five hundred rupees every month. But he doesn't pay you a single paisa. You don't care about your own son, yet you expect me to care about that miser. What is it to me whether the old geezer lives or dies?' Rukku screamed. Still, Venkata got Shakuntala to make some rice-gruel and took it to Sheshanna's house.

I had sat up in the bed now. Rukku came and stood before me and started to cry. According to her, Subba was under the influence of inauspicious stars. He wanted to go to Bangalore or Mysore to become a mechanic. Why shouldn't he also prosper like Sheshanna's son? He didn't lack brains. At least, as a favour to my childhood friend, I should take his son with me to Mysore and set him up there in some job.

I was afraid. If I took him home with me, my wife would not put up with his antics. Still I promised Rukku that I would do something for him. I'll get him a room on rent somewhere, I told myself. My assurance made Rukku so happy that it brightened up the whole house. Gouri and the little girl, Ganga, too pranced around. When Venkata returned, he saw the changed mood of his household, and he too became cheerful. But he didn't know of the promise I had made his wife. As if he were enacting a scene from a comic drama, he acted out a past instance of Sheshanna's stinginess, without showing the least bitterness toward him:

Venkata had just then bought some medicine for him. Again and again, Sheshanna counted the change Venkata had brought back. Seeing Venkata mimic Sheshanna's cough and count the coins with shaky hands, even Rukku laughed. When Sheshanna started counting once again, Venkata asked him, 'Anything wrong?'

'This quarter seems all worn off,' said Sheshanna.

'It's a good coin. It'll still pass,' said Venkata.

'But why take a chance? Go back and pass this off, and bring me another quarter, will you?' Venkata imitated Sheshanna's feeble, raspy voice.

'Do you want me to go right now?' asked Venkata, having just walked three miles from the town. 'Is there anything else you want done in the town that cannot wait till another day?' Sheshanna's ashen face then showed supreme satisfaction.

'I knew that he wouldn't have been able to sleep. So, I gave him a different quarter I had with me,' said Venkata and took out from his pocket the worn quarter he had been unable to pass off. 'When he dies, throw it on his corpse,' Rukku said angrily, and got up and went inside to get supper ready.

∽

Since childhood, I was very fond of patrode. But now something had happened which would make it impossible for me to eat Rukku's patrode. I couldn't help noticing that Rukku was crying uncontrollably while Shakuntala and Venkata tried to unsuccessfully to console her. Soon I learned what had happened: she wanted to serve me the kheeru in the silver cup. So, she went to look for it in the brass trunk in which she kept all her dowry items she had brought with her when she got married. When she opened the trunk, what did she find?

The gorochana kept for her future grandchildren, some nutmeg, dried ginger, kasturi pills, a rudrakshi berry, dried pomegranate shell, a block of sandalwood, soap-nut for washing jewellery—everything else was gone. All those pieces of jewellery which, despite their being poor, had been saved from being pawned away because Rukku had the foresight to put them away for the girls when they would get married—earrings, ear chains, a four-strand necklace, four bracelets, a waistband, an ornament of floral design for the braid, a nose ring, a pair of anklets, a coral chain, two silver bowls, three silver cups, a silver cup used for puja, a silver pitcher, a silver spoon, silver boxes for kumkum and turmeric powder. Everything that had been put away, wrapped in a piece of an old silk sari after the Gouri festival, had now disappeared.

Venkata had been pressing me to eat the patrode pretending that nothing had happened, when Ganga, the youngest girl, came running and told her father anxiously: 'Mother is crying. Subba has stolen all the jewellery. Everything was there when Mother opened the trunk on Friday to get the pomegranate shell to make medicine for your stomach pain. You remember, the day before yesterday, Mother went to the pond to wash clothes and Shaku and Gouri also went with her? That same day Subba came to me and handing me a wet strip of banana fibre, told me: 'Go, string some jasmine flowers, I'll sell them for you in the town and bring you some money.' I went to the backyard wondering why Brother was being so nice to me that day. When I got back, he was doing something in the room. I told myself that he must have shut himself in the room to smoke a bidi.'

Neither Venkata, nor Shaku, nor Gouri spoke. Shaku went inside to comfort her mother. 'We will find it. Where will it go? He must have pawned it. You eat,' Venkata said urging patrode on me. He finished eating quickly. After I went through the motions of eating, I went out and sat down on the front steps. Thinking 'what hardships for this innocent creature!' I looked around me for any sign of Subba. From where I was sitting, I could see one or two houses in the distance, a temple and a trail made by the walking feet, another path leading to town. Further on, a green hill. The air was permeated with the fragrance of yellow-stemmed parijata. All over the front-yard of the house were flowering plants. The moonlight I had failed to see in

Venkata's massage had now filled the flower garden. I could hear Rukku crying and whimpering inside: 'Oh! How am I going to see my daughters married? Why do you make my womb burn like this?'

Venkata came out and stood near me. 'Ah, the moonlight!' he said. Probably he was seeking me out while waiting for his wife's sorrow to subside. Maybe he also felt uneasy thinking that I might be distressed. It pained me to see my friend so uncharacteristically quiet. 'Come, sit,' I said.

'Nice fragrance of parijata, isn't it?' he said. I smiled and motioned to him to keep quiet. I am not good at comforting others. Still, I went inside and urged Rukkamma to eat. She burst out weeping in front of me. When I came out, Venkata, who was pacing to-and-fro in the garden, said, 'You know, the garden is our Ganga's delight.'

Far into the night, nobody seemed able to sleep. It is possible, I thought, for anyone to be faced with a situation like Subba's. Anyone but an utterly harmless person like Venkata. Who knows what would have become of me if I too had to remain rotting in this village? Because I dared to defy my father and reject the ways of my family, I was able to grow and become what I am today. But how is it that such impulse is brought on in this family too? Venkata seemed cowed by his son. His clowning, his massaging, his altruism—nothing seemed to be of any use here. This very moon, this plant, this tree, these birds have nurtured a nature like Venkata's as well as inexplicable violence like Subba's. Can Venkata's nature take it, stomach it? Or just spit it out? If so, the clowning of an escapist is pitiable, discomforting. All the same, I couldn't just brush aside my childhood friend who had just begun to resuscitate my waning love for humankind. The image of Venkata standing, like an Ashtavakra, with folded hands, cowering before his menacing son was still troubling me. With a stone in his raised hand, Subba had seemed like a barbaric caveman whose indomitable brute strength was about to explode. This barbaric defiance and denial seemed the very source and vital energy for the creation of nuclear weapons and poison gas. It was born, of course, out of the rejection of Venkata's narrow and insipid world. I know it, for I, too, had kicked my parents. In a state like Venkata's, one can only blossom like the parijata and then wither away. In that state, there is no movement.

My imagination had probably exaggerated it when, before falling asleep, I thought of Subba as the image of movement. 'What is so heroic about stealing?' I later tried to temper my thoughts. But, what I saw, just before daybreak, when everyone else was asleep and, outside, one could clearly see everything dew-drenched under the starlit sky, still weighs me down.

Hearing some sound from the garden, I got up and went out to see. It was the sound of a tree being cut down. 'Who's there?' I called out and was about to go down the front steps when Subba, raising a scythe in his hand, in the dim light, cried out, 'If you come near, I'll cut you to pieces.' I stood still. With his hair dishevelled, teeth gritted, cutting down the parijata tree in the morning twilight, he appeared like a rakshasa to me. He had already cut the flowering plants and shrubs down to the ground. Only the rugged and knotty parijata tree had still withstood the sweeping strokes of the scythe. Venkata, who had got up after me, ran toward Subba. Subba raised the scythe and would have brought it down upon his father had Venkata not ducked in time and ran back calling out 'Mother Goddess!' I tried to restrain Rukku who squirmed in my clasp and shouted to her son, 'Come, cut me up! Kill me! I gave birth to poison and I'll die by swallowing it!' Freeing herself, she ran and stood before Subba while her daughters tried to stop her. 'Don't! Don't you dare me! I'll chop your head off!' said Subba raising the scythe. We all stood there, eyes closed, frozen. When I opened my eyes fearing the worst, Subba had jerked out the hand that held the scythe from his mother's grip, and, shouting curses, was walking away past the fence-stile. He walked briskly towards the town and was soon out of sight. Rukku still stood with eyes closed as if she expected the scythe to fall on her at any moment. Venkata dragged her by the hand into the house. Seeing the garden all razed to the ground, Ganga began to cry and, looking at her, her elder sisters cried too. I sat down on the mound of earth, my senses all numbed. No comforting words were left in me. But I, who thought that all that had happened had left Venkata devastated, was in for a surprise in the morning.

∽

No matter who dies or how dear the person, life's routines go on, don't they? Even though the house looked as if there had been a death in the family, Shakuntala had made the morning coffee. I cleaned my teeth with the ashes of paddy husk. Having had his early morning bath, Venkata was making the sandal paste for worship at the riverside temple. Only Rukku had taken to bed. Gouri hurriedly milked the cows and sent them out of the shed, for the cowherd boy was already there to take them for grazing. I sensed that something inside Venkata had died, and not being able to look him in the eye, I came out and sat on the front stoop but couldn't bear the sight of the ruined garden and so went around to the backyard and stood there under the pomegranate tree.

Near the fence stood Venkata in his bandy-leg posture, with no clothes on except his loincloth. What is he doing there, standing and looking so engrossed? I wondered. He couldn't have gone out to relieve himself, because I didn't see his sacred thread over his ear. Besides, he had already finished his morning ablutions and done his morning prayers. I watched him, standing crookedly by the hedge, motionless, almost naked, engrossed. The green fence-hedge facing him was tall, so he couldn't be seeing anything over it. I walked towards him softly without making any sound, and stood behind him. Still, Venkata didn't know I was there. Curious to find out what he was looking at, I followed the direction of his gaze, peering at the hedge and scanning its leaves and flowers and everything else that came in the range of my vision. What came in sight was a grasshopper. For a moment, watching my friend, simpleton Venkata, looking fascinatedly at this humped, bent-legged, gaunt, green, an angular, Ashtavakra-like insect, I was amused; but only for a moment. Pressing down its bent legs, the grasshopper sprang and hopped away. The moment it sprang, Venkata's half-shaved head shook as if he just came out of a trance, which I was glad to notice. Turning around and seeing me there behind him, he beamed an innocent smile and said, 'Stallion of the sun!' I looked into his fascinated eyes and my mouth fell open.

'Stallion of the sun!' I said.

Translated by Narayan Hegde

JARATKARU

Jaratkaru, a great sage, descendant of Bhrigu and father of Astika, had taken a vow of lifelong celibacy. One day, on seeing the spirits of his ancestors hanging upside down in a cave, he asked, 'Who are you? What is the reason for your hanging upside down?' His ancestors replied, 'How shall we explain our predicament? A descendant of ours, named Jaratkaru, has been born into this world. Because he has remained unmarried and therefore childless, we are in this state.' Jaratkaru said to them, 'I am that Jaratkaru. I will release you from the sorry state you are in. But, I will marry only that girl whose name is the same as mine.' To this the ancestral spirits agreed. Jaratkaru then went looking for the girl. He came to know that the younger sister of Vasuki, the king of the serpents, was named Jaratkaru, so he went to him and asked for his sister's hand. Vasuki, the serpent-king, agreed and gave his sister in marriage to Jaratkaru. Then Jaratkaru brought her with him to his hermitage.

One evening, Jaratkaru was asleep. Fearing that it was getting late for her husband's evening prayers, she hesitantly woke him up. On waking up, the sage got angry with his wife that she had hindered his sleep and insulted him with her carelessness. Then, without paying any heed to the entreaties of his pregnant wife, he left her and went to the forest to take up asceticism. There, having emaciated himself in body through the practice of austerities, he came to be called Jaratkaru. His wife gave birth to a son named Astika.

I

Thimmappa would become incensed that his mother, her shaven head covered in her widow's red sari, would make the rounds of the neighbourhood talking about her son's birth as if it were a holy event because, according to her, she had conceived him through the blessings of Thimmappa, the God of Tirupati, which is why he was named after him. When he was about ten years old, his father already dead, his mother had taken him to Tirupati. There, she had made him go through a grand ceremony of wearing the sacred thread, and after making him take three dips in the holy pond whose water cleansed the sins of anyone bathing in it, had made him stand briefly in obeisance before the dazzlingly decorated idol of the god—which had made him puke. Also, on his way to Tirupati, something else had happened—an experience which made him feel as if his very body had undergone a transformation.

Lying under the seat of the crowded train, he was half asleep and quite uncomfortable. Like him, there were many others—women, children, old people—who were lying motionless in various stages of sleep. The rancid smell of the leftover food which the travellers had brought with them in baskets and which was now going bad, the odour of their bodies sweating in the sweltering heat, the stench of the children's urine—in the midst of this unbearable putridness, he felt a hand groping him eagerly and it felt good. He had no way of knowing whose hand it was because of the position in which two women—one old and the other young—were sleeping next to him. The more excited he became by the ministerings of this anonymous hand, the more busy the hand got, creating in him a new sensation he was hitherto unaware of. Unable to bear the excitement any longer, he stood up.

The sun was just rising. Suddenly, a bald, tall hill in the distance came into view through the train window. A red ball of a sun atop the hill. Thimmappa at that moment lost his sense of where he was. Everything before him went dark. The same hand was caressing his leg in a tickling manner, pinching it here and there softly. Thimmappa shook his leg off and looked for his mother. In a corner of the train, her sari pulled over her shaven head, her prayer-beads in her hand, she sat meditating. Like a turtle hidden snug in its shell, she had made herself a little room in the corner. Maintaining her ritual purity and appearing immaculately clean even there in the train, she motioned to him to come near her. She made him sit next to her and gave him beaten rice to eat. Though hungry, he didn't feel like eating; he felt unclean.

II

According to those who admire his writing, Thimmappa is tormented by the notion that nothing has any meaning because God probably does not exist. At least, that is the meaning they find in his cold, unemotional writing which, with hardly an oblique glance at the reader, only stares into nothingness.

Thimmappa has no memory of seeing his father. He grew up looking at a father who meant to him little more than a fading picture—of a man in a turban and an embroidered shawl—which hung in the middle hall of the house. As he grew more and more distant from a mother who brought him up—while herself living on one meal of rice-gruel that she cooked daily, fasting so rigorously on the eleventh day of the month that she wouldn't even swallow saliva, and observing her ritual cleanliness—his verbal creations were turning into sculpture-like expressions—harsh and self-luminous.

When he was a child, the only time he felt his mother to be a woman was when she remained outside the main part of the house during her monthly periods. In the ten years since she stopped getting her periods, he grew to reject her ardent but silently wilting fervour at making God an actuality for her son through the rigorous austerities of her widowhood. He had gradually lost both his childhood affection and, later, the feeling of indignation he had for his mother.

His mother knew that because of the rigours of her orthodoxy as a widow, no educated girl that might be attracted to Thimmappa would agree to live in the house. Thimmappa didn't want to get married either. But this rugged hermit put all her family gold and jewellery in a big iron trunk, put a lock on it, and guarded it like an old serpent guarding a treasure. She would do her daily prayers sitting right beside the iron trunk. A portrait of the saint Raghavendra Swamy hung on the wall. In the corner were the grass-mat she used for sleeping and deer-skin covering.

She kept guard over the jewellery for the sake of her future daughter-in-law. The priest who saw her son's horoscope had predicted that in only a few years the present troublesome period of his life would be over and his prospects would be auspicious. According to him, her son's main trouble was his desire to renounce the world and become an ascetic. Her son, who drank himself stiff daily, who didn't seek any government employment or anyone's favour, who didn't hanker after anything, didn't show affection to anyone, who ate forbidden food and drank forbidden drinks in the company of prostitutes, seemed to her a pitiable child that had lost its way on the path to sainthood. She, the daughter of a Sanskrit scholar from Udupi, was convinced that her son's verbal creations were nothing but the supplications of a defiant devotee.

III

There was hardly anyone who did not feel humiliated by Thimmappa's cruel insights. Stripping down mercilessly all those whom we would consider noble, refined, and progressive, he would expose the inferno of self-love in which they lived. Not that he enjoyed exposing people thus. His creations were wrought like the musical brass that gave no impure note; they would resonate only when polished bright.

Was it hell which Thimmappa had created for others? The question bothered his admirers. There were also those who criticized his writings as sick. In order to convince themselves, they told each other: 'Consider the income that this Thimmappa has! Doing nothing, he gets at least ten thousand rupees monthly from his mother's ancestral property. This was the fortune amassed by her grandfather when he was the diwan, chief minister, of the princely state. If Thimmappa had to work for a living, then his melancholy, his infernal vision, and his pitiless insights—all would have had a historical reality.'

To those who like him, he resonates differently. In the dark cavern of his verbal patterns there flashes suddenly a message of divine light. The calf of a water-buffalo prances about in the morning aimlessly, with its tail turned up. Distorted faces smile Buddha-like. Flowers appear dilated as in a dream.

IV

In his house there is a girl who cooks for him and waits on him. But his mother, who sits praying curled up next to her iron trunk, eats only the rice-gruel cooked by herself. For her cooking, she has a separate hearth of firewood. The water she uses comes from a well in the backyard. For Thimmappa's convenience, there are gadgets such as a refrigerator and gas stove. A room in a corner of the large compound of their bungalow has been given to the girl who cooks and her mother for their use. His mother provides food, clothing, and shelter to both.

The girl, called Kamala, has studied up to the Secondary School Leaving Certificate. She types all of Thimmappa's writings herself. She dusts his books and arranges them neatly; washes his clothes bright and irons them. Kamala adores him. If he vomits after getting drunk, she cleans it up without feeling disgust. She wears the two saris she owns alternately, taking care to hide the torn parts. Always she appears spotlessly clean. Applying coconut oil lightly to her dark hair, she combs it and wears it in a loose braid. She wears either jasmine or champak or some other flowers in her hair always, and through their fragrance, gives a hint of what has been flowering in their large compound. Full lips, a nose on the pudgy side, cheeks filled out; eyes like those of a deer, and oil-dark complexion—Thimmappa thinks that the girl's body is as nimble as her mind is dull. She is not an object that lends itself to be pitilessly analysed by his perceptive mind. But he has realized that just as he should keep a distance from his mother, for his own stability, it is necessary to reject the girl's worshipping of him as well. Through this stability alone and by rejecting the comfort derived from false devotion, by rejecting the insincerity of pretentious love as well as the domestic security it offers, could he hope to perceive the reality of human beings living in the hell of self-love.

Still, his curiosity got the better of him one day. His sexual desire, which had lost its keenness in the company of prostitutes, was now aroused because he was alone with Kamala and his mother had gone out having announced within his hearing that she was going to the shrine of the saint Raghavendra Swamy and would return only after finishing the night prayer. Thimmappa, who was writing at his desk, lit a cigarette and noticed Kamala who stood there in his room dusting the books. He got up, stood facing her, asked her dispassionately to have sex with him. Her head bowed, she consented. When he started to undress her, she felt shy and became anxious that her bashfulness might stop him from going any further. Lying with him, she even appeared to be enjoying it. Afterwards, when he offered her money, she turned pale with fear and started crying.

Thimmappa had not expected this. He felt so disgusted his hair stood on end. It scared him because in the world of stark reality which he was pursuing so relentlessly there was no place for what he had felt just now. After this incident, Kamala too, like his devout mother, seemed to him to be eager to make him see the reality of God. Seeing the possibility of himself becoming drawn into the web of life, mired in self-love, forever conceiving, forever giving birth, he became perplexed.

When the body craved, he went back to the streets where he could drink, eat, and seek gratification of his urges while at the same time feeling disgusted about it. It would be now more than two months since he started coming home after having gotten rid of the urges, all spent so that he wouldn't be attracted to Kamala any longer.

V

Again today, after sleeping in the dark with some woman as if it meant nothing and gulping down a glass of whisky, he sat in the car smoking a cigarette and thinking why he had done this. Isn't it because my writings stand apart from me and are therefore thought to be greater than myself? Yet, it's only the self-haters who are also self-lovers whom these creations impress. Today he felt more disgusted than ever about all this stuff that came out of his self-stimulation. He thought that the prostitute who immersed herself in her calling, just like his mother who had been withering away for the sake of God, was in a higher state of purity.

Next to where he had stopped the car was a city trash bin into which all kinds of things—broken bangles worn by the prostitutes, discarded sanitary napkins, used condoms, and plastic pieces—had been dumped. Expecting to find something useful even there, some dishevelled beggar-women were picking and sorting the trash with their hands. Thimmappa felt like vomiting. It was the fear, he thought, that desire for women and devotion to God would make him forget himself which had caused him to stand apart from everything and to write like this.

On the seat of the car there was a notebook that contained his recent pieces. He had suffered much agony writing them. The writings were born out of his need to express all his emotions fully and uninhibitedly, which he intensely experienced and hated at the same time. He threw the notebook with those writings exploring the Jaratkaru-state of man into the trash bin. The cold hatred in those writings was all a pretension and so the trash bin was to be their natural destination. He wished to live without having to create, shining like a diamond, unto himself. With that thought he felt light and drove home.

VI

Inside the compound of his house were many varieties of flowers his mother had cultivated with great care: champak, evening-jasmine, parijata, hibiscus, bilva, tumbe, round jasmine, needle-jasmine, ratnagandhi, and nanja. Many of these flowers were used for decorating the household deity as part of her daily worship. Some went to decorate Kamala's braided hair and to the shrine of the saint Raghavendra Swamy. What was left over would be distributed among neighbours as offerings for their deities.

The diwan's bungalow, its walls coated with lime, had become dilapidated over the last hundred years. All around it were haphazardly scattered, crowded, box-like dwelling places built by his mother for rental income. The domestic problems of those tenants, their struggles, their love intrigues, their pettiness—which Thimmappa as a child had heard about from his rigidly orthodox mother who herself remained aloof from such things—became the material for his writing. The very rental income from those struggling and grumbling tenants also became the wealth that enabled him to be brought up in comfort all this time. But now nothing in the compound, except the trees and the birds that visited them, held any interest for him. Like those familiar tired-looking faces in the compound, his creations too were becoming lustreless.

Wondering why there was still light in Mother's room though it was past midnight, Thimmappa unlocked the door and let himself into the house. Kamala came out of Mother's room and stood with tears in her eyes. She seemed frightened. Thinking his breath might smell of liquor and garlic, Thimmappa lit a cigarette at a distance from her and asked, 'What's the matter?'

'Mother's speech has stopped. She is waiting for you,' said Kamala holding out a copper vessel in her hand for him to take. It contained holy Ganga water meant for the dying person to drink. The fresh tulasi leaf which was stuck with sandalwood paste to the outside of the vessel meant that his mother had worshipped the holy water just that morning.

Thimmappa threw his cigarette to the floor and stamped it out. He didn't touch the vessel that was being held out for him. He went straight to the bathroom and cleaned his teeth with the ashes of rice husk which his mother used. When he was a young boy, she used to clean his teeth herself with the mixture of camphor and the ashes of rice husk. She used to clean him—armpits, behind the ears, the groin—all over with a mixture of lentil flour and soap-nut.

From the water tub he scooped up cold water in a copper pail and poured it on himself. Shivering from the cold, he dried himself. Then he went into his room, put on the red silk cloth worn on holy occasions, a cloth he had with him since childhood, and entered his mother's room. For a few years after he started wearing the sacred thread, his mother wouldn't let him eat food unless he removed his shirt and wore this silk cloth. It was now faded and torn in places. He took the vessel containing Ganga water from Kamala and sat down on the floor near his mother. Knowing she was nearing her death, she must have laid herself down on the bare floor beneath the portrait of the saint, Raghavendra Swamy; or Kamala must have helped her lie down. She had grown so weak and emaciated.

Her breathing was so heavy that it sounded as if a log was being sawed. He had not imagined that his mother, who, for the sake of making him realize God, had allowed her youth to wither away, had disfigured herself, and had been waiting in her old age to fall to the ground, would have any life force left in her for death to destroy. Exhausted as she was, she looked as if she was holding on to life just to see him. Thimmappa, who had not addressed his mother directly in years, now called out to her, 'Amma'. Half-opening her eyes, she stretched out her hand with difficulty. He was embarrassed at the thought that Kamala saw him holding his mother's hand. He brought the vessel containing the holy water near her mouth. Mother stretched out her other hand and held Kamala's hand in it. With just her eyes she appealed to Thimmappa to take Kamala's hand. Apprehensive about all this display, he took Kamala's hand in his left hand and with his right hand tilted the vessel to pour holy water into his mother's mouth. Opening her mouth three times, his mother swallowed the holy water and died. Kamala closed her eyes, folded up the legs. She made wick lamps out of the split halves of a coconut and placed one each at the head and the foot of the dead body. Applying oil to the big toe, her eyes pleaded with Thimmappa also to do that. She put grains of rice in the dead person's mouth and requested Thimmappa to do the same. Embarrassed that Kamala's sorrow, which she was suppressing silently through these rituals, might make him cry, Thimmappa went into his room and lit a cigarette.

Now, Kamala began to cry. She cried loud enough to be heard by her aged mother. Her mother came running; she beat the ground with her hands and cried so loudly that the neighbours heard her. The neighbours came running and in turn, with their crying, caused people to gather out in the street. They all started praising his mother: her religiosity, her rigorous practice of ritual cleanliness, her knowledge of Sanskrit lore, her helpfulness to others, her pride in her family, her love for plants and trees, and how proud she was of her son's fame, having brought him up all by herself. While people were doing their duty thus by praising his mother before him, Thimmappa sat attempting within himself to become hard and serene.

VII

The events that ensued should not be taken to mean that they offered the solution to the predicament of Thimmappa's Jaratkaru state. In his writings, Thimmappa tried to stress unsuccessfully that the alternative to the predicament of a Jaratkaru state would be the compassion which the Buddha attained on realizing that life itself is sorrowful. Whether in the disgust he felt at Tirupati, or in challenging his mother's harsh asceticism, or in deliberately choosing to associate himself with the sordid in order to reject the superficiality of genteel life, he had come to the realization that real self-awareness is not attainable merely through his verbal creations out of these reactions. Therefore, all one could say for now was that, perplexed by the events that followed, he mellowed.

Two days after his mother was cremated, Kamala came to him in the morning and seemed as if she wanted to tell him something but hesitated. Without the usual flowers decorating her hair, she looked like an ascetic in mourning. Thimmappa was smoking cigarettes and feeling disgusted with the words that were refusing to take shape within himself and with those trashy words that did take shape. Looking up towards Kamala, he asked 'What is it?'

'Mother wrote a letter to you and asked me to give it to you after her death,' Kamala said with tears brimming in her eyes. Thimmappa said nothing, but waited for her to give him the letter. Kamala said that it had been a month since the letter was written. He told her to bring the letter; she did not move, but gave him the key. Thimmappa went into his mother's room and opened the big iron trunk which was secured, in the old style, with metal straps.

The trunk was filled with old-fashioned heavy silk saris from the time when her husband was still living: the kind of saris used to decorate the images of goddesses Madurai Meenakshi or Kolluru Mookambike. The saris gave out a smell of dried kedige flowers which used to be supplied to Mother by a man from their ancestral village. In a corner of the trunk was a brass box brought from Kerala during his great-grandfather's time. It contained several things: a piece of baje that cured many of his illnesses when he was a child, nutmeg, gorochana, kasturi, a saligram like blackberry reputed to be from the time of the Vijayanagara empire, the paste made from which could be taken thrice daily as medicine. Thimmappa had seen people from the neighbourhood as well as from his ancestral village come to his mother in emergencies to ask for this berry which was considered a panacea for all illnesses. In addition to these medicines, the box contained his waistband and a pair of earrings, both made of gold. Another sandalwood box had in it jewellery Mother had been saving for her future daughter-in-law, all the time guarding it like a serpent. Thimmappa picked up the letter smeared with turmeric paste and placed on top of the sandalwood box and started reading it:

'Blessings on you, my son! May you live for ever! The contents of this document penned by me in my own hand on this eleventh day of the month of Kaartika in the year Prajotpatti are to be carried out by you when by the grace of God I am dead. As my son, you are to perform all the funeral rites upon my death. Or else, there will be no salvation for you. It is not important that you believe in the rites performed for the mother who gave birth to you. Who knows, you may even be inspired by our saint Raghavendra Swamy into believing. Even otherwise, the rites must be performed. Moreover, the present inauspicious period of your life is about to end. By the grace of God, daughter Kamala, may she live for ever, is carrying your child in her womb. I decree that all my property, movable as well as immovable, which I have inherited from my grandfather shall go to that child. From the time the child is born, until it grows into adulthood by the grace of God, Kamala shall manage the property on the child's behalf. She shall take care of you in every manner that would be pleasing to you. I am writing all this down as commanded to me by the saint Raghavendra Swamy who appeared in my dream. The Saint who knows the past, the present, and the future has assured me that you will carry this out. I give my blessings to you whom I conceived by the grace of God Venkateswara, and to daughter Kamala, and to the child about to be born. May you be granted long life, fortune, and happiness. In God, your mother, Rukminiyamma.'

Thimmappa put the letter in his pocket and came out of the room. He went into the kitchen and stood before Kamala with a questioning look on his face. He understood just by looking at her face that she didn't know what was written in that letter. Still, he asked:

'Did Mother tell you what she wrote here?'

She shook her head to indicate 'no' and, her eyes filled with tears, she bowed her head. With the loose end of her sari, she tried to suppress a sob.

'How many months?'

Kamala shyly held up three fingers roughened by washing dishes. She pulled the edge of her sari over her shoulders and stood there bashfully scratching the ground with her big toe. 'How did mother come to know?' Thimmappa's voice had become gruff without his knowing it.

But there was no need for Kamala to explain. For some time now, Kamala had not sat out and sent her mother to take her place in the kitchen as she used to do every month when she would have her period. Instead, she had gone to the kitchen without missing a day the whole month. This had not escaped the sharp eyes of Thimmappa's mother who had guessed the reason. Thimmappa became uncomfortable thinking that Kamala, who stood before him looking guilty, might break down any moment. He went into his room and sat at his writing desk trembling. The sudden thought that came to his mind made him feel disgusted at himself. For a moment, he had wanted to tear up his mother's letter, have Kamala's pregnancy aborted, and give her a lakh or two as well as all of Mother's jewellery and thereby set himself free. The next moment, he realized he had himself become the true picture of the man whose self-loving, loveless condition he had been exposing. Even if, in his self-hatred, he obeyed his mother's commands faithfully, he would still be unchanged because those desires in him were inborn. Disconcerted by this realization, without telling Kamala anything, he got into the car, went to a lawyer of his acquaintance and asked him to get his mother's letter registered as a legal document. He brought back with him a photocopy of the letter. He saw that his coming back home so early had pleased Kamala and that in her happiness she was getting ready to make coffee for him.

'Don't make coffee for me. Get me a glass of brandy,' he said. Showing her which glass to use for which brandy, he poured some brandy into a glass himself and gulped it down. 'Here,' he said to Kamala, giving her his mother's letter. Kamala who stood there demurely, her big eyes showing no expectation at all in them, took the letter in a shaky hand. Seeing that she was hesitating to read it, he said, 'Go to Mother's room and read it there.'

VIII

The entire community took it upon itself to conduct the funeral rites for Mother. The old family barber, who used to shave Mother's head, came and established himself in the courtyard as someone who had a role to play in the ritual. He was followed by the Brahmin who supplied the cow to be given away in charity, another who prepared the paraphernalia such as the sacred grass, sesame seeds, etc., required for the ritual, as well as the dedicated Brahmins with courage to become the recipients of the inauspicious gift to be given at the funeral. Ritually alternating the position of the sacred thread he had worn as required of him, he went along performing all the rites necessary for Mother's salvation. All his ancestors, arriving in the guise of crows, ate the ritual offering of the rice ball by pecking at it. Eating thus, they invited more crows to join them.

As it was getting dark, the screaming of the devotees of Ayyappa began to pierce the silence of the night. It continued until daybreak and then was joined by the call for prayer from the mosque. As he came out of the compound after thus suffering the shrill clamours of devotees, the sight of children in tattered clothes, sitting in the cold, defecating in the streets hit his eyes. Written all over the walls along the streets, on the lamp posts, and on the tar-blackened roads were political slogans, words advertising drugs to increase your sexual potency, exhorting you to eat this, drink that, apply this to your skin, wear that, chew this, kill these, wipe out those, topple that one, denounce this one, build for the future, join, boycott....

Thimmappa feared that he would drown in this cacophony of gods, children, the disgruntled, and the hallowed. He became concerned that he might lose the lustre and the purity of his inner voice. He marvelled at his mother who used to walk these filthy streets barefoot without losing her sense of personal purity to go to the shrine of Raghavendra Swamy.

IX

Thus growing disgusted with the meaningless phenomena of the universe, Thimmappa drove around in his car from one place to another for two months and, finding no comfort, returned home.

The house was gleaming, having received a new coat of whitewash. Mother's old saris were all hung outside to be aired. Kamala's pudgy nose wore his mother's diamond nose stud. There were diamond earrings in her ears. Fresh jasmines were strung in her loose braid. On seeing

Thimmappa, she felt thrilled as though her prayers had been answered. The edge of her sari covering her shoulders fully, her turmeric-smeared cheeks and the vermilion-dotted forehead affirming her status as a married woman, she stood in the inner veranda of the house. At night, she came and sat next to his bed hesitantly; poured brandy for him. When he asked her to lie down, she lay down with her legs curled up. Later that night, Thimmappa had a dream. A woman is lying naked. Her legs are drawn up making her thighs spread wide. Her vulva is open like an enormous two-petalled flower. But her hands are covering her face. Her hair is heaped all over her head like a shrub. In his dream, he cried out in agitation, 'Amma, Amma'. The face remained covered. He felt scared, disgusted, and nauseous. He recalled all the prostitutes he frequented and began calling out the false names they had given themselves: Laxmi, Lalitha, Ragini, Komala, Margaret, Lilah, Kamini, Lasitha, Subhaga.... The face was still covered. Between the splayed thighs, the vulva remained still open. He called out, 'Kamala'. Kamala, who was sleeping curled up next to him, pressed her warm face, like a cat, to his cheek. Half-awake, his dream over, Thimmappa remembered his feeling of nausea; also remembered Kamala vomiting that afternoon, and, in her present craving, her eating moist clay which she had hidden in the loose end of her sari. Her slightly swollen belly was pressed to his. A life that was distinct from his own was taking form there. Looking at this in his half-asleep state, in that languorous moment of entry into deep sleep, his body received the warmth of her body.

Translated by Narayan Hegde

AKKAYYA

My childhood friend, Srinivasa, a professor of English in Philadelphia for many years now, has made a name for himself in university circles with his recent book on Henry James. Actually, his name is not Srinivasa. I have concealed his identity to avoid causing him any embarrassment. And also because I suspect that even though I write this as his story, my own self-importance might creep into it. Besides, this is not entirely his story either. It is also the story of Akkayya, his elder sister, who was responsible for his 'philosophic awareness explosion'. Someday, when he sheds his inhibitions, the way a snake sheds its skin, he may write this story too, and it might come out quite differently. (By the way, 'awareness explosion' is his phrase.)

In his middle-school days, Srinivasa was a real rogue. He would pick pockets just for the fun of it. You could hide your pen or your money in any of your pockets and he would lift it without your realizing it. Of course, he would give it back to you after some teasing. He would make you say all sorts of shameful things about yourself—I am a dog, I eat your leftover food, I'll clean your ass, I'm your slave, I'll do whatever you say…and, just as you were about to break down, the rascal would graciously accept an eraser or a pencil as a bribe and hand you back what he had stolen. You could not even confide in anybody about your humiliation, because if you did, your pockets would never be safe again.

Once this fellow even stole our headmaster's pen. That is quite a story. None of the boys, even after receiving a beating, would disclose that it was Srinivasa who had done it. Finally, as if he could not see them being punished, he gave himself up. In all humility, Srinivasa bowed before the stern headmaster, who stood there in his jari-edged turban, and spoke in such a way that all of us burst into laughter, despite the headmaster's presence.

'Sir, I found the pen near the kake bushes behind the school… that spot where you usually go to piss, thinking nobody can see you.

You probably did not notice but the pen fell down while you were pulling out your janiwara from under your coat to put it around your ear. You must have been in a hurry to piss. If you had sat down to do it, instead of standing, you might have spotted the pen on the ground. But then, you were afraid that your jari turban might fall into the piss. Besides, untying the dhoti to piss is such an inconvenience.'

He gave a good imitation of how the headmaster would pull out his janiwara and put it around his ear. He ran his hand inside his vest, as if he was looking for his janiwara and pulled out the Blackbird pen. The way he uttered the word 'inconvenience'—in the same grave tone the headmaster had used in class the previous day—and the humble and scared-to-death manner with which he gave the pen back were enough to make him the darling of all the boys, and even of the girls, who were all so shy. The headmaster, though glad to get his pen back, was still furious and he raised his hand to hit Srinivasa. But he seemed to be in a dilemma: he could not bring himself to slap the boy who had returned the valuable pen, nor could he forget his own position of authority. Under the raised hand of the headmaster, Srinivasa cowered as if he feared for his life and pretended to collapse to the floor. Shielding himself with both hands, he moaned, 'Sir, sir, don't,' making us convulse with laughter.

This Srinivasa is a very dignified person today—much to the surprise of all those who knew him in his childhood. His father, a wealthy landlord, had died when he was still a child. Srinivasa was the last of twelve children. After their mother died, the eldest daughter became Akkayya—big sister—to the rest. It was Akkayya who had brought him up with loving care. Hers is altogether a different story.

She was married even before she reached puberty, to a rogue who traded in buffaloes in Hubli. It was not known then that he already had a mistress. He harassed her, a motherless girl, saying that the gold and silver she had brought with her as dowry was not enough. One day he branded her back with an iron rod—even kicked his mistress who tried to stop him before sending his innocent wife back to her father's house. Her father quietly accepted this as his fate. Dark circles formed around his eyes, his head turned grey, his back bent over, and he was troubled by a racking cough. He aged rapidly.

Every morning Srinivasa stepped out of this sorrow-stricken household, his bag slung on his shoulder. Sitting on the stone platform under the peepul tree, waiting for the school bus, he would enter a world of his own—a world filled with mischief and playfulness. His bag was always full, but not with books. It held things like a packet of kodubale wrapped in a dried banana leaf and tied with a string of banana fibre, a slingshot, cowrie shells with which he played with great skill, channemane beads to be given as gifts to friends, pieces of raw tamarind which would pass from one hand to another in class, undetected by the teacher. This sour tamarind made our teeth chatter and our mouths fill with saliva as we slurped and sucked it, turning the whole class into a jungle of noisy little animals.

Srinivasa's roguishness reached its peak when he started smoking bidis. He would hide the bundle in a hollow of some tree. He felt it was all like a great adventure to sit hidden behind haystacks with friends and light bidis, and to blow out smoke rings from his mouth or exhale smoke through the nostrils. One day, a haystack caught fire from a half-smoked bidi carelessly thrown onto it. Within no time the fire had spread to a thatched hut nearby, leaving the poor people who lived there homeless. Guessing the cause of the fire, Akkayya took Srinivasa aside to a dark corner behind the staircase. 'Why did you do it, Tammayya?'

Srinivasa did not answer. But that night, she heard him talking in his sleep and her suspicions were confirmed. She did not tell anyone about it but sent for the owner of the hut. She gave him two of her gold bangles, and told him to use the money to build himself a new hut. Later she was taken to task by her father and her grown-up younger brothers for being so generous.

After the bidi episode, Srinivasa got involved in the freedom struggle. As a young leader, he became quite an expert in protest activities like cutting down sandalwood trees and toddy palms. I still haven't forgotten the jingle he would sing in those days.

Kasturibai, Kamaladevi
To go on strike with you, we are ready

I used to spend the holidays with Srinivasa in his house, so I knew everything about him, even his anxieties about his nocturnal emissions. He underwent a transformation in college, where we were again classmates. Like a caterpillar changing into a butterfly, he turned into a big scholar. It was he who made me a writer. It was from his harsh and angry views about the obscurantist Hindu beliefs that I got my inspiration at that time.

At the centre of all his mental turmoil was his Akkayya. Though I knew it all along, Srinivasa, all serious and dignified now, would not admit that his affection for her stemmed from the fact that she had brought him up with the tenderness a cow lavishes on her calf.

Srinivasa's bitter anger was directed at his elders who had got her married as a child to an unknown man and deprived her of any opportunity for personal fulfilment. The blind faith and slavish adherence to tradition that had stifled their liberal instincts became the focus of Srinivasa's dialectical analysis. That sort of thinking, which everyone takes for granted now, was very exhilarating and liberating for us. At the centre of such a way of thinking would be either a widow who had to have her head shaved or the kerosene-induced burning of an innocent bride for not bringing sufficient dowry. Or later, when we were doing our MA, it would be an impoverished tenant, a Harijan wrapped in a coarse kambali, or the revolution in China.

It was in those days, when we were seething with anger and bubbling over with the promise revolution held for us, that Srinivasa narrated an absurd incident and made me write a story about it. It went this way....

Srinivasa's elder brother came to know somehow that the man who kept the paan and cigarette shop in front of the famous Gopi Hotel in Shivamogga was Akkayya's husband, the man who had branded her and driven her out. With the help of the police, Srinivasa's brother got him arrested. At the police station, the man calmly admitted that he was indeed Akkayya's husband. He was prepared to atone for the wrongs he had committed against her. What made him do so was not any feeling of remorse. Abandoning his wife before the marriage was consummated had deprived him of a Brahmin's privilege of receiving dakshina from others. To set things right at least now, he decided to go through the consummation rites as decreed by tradition. It did not matter that Akkayya was past her menopause, or that her loafer of a husband, his face bloated by drinking not less than a bottle of country liquor every evening, had lost all his teeth and had become consumptive because of chain-smoking bidis. The ritual consummation of the marriage, which had not taken place, had to happen now.

On his way to the house, in the car, the wretched Brahmin complained that his father-in-law, now dead, had not given him the gold that was his due. At the temple, as was the custom, he saw his wife's face reflected in a bowl of oil. Wearing a jari turban, a bridegroom's basinga tied on his forehead, with agni as witness, he accepted Akkayya as his wife all over again. That night he lay down by her side. But she jumped off the bed and came out, kicking and running. Covering her mouth with the pallu of her sari to hide her shame from her younger brothers, she mumbled, 'He tried to touch me all over. It was disgusting.'

Srinivasa had narrated this incident as a scathing criticism of the Brahmins who lived a life of rituals. So, when I wrote a story based on this, he had not liked the humour I had introduced in it.

My readers should keep in mind the events I have already narrated when they try to understand my feelings towards him when I met him many years later in Philadelphia. Had he not been a stringent critic of the orthodox milieu he was born into, he could have continued to live in it enjoying his share in the ancestral property, driving a car, even sipping scotch whisky daily in the company of wealthy men of other castes, and eating chicken. He could have continued wearing a janiwara underneath his Western clothes. Nobody would have bothered to question all this. Isn't that how we all shed our orthodoxy?

But for Srinivasa, to live like that would be living in bad faith. So, to make his rebellion authentic, he started eating meat. Then he fell in love with a Punjabi doctor and married her, not heeding the protests of his not-so-educated elder brothers. But his Akkaya neither approved nor disapporved. As a wedding present to Srinivasa's wife, whom she hadn't seen, she sent the few pieces of jewellery she had with her. And, of course, her mother's toe rings. But, how could the doctor, who was accustomed to wearing shoes, possibly wear those thick, thrice-coiled rings on her toes? Akkayya died without seeing her.

All this is my speculation, of course. I think Srinivasa did not bring his wife to meet even his beloved Akkayya because he thought that the atmosphere at his home may not suit his Delhi-bred wife. His shrewd and worldly-wise brothers, as is usual in such cases, were pleased that their brother had not come to demand his share of the property, and sang his praise in front of others. Everything seemed fine.

After his marriage, Srinivasa became distanced from his language, his home, his people. Once you are so alienated from everything, what does it matter where you live? Thirthahalli, Delhi, Philadelphia—it's all the same. He settled in Philadelphia. His wife became a very successful physician. After their first child, a daughter, was born, his wife did not want to have any more children lest they interfere with her career.

The three of them live comfortably in a huge brick house, which they had got custom-built, with four bedrooms and a swimming pool. As a professor, Srinivasa also earns well. The slight regret about having moved away from his roots has made him a very sensitive man. This sensitivity adds new flavour and sharpness to his writings and thoughts. Without these, who would care about him in America?

I am not saying Srinivasa is heartless. Readers should excuse the occasional jibe that creeps in—it is a habit with me. At least, he visits his home once a year. But his poor wife is not able to do even that. When she finds a little time, she has to visit her brothers who work for multinational firms. And if she has some more time, she should spend it with her aged parents in Delhi, shouldn't she? We all have our own difficulties, don't we?

Only once did Srinivasa take his daughter to his home near Thirthahalli—a rambling, dark house with a tiled roof. It was not a happy experience for him. This teenager from Philadelphia, made to go through an elaborate bath—complete with the slimy hair cleaning mixture made of matti leaves and shikakai powder—by a loving Akkayya, and then having to eat patrode and be confined indoors all day with the womenfolk, had a big argument with her daddy. Akkayya, poor thing, could not understand a word but was thrilled to hear her niece speak such fluent English. She had admiringly thought that the girl was like her father, just as obstinate. In her joy, Akkayya had gone near her to put coconut oil in her hair and plait it. The girl had stared angrily at her, saying rudely, 'Don't, please! Excuse me!' Akkayya was baffled and, not sure what to do with the fresh jasmines she had strung together for the child's hair, had quietly put the flowers on the household deity in the puja room.

As they had been informed a week ahead about my arrival, Srinivasa and his wife had made themselves free for a whole day—his wife, until the evening—for my sake. They picked me up from the airport and took me home in their car. That evening, formally inquiring what I wished to drink, he, who knew my tastes all along, poured some scotch into a glass, added ice cubes and handed it to me. As if to recreate our past intimacy, and to impress on me that he had not changed, the bastard poured out a scotch for himself too, and said, in the singsong style of a character from a Yakshagana play. 'In this evening hour, when the cows come home, and the birds in flocks return to their nests, what better drink can a man have than this?' He sat down on the sofa facing me and toasted, 'Shiva, Shiva.' I glanced around. It was a luxurious house, like all other houses there. Only the decor was different. To proclaim their difference, they had Italian furniture and Mexican statuettes in their living room. But in Srinivasa's library, the wall, wherever it was exposed, had pictures from our hometown—including a Ganesh Bidi calendar. What attracted my attention was the scene of the Mysore Dasara which he had got painted on the wall. Though the pageant in Mysore these days does not have the maharaja riding a caparisoned elephant, the painting on the wall of Srinivasa's library included the royal procession. On another part of the wall was a picture of an areca nut grove, lush green, with no hint of the chronic blight which affects areca. Anyway, these details are not so important. What particularly captured my attention was a painting which Srinivasa had made in imitation of a painting by Blake.

'You may find it sentimental,' Srinivasa said, standing beside me. He had not failed to notice that I found the painting rather ordinary. 'It's not important to me that as a picture it should be attractive,' he explained. Agreeing with him, I looked at it again—as a picture painted by my friend, meant for his eyes only. I was probably the only person he had shown it to.

It was a painting of Akkayya, plump, with a pudgy nose and

rumpled hair. She was rising upwards, her hands held high as if to clap. Her eyes were lifted to the sky in blissful rapture. Her heavy body seemed to have been made light by her two wings.

'This is not just my imagination. Akkayya actually believed that after her death, she would soar, like a bird,' Srinivasa began. I will now narrate, more or less in his words, the summary of what he told me then.

There were three points that he seemed to be trying to make. The first was to highlight an aspect of Akkayya which neither I, who had been acquainted with her, nor he had ever noticed. The second was to explain the ways in which this had influenced his thinking. Lastly, he was trying to question, through the first two, the basis of my literary sensibility, which to some extent had been fostered by him.

'I began to think about Akkayya,' Srinivasa told me, 'when I was in Manchester.' After completing his PhD, because the scholarship he received was not enough for his needs, he worked for some time as a teacher in a secondary school. In his class was a student who lived in a slum with his Irish mother. He was a lovely, curly-haired boy. But he had a speech problem and he could not do even simple arithmetic. He could draw brilliant pictures though. If you asked him a question, he would give a vague answer, and a meaningless but beatific smile. If you were to ask him, 'Where is Ireland?' he would say, 'There is a black bird sitting on the tree, eating a red fruit.' He would lead you by the hand to show you a fully grown tree in the school compound. During the lunch break, he would drink half of the milk given to him and pour the remaining half into a plate for the birds outside. He would then sit there calmly, watching them drink it.

Srinivasa was fond of this extraordinarily compassionate and friendly boy. But the headmaster of the school wanted to send the boy away to a special school for slow learners. Almost every day he urged Srinivasa, who was the boy's class teacher, to issue the certificate that was required to send the boy away. The boy's mother who brought him to school would plead with Srinivasa. 'His father is an alcoholic and has abandoned me. If you certify my son an imbecile and send him to another school, he will be branded for life. Please don't do that.' Srinivasa thought that the boy was extremely sensitive and affectionate.

So what if he was a slow learner? Srinivasa resisted the headmaster's pressure. But when he went on leave for a week, the headmaster got the substitute teacher to issue the certificate, genuinely believing that it was in the boy's best interest.

That day Srinivasa realized that, from the perspective of Western capitalist efficiency, his beloved Akkayya too, like this boy, would have been certified an imbecile, one who is mentally challenged. She would have had to spend her life in an institution meant for such people. A person who cannot survive in this competitive world is not considered normal. So, he reasoned, there is no place in this world for Akkayya, Ramakrishna Paramahamsa, and Akkamahadevi who went about naked, because they were not normal.

Once, when she had to get into a bus, Akkayya, like a scared child, hid behind a haystack. Another time a lorry was parked in front of the house. Srinivasa was a little boy then, studying in elementary school. But, because he had been to the town, he could explain to her, 'Akkayya, that is a lorry.' However much he tried though, he could not make her say lorry. Every time, she would say, Rolly and, immediately realizing her mistake, would laugh loudly. Right till the end, it was a sort of a game between Srinivasa and her.

While telling Akkayya's story Srinivasa had shed his armours of wisdom and opened up to me, making himself totally vulnerable. Towards the end his narration became awkward, like his portrait of Akkayya done in imitation of Blake. ('Awkward' is the word he used.) The way in which this man, who had not spoken in Kannada for years, had broken into Kannada to talk of intimate matters while he used English to convey his intellectual convictions had itself told me all that he wanted to say. Also, the way in which he would refer to Akkayya sometimes affectionately in the singular and at others in the respectful plural. He had depicted his Akkayya as a creature, an animal, as a mother, and as a goddess—all at once. When he was studying in college, to him she had seemed to be a cow among the cows in the cattle shed in their house. Milking the cows, giving them fodder, and bathing them, she would herself become a cow and talk to them. 'Ai Kouli,' she would say, calling a cow by her name, 'where were you wandering last evening, you big shot? Couldn't you come home before the sun set? Didn't you remember that your daughter Nandini would be waiting to put her mouth to your udders?' Akkayya would even wait for the cows to answer. While Akkayya spoke, she scratched Kouli's dewlap and Kouli would stretch her neck, breathing loudly, her eyes closed; sometimes she would look at Akkayya with melting eyes. She would bend her hind legs slightly and offer herself to be stroked all over. While getting herself pampered, Kouli would stick her tongue out, shake her ears, arch her tail into a bow, and when the bliss became too much to bear, she let out a bellow, 'Ambaah.' That was how Kouli answered Akkayya's every question and, whenever she got the answer she was waiting for, Akkayya would respond, 'Is that so!'

According to Akkayya, in a previous life, Kouli had been her little sister. In another former birth, Akkayya was the mistress of a Gowda's household and Kouli was a cow who grew up in this family, and died giving birth to her calf. Going still further back, Akkayya said Kouli had been a gopi in Gokula and she herself a cow who, blissfully listening to Krishna's flute, would become heavy in the udders from which milk would ooze out. Thus, there had been a continuous relationship between Kouli and Akkayya throughout their several lives as humans and cows. Akkayya believed that Kouli recalled her previous lives while she urinated or chewed her cud. But then, both she and Kouli would sometimes forget all this: Akkayya, when she became involved in her brothers' antics; Kouli, while suckling her calves of this life. Kouli's horoscope had been cast, too. She was born under the star hasta in kanya lagna—the same star of her previous life—but this time, in its second quarter.

There were fifteen cows in the cowshed. Akkayya had names for each one of them. For her, they were beings who found themselves in her cowshed because they were bound to each other by some relationship of their past lives. One among them, a vagrant cow, had been a butcher in a previous life. One day, just as he was about to bring down his knife on a plump piglet, he looked at its snout and, overcome by pity, threw away his knife. Having atoned for his karma in that birth, he was born a wayward cow in the next. Akkayya would tell her brothers' grandchildren many such stories at bedtime.

Akkayya knew the day and time of birth of each cow in the shed, she knew the life histories of all of them. She remembered even the dead ones. Whose horns looked like what, what was their colour like, which one gave how much milk, which one used to kick people, which one refused to suckle her own calf.... Akkayya would talk as if to herself, for hours on end, while dry curing the banana leaves or peeling the areca nuts. She could identify and describe each cow's characteristics and delve into their previous lives, whether they had been human, dog, or bird. Often, these descriptions were not meant for her brothers, not for their stuck-up wives, and not even for their innocent children. These were for Pilla.

Pilla was a servant who helped in the cowshed. He was as old as Akkayya. His son, who worked as a teacher in the town, did not want his father to live with him. And neither did Pilla. The name that the son assumed after he got an education was different from the one his father had given him. Pilla was happy for his son's good fortune, he was happy that his son sent him money every month. But he would not even think of retiring from his chores in Akkayya's cowshed, though he always did as his son said. If his son said that they should not call themselves Holeyas, untouchables, he said, 'Fine.' If the son said that they should call themselves SCs instead, he again said, 'Fine.'

According to Akkayya, Pilla was a saint. In a previous life he had been her husband's younger brother. Both had suffered because her husband felt that her love for her brother-in-law was excessive. When the brother-in-law had chickenpox, his face got all swollen and nobody would come near him, she had nursed him. But he died even before he was married. Thereafter, he was born a Byari—a Muslim trader from Kerala. She was his cart horse and would eat grass and horse-gram from his hand. Owing to their karma, in this life he was the cow dung picking, saintly Pilla, and she the mistress of the house.

As Pilla had no feelings of attachment to anything, he was not going to be reborn again. Sitting in front of the fire in the bath house and warming herself, Akkayya herself told him all this. Pilla just said, 'Fine,' as he would to everything else.

The story of Pilla made my eyes twinkle. My childhood friend who noticed it yelled, 'Shut up and listen, you useless creature!' He was laughing too, and poured some more wine in my glass. We were eating Chinese chicken and so the wine to go with it had to be white.

'Did you like the wine?' he asked. 'You and I sitting here, drinking Italian wine, eating chicken in this Chinese restaurant while talking of Akkayya; your painting, that Blake-like picture, all without giving up your lifestyle—on the whole, all this does not seem authentic, and I am using your own word here,' I said, enjoying the taste of the wine. Even there in America, a Chinese ambience had been recreated in the restaurant—through its paintings, its lanterns, and its unintelligible calligraphy. 'The India that you have been creating is also like this restaurant. Remember how you teased and tortured our headmaster before giving back the Blackbird pen you had stolen? You rascal, what happened to the great spirit you used to have then?' I said theatrically and laughed.

But what I said did not seem to have interrupted his thoughts. My teasing got him worked up even more and he told me another story about Akkayya.

It too was a story about the relationship between Kouli and Akkayya. One evening, Nandini, Kouli's calf, did not come home. Akkayya stood near the cowshed and for a long time calling out for Nandini in a voice she used specially for this purpose. 'Call your daughter,' she told Kouli. Kouli too called out pitiably, 'Ambaa... Ambaah.' But there was no trace of Nandini. 'Probably your daughter needed to be with a bull. Or perhaps she went into someone's paddy field and got herself impounded. I'll go and look for her,' Akkayya murmured before disappearing into the nearby forest. She did not come home all night and returned only the next morning around ten.

'Do you know what she looked like when she got home?' Srinivasa went on to narrate the rest of this incident from his college days.

'She spent all night in the forest, wide awake under a mango tree. By morning, Nandini had materialized before a dozing Akkayya and was sniffing her. Akkayya opened her eyes and scolded her left and right. As she scolded Nandini, she looked up and what did she see? A tree full of baby mangoes, just right for pickling. Stay right here, she commanded Nandini. Like a little girl, Akkayya climbed the tree and carefully plucked bunches of mangoes by their stem. Their sap dripping, she wrapped them in the loose end of her sari, and tightly holding its end in her left hand and grabbing the rough trunk with the right, she slid hesitantly down the trunk. Then, holding the mangoes wrapped in her sari and with Nandini by her side, she reached home panting. Once home and bathed, she straightaway got busy with washing the baby mangoes one by one and salting them.'

Srinivasa said he had been standing outside when Akkayya returned home. Her hair dishevelled, her eyes smiling, her pallu filled with baby mangoes, with the black-coloured Nandini walking next to her—she had appeared to him like a fierce forest goddess.

He went on to another story about how one night she fought with and triumphed over Yamadharmaraya, the god of death, and became a jagatjanani. The story goes like this:

After Nandini, Kouli almost died giving birth to twin calves which were stillborn, but she became pregnant again. By way of precaution, Akkayya prepared every kind of medicine known to her, but it didn't seem as if she would have an easy delivery. The night Kouli was in labour, Akkayya must have somehow felt that she might die without being able to deliver.

When everyone had had supper, she went to the cowshed. To ward off the evil spirits, she made a charm and circled it around Kouli who lay there, helplessly. Hands on her waist, Akkayya appealed to Yama. 'My Lord, please let her grow old and then die. Take us both at the same time, just as you have been doing in every one of our previous lives. I beg you, do the same this time as well,' Just then a lizard made a sound that Akkayya understood as Yama's refusal of her request.

She went straight to the door of the cowshed and sat on the threshold, her legs stretched out. Shaking the broom she held in her hand, she said, 'If you are coming here to take her away, you will have to deal with me first. Do you see what I have in my hand? This broom has been dipped in Kouli's dung and I will thrash you with it. I will become Maari and haunt you.' Holding the broom in her hand, she sat up all night. By morning, Kouli was licking a newborn male calf, which was trying awkwardly to stand up and reach its mother's udders.

It was midnight when Srinivasa and I returned to his house. There was no need for anyone to let us in. The garage door was operated by remote control. Srinivasa's key opened the main door quietly. The library was open. His wife, who must have come home tired after delivering babies, and his daughter, back home from her date, were probably sound asleep.

After we sat down, Srinivasa poured cognac in two glasses and gave one to me. Savouring his drink, he said softly, 'Your understanding is right. I started saying all this to set you thinking in the right direction, to tell you not to look at life in India from a Western point of view. I cannot tell this to others. Even my wife and my daughter are outsiders to that world of mine. I could write about such things only as an academic discourse before, but that is the kind of writing which is taking place in our circles nowadays. See how ludicrous it is! But I don't feel that way when I talk to you. Do you know I have begun to realize all this only lately?

'In the beginning I didn't think that Akkayya talked much. Then, after my coming here, I began to marvel as to how much she used to talk. The way she died was also strange. At night, after supper, it was her habit to sit in front of the fire-place of the bathroom outside the house. A big log would be burning there all the time. She would have plenty of jackfruit pits in her lap. Pilla would sit at a distance from her, his bottle of country liquor hidden away behind a bush close by. Akkayya would be talking and at the same time roasting the jackfruit seeds in the hot ashes. As they got roasted, she would give them to Pilla. Biting into the seeds, Pilla would quietly go behind the bush to quickly take a few swigs, fart, and come back to sit before the fire. Akkayya would be talking to him all through his disappearances behind the bush and he would go on saying, 'Hm, hm.'

'Hadn't Akkayya always said that this Pilla had no more births? But it was Pilla who survived her by three months. One night, while sitting in front of the fire and talking, she dropped some freshly-roasted jackfruit seeds into Pilla's hand and then just closed her eyes. Pilla waited for some time and, because he was not supposed to touch her, he called out, "Amma-re, Amma-re!" When there was no answer, he went into the house shouting, "Masters, Masters!" and woke up my lazy brothers and then stood silently....

'I was not there when Akkayya died. I was getting ready to leave for France to attend an important seminar on Orientalism. I cancelled my trip and went to my hometown for the funeral rites.'

Finishing the story, Srinivasa was silent for a while. Then, 'Your scepticism towards me is understandable,' he said. 'You could say, if you want to be kind, that all the theories I conceptualized in the course of my successful career are either in order to move away from this world of Akkayya, or because I thought I had already moved away from it. That is how I first became a progressive Marxist, then a liberal, and now a post-modernist. I cannot go back now, nor can I be a neocolonialist badmash, claiming that her world is all false.'

Because it was winter, Srinivasa stood in front of the electric heater in the library which glowed like a blazing log of the bathroom fire back in his hometown. He had removed his tie and unbuttoned his collar. The jeans and the tweed jacket he was wearing gave him a youthful look. He didn't have an awkward paunch like I did. His was a muscular body. His hair, which he wore long, and which fell over his broad forehead with a right mix of grey and black, the light-framed glasses, his soft-leather shoes—all these gave a lustre to his sadness.

A real essay was shaping up in me in response to his theoretical sadness, to its underlying mental distress, and to his worldly success. But remembering the mischief and the fun the two of us had had in those days when he used to pick pockets, and looking at his long, shoulder-length hair, I saw him as a visiting Bhagavata and enjoyed the thought of it. There were, in his library, four hats made from the fronds of areca palm. I put one of them on my head and, seeing Srinivasa's eyes light up mischievously, put another on his. The clothes he was wearing, together with this hat, turned him into a metaphor for me.

There was a ghatam in the library. I picked it up, went in front of the heater, and sank into a bean bag that softly hugged my contours, backside, and all. Playing on the ghatam, I started singing whatever came to my mind. Srinivasa also began to sway to its rhythm.

Those of you who are reading this story, you too may wish to add your own lines and join in. But, for this it would be necessary to mutilate and shorten some English words that have served us well, words that have been the cause of our misery, as well as our success. Sensitivity, for instance. A word that has been the cause of our international success, may be modified thus:

Sensiti sensiti
Sensitivity vity
Born to a minda
Sensitivity vity

With this as the refrain, I went on adding lines as they came to my mind. These are the lines I can remember now:

Seena's sensiti
Said's sensiti
Born to a minda
Sensitivity vity
(Or, in Srinivasa's case)
Born to Ford
Sensiti sensiti
Sensitivity vity
Harvard sensiti
Fostered by the white shetty
Vedic sensiti
Nurtured by the dark bhatta
Seena's sensiti
Said's sensiti
Born to a minda
Sensitivity vity

(The following should be sung as a melody)

I-can-be-neither-here-nor-there sensiti
Seena's sensiti
Said's sensiti
Born to Ford
Sensitivity vity
India's glory, great sensiti Arab glory, grand sensiti
Born to a minda, very VERY sensiti
Prostituted-itself-to-bastards sensiti
Padded-the-white-man's-ass sensiti
Seena's sensiti
Said's sensiti

Sensiti sensiti
Sensitivity vity
Born to a minda
Sensitivity vity
To slander the Brahmins
Export folklore
To flatter the Brahmins
Export vac-lore
Yajna-ritual Tantra-ritual
Funeral-ritual
Wedding-ritual

(Hereafter in the Harikatha style)

The pimps (minda) themselves setting it up, themselves heading it, editing it themselves, and later the pimps themselves inviting the Indian monks through offering them scholarships, and training them in their land of penance such as Chicago, Harvard, and Princeton, sending them back with PhDs, inviting them again and again.

Our Srinivasa Joisa suddenly remembers the smell of the cowshed from his past life and is all upset

(The following is a dance song)

Agonizing, teaching, seminar-hopping project on Gandhi
Budget from a minda
To slander these minda
Funding from Ford Lo! A book is born!
Seena's book
Said's book
A Kannada book
Born to the minda
(Now melodiously)
What sort of book?
I-am-that book
I-can-neither-be-here-nor-there book Hara Hara book
Who-am-I book Hari Hari book
A chaste book
Though born to the minda O, sensiti sensiti

Sensitivity vity
Out of the bastard
Out of the Nobel Foundations
Loafer's Bofors' guns. Ah, a book! A book born to the minda
O, the book

At a climactic moment I stopped playing on the ghatam, stood up and, like a prophet, declared:

If there is a Ford, only then can you afford to say

Both hands raised, making quotation marks with my fingers, I started singing again with Srinivasa also joining in:

Ayyo...I can neither be here
Nor go back there

We hugged each other and laughed, and laughing, I looked up and liked the picture of Akkayya that Srinivasa had painted. And I said to Srinivasa, both of us in the hats made from areca fronds, in our trousers and jackets and our middle-age gravity, dancing like clowns—dear readers, please note that I could say the following to my friend only in English—You see, it's precisely because your painting and your words on Akkayya are awkward and absurd, they felt authentic.

Just then, out of habit, I felt my hip-pocket and found my wallet gone! Till early morning, we were in front of the heater, laughing and joking.

Translated by Narayan Hegde

KAMAROOPI

1

Helen is still a tender young girl. She is dancing flirtatiously in front of a mirror with steps picked up from the street. Thinking she was alone while she enjoyed watching her body's twists has made her uninhibited. She is three parts a child, and one part woman. 'Don't disturb the hussy's concentration—the woman who will cause the destruction of the very towers of civilization is rehearsing,' says Yeats.

A schemer who I bumped into is now becoming a tale.

2

One fellow appeared suddenly and started glancing around. His eyes flit from one unoccupied sofa to another. They stop roving for a little while as he looked—in the wall mirror in front of him—at his moustache, his neatly brushed-up hair, and me, who had started to watch him. He tried in vain to open his eyes wide so that they would look attractive under his heavy brows. His eyes veered to the left and settled on the white telephone on a square glass table which materialized suddenly under a photograph of a smiling, toothless Gandhi. He stood still in front of the telephone and Gandhi like a bee which buzzes in from nowhere, flies around aimlessly, collides with things, and then quietly settles down somewhere. He flung his briefcase on a red sofa and looked at me. That is how each of us became a tale to the other.

3

It was while I was waiting alone for my flight at the Hyderabad airport lounge that I sighted this character. A tight white bush shirt and white trousers—both of them khadi. Though there were no signs on his face of the class of respectable men who merited the VIP lounge, his khadi his khadi explained his audacity. Must be of my son's age, I thought.

It's not easy though to guess the age of a man with sallow cheeks and greedy wandering eyes.

It must have been the influence of reading Kundera and his all-encompassing sensibility—I couldn't ignore his request made in free flowing but broken English. Thrusting a cheap camera in my hands, he described how I should hold it, described how I should hold it, at what angle, and how steady I should be in snapping him just as he takes up his pose. What I first saw in his indifference to reaction was a comical shamelessness even as he tried to close his lips over his slightly protruding teeth before the camera clicked and hurriedly explained to me what he wanted. As he spilt out his words, his own brand of English, he seemed to be sure that I, a stranger, would obey him.

'There, mister, there under Gandhi's photograph. I am there on the sofa picking up the receiver, smiling and talking, working up the necessary mood. That's when you should take a snap making sure that Gandhi's photograph, the red sofa set, a bit of this green carpet, the rose in the vase, and my smile are all in focus.'

One-eyed, I clicked the camera politely. Encouraged by my willingness, he had his image taken in various poses to match his many metamorphoses. Once he guffawed as he said 'Cheppandi, go on,' holding the phone pressed to his ear. He is now in the house of his brother-in-law who is the personal assistant of a Minister of his own caste. The fellow is so close to the Minister that the latter is having his bath in his house.

He might have wanted me to submit to his will or he might have wished for a mood needed for his success in life to glow obviously on his face. Anyway, offering relevant details in this regard in English, Telugu, and Hindi, he had me register each of his moods in its purest form.

In the last picture of the reel, he is listening to the phone and taking down notes. (By now, he had taken out a packet from his briefcase and applied vermillion to his forehead.) The Minister himself comes in at that moment. He lifts up his hips a little and motioned with his outstretched hand to ask the Minister to be seated.

Thus he had his dreams for the future materialized thanks to my willing artistic curiosity. Rising with the briefcase in hand, he took out the reel from the camera, and safely tucked it into its case.

4

He wouldn't leave me, the Shani. Even as I desired to get into my former state using the pretext of reading Kundera, he sat down next to me and took out his wares from his briefcase. The mirror in front of us and my polite nature—they must have appeared ideal for blowing up his ego. Not knowing the antecedents of his desire to sprout by rehearsing his role in my eyes, I was curious about his story. He started blowing his own trumpet after finding out who I was. He didn't know what I thought of him but he had seen many like me in the Minister's chambers. The snaps I had taken were nothing other than those of his beaming routine states of being. 'Look,' he said and opened the album.

In one of the pictures, he is there garlanding Fernandes. It was of the time when he was, in his patriotic fervour, a member of an inconsequential party and gained nothing. In another, he is in the vanguard of NTR's Chaitanyaratha*, hands raised and shouting slogans. That was of the period when a leader of his own caste joined Telugu Desham Party to become a minister and so he too had to be with him. In another, he is there with his moustache and head shaved, looking like a gnarled root. That was when the president went to Tirupathi with his leader and had his head shaved. He had followed suit.

The rest were all xerox copies. Recommendation letters from some minister or the other to people suggesting that the applicant be considered for employment if possible. They had to pass through his helpful hands and he showed in support letters from the ministers of Andhra Pradesh and the Centre. He is now in the Congress party, a secretary of the Youth Congress, and president of the backward cell. He is the brain behind all the ministers of his caste and had scripted all their speeches. His brother-in-law was so close to the Minister.... His brother-in-law, whose English wasn't very good, leaned on him heavily...I had all the details within a few minutes.

At first, he appeared to be one of those comical figures who attract writers in search of stories. As he introduced himself stretching out his

*Refers to when the Telugu Desam party founder Nandamuri Taraka Rama Rao travelled over 75,000 kilometres in a Chevrolet van in the run-up to the elections in 1983.

hand, he said, 'Mr Shankarababu Youth Congress leader, nominated by my minister to be an invitee at the All India Backward Cell.'

5

'Do you know that my heart was filled with hope when I saw your outfit? People who have got on in life like me don't even visit their wives without a suit on.' He stood up laughing. I decided never again to wear pyjama and kurta. He wandered round the lounge fictionalizing me. I must be one of those that have got on. One look was enough to size up anyone. The blessings of those above was needed too. I, who was coolly waiting for the Delhi flight, had appeared a friendly man to him. Can talent alone help get on in life? One needs too the blessings of those above. He knew that I was a very friendly man. No agitation whatsoever while I waited for the flight to Delhi. Our prime minister knows how to use people like me. He is waiting too with his hands at the back. (He turned around to show how he was waiting.)

Mr Shankarababu must have sensed that my attention had started wandering. He showed me a greeting card from Rajiv Gandhi in which the words that looked handwritten but had actually been printed. He could see in the mirror that it didn't have the expected impact on me. He then took out a large wedding photograph. What I saw in it was different from what he wanted me to see.

The bride in the picture was a beautiful dark-complexioned girl with thick plaits of hair flowing over her chest. Though every limb of her body was covered in shining gold, she looked to me to be an damsel from heaven, now under a curse. In her front was a pot-bellied man with layers of fat on his thick neck. With his dyed hair on his balding head and a shining jubba clinging to his belly the VIP looked like a lusty libertine. It was obvious from the way he kept his hands folded that he was waiting for the click of the camera. The bride had bent her head a little and seemed to be noticing nothing. My imagination grew, making her into a myth where an evil eye had turned her into a stone idol.

While Shankarababu was eager to let me know about the fat man, I started probing about the girl who seemed to be under a curse.

'What is your sister's name? Tell me about her education. You don't need to tell me that the happy-looking man standing next to her is the lucky personal assistant of the Minister, your brother-in-law. Yes, I guessed that he was your Minister. You didn't have to tell me. Has your sister any children? What are their interests?'

But he was there, standing with his hands at the back, telling me about the Minister. He doesn't ever drink coffee before performing puja. His jubbas are made by the best of tailors. The Minister was grooming him to be among the second line of leaders. He wished to let a man of his own caste grow. It was the Minister who bore the wedding expenses. He has been a member of all the five cabinets. Even the Naxalites are scared stiff of him. The whole of the backward class loves him. 'Saroja, make me a cup of coffee,' he would say and come straight into the kitchen.

I became more curious as the last sentence was in the past tense. While I faced the flood of his narration wishing to raise the matter of his sister, he spoke about the Naxalite menace as if he was addressing an assembly. He had scripted a speech for the Minister: 'It was not possible to tackle the Naxalite menace saying it was a simple law-and-order problem. The backward castes need justice immediately and so on.' Imagine! His own mother, a religious person, had started praising the Naxalites. His sister too was ready to join them....

I fixed my gaze on his wandering beady eyes which occasionally turned to the mirror, and asked, 'Which sister?'

He sat down suddenly and took out another photograph from his briefcase. 'I took it, she didn't know.' He smiled as if to encourage the shift in my attention.

Her thick shining hair thrown over the chest to dry, she was unadorned—without even her earrings perhaps. She seemed to have come out of the bathroom, clad in an everyday handwoven sari. She looked just like Panchali with anger flaming at the nose-tip, and unlike her elder sister, a gentle goddess under a curse. Startled by the camera flash, her stern eyes seemed ready to set her brother on fire. Dark face, black hair, and shining eyes—she was a dark cloud, I thought.

'This is Geetha, the younger sister. She used to sweep the yard and wash it and cover it with rangoli patterns. She is now a revolutionary, busy organizing our people, shutting down toddy shops.' Shankarababu laughed sarcastically and tried to draw me into an elaborate analysis.

6

They could have been anyone's thoughts. Shankarababu had no concern either for the deficiencies in human affairs or black spots in history. His was the confidence of people who like him had their hands on the wheels of history. Don't you want democracy? Can democracy function without elections? Don't we need funds to conduct elections? Where do they come from except from black money? In the same way, Don't development projects need funds? Where can they come from? Isn't most of it generated from the sale of liquor? Where do these Naxalites get guns for their revolution? From drugs, from Pakistan and China. Would Lenin have had his revolution but for the treachery of the Germans? Was it not Birla who gave money to Gandhi? How did he get his money? It didn't fall from the sky, did it? People like you pride yourselves on having been educated in England and America. They had wealth because they bled the poor countries dry. Take for example the hospital that Sai Baba builds or the treasury of Tirupathi Thimmappa....

He started laughing to himself when he noticed that I stayed quiet without getting into an argument. 'What, sir, you become silent just as I was practising my English in the presence of people like you? I haven't gone abroad like you. I have picked up my English by reading whatever I could lay my hands on—*Sunday*, *India Today*, *Financial Express*. Our office gets even the *EPW*. You might not have been impressed, but I am my Minister's brain. If I had prepared for him a brief about what we just discussed, and made him speak from it, I am sure that political scientists like you would have started making a serious analysis of the issue. You would have even written about it in the *EPW*.'

I didn't relent even though he had transformed himself into an ardent learner.

'I asked you about the first of your sisters. You didn't tell me anything.'

'What shall I say, sir? It was my bad luck. She died within a month of her wedding.' Casting his eyes down, he continued in a low voice, 'She committed suicide. She is the cause of all my problems.'

It was nothing but illusion on my part to think that his real self could be talking to me for at least a moment. What did he want of me? Within a few seconds his eyes had started flitting from the mirror to the sofa and back. His exposition was neat. Saroja must have been mentally ill. Their family was uneducated. His mother failed to recognize this problem. He was busy with social service on all days. The girl hadn't lacked anything. She had the Minister coming into the kitchen asking for coffee. No in-laws to bother her, either. A countless number of saris and jewels to cover her....

My voice shook as I said hurtingly, 'You know why she died. If you want to continue to talk to me, tell me the truth.'

7

There was a change in his gestures and he dropped even the little humility that should be there in a stranger. With an assured air of familiarity, he stood opposite me in the manner of facing a large audience. Glancing sideways at the mirror, he spoke as if I was anyone.

He had been surprised to find that I was talking like his other sister, Geetha. 'Is there anyone who has got on in life without compromising with principles? Let's take you for instance.' He went on with his poor English. The conceit in his words seemed to wish that I saw this as an occasion for him to rehearse his English and also hope that I tolerated the hard truths he shared.

'The Minister is at his table. He is in a corner watching everything. For instance, you. If it's not you, it's someone of your class. You come in, stand there, and bow as you greet the Minister. (Shankarababu grinned as he stood in front of me with folded hands.) The Minister lifts up his face slowly and his eyes suggest that you be seated. (Shankarababu sat down on the sofa in front like one who has done something wrong.) You have now a problem. English or Telugu? If you launch into Telugu, you are suggesting that the Minister doesn't understand English. And so, it will be in English.

'"Sir, your analysis of the Naxalite menace was absolutely great. People like us with a doctorate in Political Science aren't blessed with an insight like yours." (Shankarababu spoke now in an altered voice. He pointed his fingers at himself and said, it was this poor soul that wrote the script of the speech.) The Minister beams in pleasure without any compunction, cleans his glasses, and puts them on. "What can I do for your?" he asks in Telugu so that there is a touch of easy familiarity. You then come out with your request. There is a lot of clearing of throat before you speak. (Shankarababu was mimicking the way I speak.) "Sir, I should have been appointed the chairman of the Public Service Commission the last time the post fell vacant. Our chief minister has no interest in the welfare of the backward people. Not a single backward vice-chancellor in any university, sir. You too shouldn't forget them. You are our only hope. You must give me a chance in the PSC."

'The Minister smiles gently. (Shankarababu speaks in a gruff voice, mimicking him.) "Hand over all the details to my PA." He folds his hands suggesting that you may leave. It is then that even an upright person like you goes to my brother-in law's chambers. He is there, seated like this.'

He took out another surprise from his briefcase that had been reserved only for me. The picture shows his brother in-law sitting on a red sofa with a white phone at his ear. By his side a garland of flowers and on his forehead vermilion. Behind him though, a photograph of Gandhi at his spinning wheel. The brother-in-law too might be saying, 'Cheppandi, go on.' Shankarababu must have caught him in real action.

The brother-in-law doesn't know English. He asks me to sit down in a gruff Telugu. He asks me to visit him at home with all the details. Shankarababu's eyes rise in a question, 'You know why, surely. No? How did you manage to get on if you are that thick? Can you get anything at all these days without dispensing money? Tell me, who had the upper hand in the bank scam? Was it not the South Indian Brahmins before? Get on, get honour, get honest. They are the only three degrees of the times. I am still working for the first one. You have already got the third. My brother-in-law will catch up with you soon. He is thinking of building an orphanage in his village, the rascal....'

Talking in this manner, the lean-bodied one started wandering lightly round the lounge, a bundle of boundless energy, while I sat there, ponderously. There is a proverb which says that a man who has jettisoned all thoughts of honour is the equal of God.

8

He was a pest, the Shani. It was only after he had gone that I realized why he brought up the matter of the little girl Ameena and had drawn me to his net of betrayal in order to weaken me. Before he left, his new and overpowering form had tried to evoke compassion in me.

'It's true that Ameena was forced to marry the rich old man from the Gulf. If she had said that in court, her father would have gone to jail. A poor rickshaw-puller with a house full of girls. What could they have done if he had been sent to jail? They would have turned to prostitution. No other way. The powerful and moral members of the upper caste don't understand their plight, do they? But the girl knew what was in store. "I had given my consent to the marriage," she said. Poor thing! That is what is meant by sacrifice. Brother, it's easy for you and me to sit comfortably in the airport lounge and talk about ethics. It's a different thing altogether having to sacrifice one's whole life for the sake of a poor family....'

Shankarababu's face was serious as he looked askance at the mirror and spoke with a choking voice. His face changed later as he looked into my eyes. There was a spirit of camaraderie as all his teeth bared under his heavy moustache. His eyes shone with a restless desire for the good things in life. He moved close to me and I caught the heavy scent of some cheap oil on his hair. He placed a hand on my shoulder, moved closer still, and whispered into my ears.

'Some girls have a desire for old men. No, mister?' He stopped, looking at me, still savouring the way he pronounced the word 'Mister', and winked. He lit a cigarette and tried to offer it to me. The same age as my son, perhaps, this lecher seemed like a wicked old man. He then sat there whistling as he smoked.

I am ashamed when I think of why I suffered him for so long without kicking him out. I am apprehensive about this passion in me for fictionalizing things which can easily overpower me. A man with a family is in danger if his desire for artistic pursuit makes him see and portray everything and realize and tolerate everything that he imagines.

It was when I was afraid as the dirty fellow sized me up with his eyes that I remembered the poems that Yeats in his old age wrote about his irrepressible libido. The lecherous old man, as old as the man in the sky, tells the girl: 'The boys with pimples on their faces may get pleasure but, in their hastiness, they are incapable of giving pleasure. Come, sleep with me and enjoy yourself.' Shankarababu was staring at me with an easy familiarity and drawing at his cigarette in such a manner that I felt disgust at the drooling poet who was forced to pen those lines.

10

Thank heavens, the story is not ending here. Shankarababu was agitated before he rushed into the lounge. Maybe, I haven't understood why he was in such a state. Let me summarize the story he narrated.

His father was a house construction worker. Both his parents earned for the family. While his father's earnings went for his drinks, it was his mother's that fed the family. It was thanks to her that his sisters and he went to school and grew up.

His father died as a result of a damaged liver. (This part of the narration was in a low voice. The rest was narrated with Shankarababu standing with his hands at the back so that I would be impressed with all his achievement.) He got his inspiration from the Minister who belonged to his caste, became his brain thanks to his own intelligence, provided all that was needed for the family and everyone in the family prospered. It was the Minister himself who took interest in getting his sister to marry his personal assistant. His brother-in-law couldn't have hoped for a better bride than his sister as very few in his community were educated. Nor could have Saroja secured a wealthier bastard than his brother-in-law for a husband. (It was Shankarababu who used that word, bastard.)

Shankarababu is now in a fix. That bastard is now obsessed with a single thought. It was that he should have Geetha as a second wife. The Minister also desired the same. He wished to prepare him for the second line of leadership, right?

He was in no position to bring up the matter in the house. No one but a member of his caste would use the words his mother did to castigate both the Minister and his brother-in-law. His mother was sick—a weak heart, high blood pressure, and diabetes. The sky doesn't rain money, does it? It had to come from the brother-in-law. I don't want any of the bastard's ill-gotten money. I will clean the dishes in the neighbours' house and earn money', says the mother. 'I will join my people in Nellur and organize a revolt', says Geetha. A timid girl, she shared his mother's bed at night. She kept bad company at college, that was the problem.

The brother-in-law was fed up waiting and asked him to stop coming home. Even that corrupt Minister had stopped talking to him. Shankarababu had put aside his self-respect and gone over to his brother-in-law's posh bungalow the previous morning. The brother-in-law was performing his puja. The bastard doesn't have his coffee before his puja. Shankarababu stole into the kitchen, poured himself a cup of his favourite filter coffee, and waited. Saroja was a deft hand at making coffee. She was like a Brahmin in everything. The bastard had vermillion and sandal paste on his forehead as he came in his neatly pressed trousers and shirt—the outfit he needs for his daily collection. He cooled down when a cup of the aromatic filter coffee was placed in front of the sofa. 'Have you got Geetha to agree?' he asked. The Minister would dismiss him from service, his mind is set on it, Shankarababu said sobbing. He shed tears as he spoke of his mother's illness. (I had my doubts that the fellow was out to win me over to his side by caricaturing his brother-in-law and himself.) 'Geetha will surely agree. She believes in the revolutionary changes that our Minister has planned.' Shankarababu had lied freely and got a bundle of a thousand rupees from the depraved miser for his mother's treatment. They were crisp, stapled notes. (Black money is always very clean, brother, Shankarababu joked and carried on.)

He went round the Hyderabad slums all day and attended to the things he needed to do. There is a young brigade that looks up to him. What terror can the naxals possibly cause in front of them? He asked his supporters to put a little scare into his sister and her friends and went home after working out a plan.

Coughing, his mother was boiling milk inside the kitchen.Geetha was reading something and taking down notes. As usual, she was in a torn sari, her hair disheveled.

'Mother', he called softly, 'here, a thousand rupees for your treatment. Brother-in-law has given it. He wanted us to get Geetha to agree.' Shankarababu got up quietly as he spoke.

Geetha stood up, her hair rumpled, looking like Chandi and snatched the bundle of notes from her brother. She rushed to the stove like a whirlwind. She flung the hot milk vessel to the floor with her bare hands and put the bundle of notes on the burning stove.

Shankarababu really looked utterly lost as he narrated the incident. A whole day's labour wouldn't have fetched his mother ten rupees. She was a woman who had suffered fighting her husband day in and day out to get some money out of him. But there she was, looking calmly as the flame licked the bundle of notes. Geetha was haughtily staring at her brother as if she desired to burn him along with the notes. His mother rested both her hands on the floor and sobbed silently. She had lost her mind, he was sure.

Perplexed at first, Shankarababu couldn't stand it any longer. He kicked at the stove and held the burning notes firmly in his hands. He wiped the blackened notes with the cloth mopping cloth and pocketed the still crisp notes.

He couldn't contain himself. Picking up the knife used to slice vegetables, he pulled at Geetha's hair trying to cut it. Oh, what strength in her body! She kicked her brother. She snatched the knife and rushed at him. Crying loudly, her mother pushed her away and seized the knife from her and started hitting her own head with it. The Brahmins next door must have heard the whole thing.

Geetha hadn't finished yet. Hitting him with a broom, she pushed him out of the house and shut the door. (Shankarababu suddenly thought of something, took out the blackened bundle of notes asking, 'They will exchange these for new ones in the bank, won't they?' and carried on.)

He spent the night in the party office reading back issues of *The Week* and *Sunday*. He went home in the morning thinking that things would have settled down.

The door was open. His mother was in bed with the cover drawn over her head. Geetha was nowhere. 'Where is Geetha?' he asked and his mother didn't bother to reply. He pulled down the cover, shook her, and asked again in a raised voice. His mother kept quiet. She wasn't crying either as she blinked her eyes. 'Where has that slut gone leaving you to die?' he shouted and banged his head against the wall. His mother said nothing. She had become a muni with her undone hair.

Shankarababu realized at that moment that a chapter in his life had come to an end. That loafer of a Minister wouldn't talk to him anymore. That bastard of a brother-in-law wouldn't let him come anywhere near him.

There was just one thing left for him to do. There was another man of his own caste, a political rival to the Minister. A granite merchant, he was a sympathizer of the Telugu Desam Party. A rich, rich man, he needed the support of young people like himself. 'It is to impress him that I had you take all these snaps, brother. I couldn't think of anything else.'

I had no more interest in fictionalizing his future. All the facets he had shown were of a piece, interwoven. I, with a single face, had seen him in his many faces.

11

He may have wells dug in places, distribute saris and house sites may plant trees along the road and imprint his small-sized backside in history, may inflame the helpless slum dwellers to strengthen his own constituency. It may be that these people with children of their own will set fire to the hut of someone of another caste. An unknown sleeping child may get burnt to death.

On some days, on a gentle morning, a respectable gentleman out on a walk with a muffler round his neck may say, 'How unfortunate! It shouldn't have happened. But if something like this hadn't happened, these bastards wouldn't have learned their lesson. Look how they have quietened down now. These things are inevitable in history.'

In the pages of history looked at in the gentle coolness of memory, Hitler was a man who loved his dog. Stalin was lost in grief when his wife died. During the gala dinners he held at the midnight hour, he would say 'Thumbs up!' and gulp down the pepper-tasting vodka and wipe his moustache. He would have the pickle-jar-like Khrushchev eat and drink and dance like a bear. He would occasionally remember the daring of his men in the Red Army and cry. Even an evil king like Chikaveera Rajendra had asked an old woman, 'Grandmother, in which of your ears did I pee when I was a child?'

12

If a miracle that manifests in response to intense prayer were to take place in linear history, what seemed an ordinary blade of grass might become sacred ritual grass. Even Shankarababu may, in his old age, sit alone one evening, picking his nose, and think of the genesis of it all. Geetha placing the bundle of notes on a burning stove, his bafflement to see his mother watching it all quietly, his own love cleansed and made pure as the crisp notes were burnt by the angry flame and Saroja raking all of this up with her death….

But at that moment Shankarababu recovered to become his own self again and looked like a honed dagger. He looked at me familiarly and laughed. Looking into the mirror, he brushed up his forelocks. Once again a fountain of enthusiasm, he started analysing the relative strengths of the parties in Andhra Pradesh and of the unpredictability of his own people.

'If I could find a Vidyaranya, I am sure I will build an empire. I am not the one to give up easily.' Picking up his briefcase he stood up and went away saying, 'Good luck!'

Translated by Ramachandra Sharma and modified for this collection by Chandan Gowda

ESSAYS AND SPEECHES

THE LITERARY SITUATION IN INDIA
Search for an Identity

I

The situation could have turned into a series of laudatory speeches in these days of seminars in India to celebrate centenaries of well-known Indian and international figures. But the secretary of the Ministry of Education which hosted the seminar to celebrate the Aurobindo centenary was a sensitive Hindi poet, who made the occasion an excuse to discuss problems of contemporary writing in the Indian languages. After the minister paid the expected tributes to Aurobindo and called upon the writers to uphold Indian culture, work for national integration, world peace, etc., we settled down to business. We had met in one of the dingy provincial capitals of North India, and among us we had writers in Hindi, Bengali, Marathi, and Kannada, and an internationally famous Indian painter.

The discussion inevitably turned to a topic that obsesses us Indian writers these days: why is the western mode of thought and writing the model for us? Why aren't we original in our treatment of form and content in the novel, drama, or poetry?

While Indian dance and music are uniquely Indian, why does contemporary Indian literature take its bearings from the literature of the West? Are we really a nation of mimics, victims of English education which has conditioned the faculties of our perception so much that we fail to respond freshly to the immediate situation in India? Should we read Brecht in order to discover that our folk theatre can be used? Why do we import even our radicalism via Ginsberg, Osborne, or Sartre? And our reaction against the West—isn't it often emotional, while intellectually we remain bound to western modes of thought?

But the language that we used to discuss these questions was English, as it had to be. And the names and examples that dominated our discussion were different from those fashionable ten years ago. In the place of T. S. Eliot and W. B. Yeats, dear to us for the impact of Indian philosophy on them, we used now the ideas of Albert Camus, Franz Kafka, Jean-Paul Sartre, and Georg Lukacs. We admired the achievement of Russian masters, who seemed better influences for us than the Anglo-Saxon writers who are anti-metaphysical and pragmatic in their outlook. Wasn't the Russian literary scene before the revolution very similar to ours, in its struggle between the Westernizers and the Slavophiles? Fyodor Dostoevsky with his metaphysical brooding was closer to the Indian temperament than the writers of the novels of manners. Still it was Shaw and Galsworthy, rather than the more poetic Synge and Chekhov, who influenced the previous generation of writers in India.

As we were discussing these questions, ironically with examples from the West rather than from our own literatures, some of which have a history of a thousand years, and quite a few writers radical and disturbing in their vision, the painter narrated to us an incident which deeply moved me. Before I relate what he said, let me describe how we dressed, which is important for the point I want to make.

The Bengali writer and a Hindi writer wore white dhotis and collarless long Indian shirts, which nearly all nationalist Indians wore during our struggle for freedom. The Bengali writer had a Marxist background (only he spoke in Bengali which was translated to us), and the Hindi writer was a Gandhian socialist of the Lohia school. Two Hindi writers and a Marathi writer, who were in their thirties and modernist in their writing, wore pants and jubba and had long hair—now the accepted attire of bohemian and artistic Indian intellectuals. (Even in this dress one looks middle class in India. The film stars have popularized it among the young of the rich and middle classes.) Only the painter looked authentically unmiddle class with his flowing hair and beard, collarless shirt and dhoti, not elegantly gathered and worn in the Bengali fashion, but tucked around the waist carelessly in the South Indian style. He could have been genuinely taken for a wandering Indian sadhu except for his powerful and well-articulated English. Perhaps a remark made by me in the course of the discussion on the search for Indian identity had prompted him to speak, or perhaps I am mistaken. Anyhow, this is what I had said.

Speaking of Kannada literature, I had observed that there were distinctly two generations of writers—those who belonged to the Gandhian era, and us. In order to clarify certain issues, I had ventured to generalize recklessly (which most of us were doing anyhow) and described these generations as 'insiders' and 'outsiders' respectively. Some 'insiders' even grew a tuft, wore caste marks, chewed betel, and, more often than not, came from a rural background. Along with their Gandhian idealism, their sensibilities bore the distinctive features of their castes and regions, and they wrote as if the English education they received was inconsequential. I had in my mind some great Kannada writers like Bendre, PuTiNa, and Masti, and I was of course rashly generalizing, for it was not unusual in the past to describe these writers as the Wordsworth, Shelley, Hardy, Shaw, etc., of Kannada. Yet I was not wholly wrong in thinking of them as 'insiders' in comparison with my generation of writers. There is no doubt we look and think differently from them. We admire their insider's knowledge of Indian tradition but reject their celebratory attitude toward Indian traditionalism. They made it possible for us to write, but we had to rebel against their conservative clinging to certain aesthetic modes. Some modern writers are, as a result, more inventive in their writing, but...haven't we also moved closer to the West in our experimentation, thus risking rootlessness in our own tradition? I raised the question, but as a practicing modernist writer myself I also tried to argue that there was no need to be unnecessarily anxious about it. We all write in the Indian languages, and this fact has a profound consequence on what we actually do in our languages, however much we expose ourselves to the West in search of ideas and forms. The 'insiders' and 'outsiders' can't remain mutually exclusive. The fact that we write in an Indian language, like Kannada, kept alive by the oral traditions of the illiterate rural people, as well as a thousand-year-long native literary tradition, which has behind it an even longer pan-Indian Sanskrit tradition, has its own influence on what its recent writers do with their exposure to the West. The medium shapes the writer, even when he is shaping it. The writer influenced by the West may think and feel like an outsider, and yet he has to be an insider to the language created by the peculiar congruence of indigenous and Sanskrit classical traditions, folk tradition, and now the impact of spreading western education. If you borrow western technology and science, its culture too is bound to influence you, and where else can the integration of conflicting strains in our life be achieved except in one's language?

I was at pains not to appear eclectic in my approach. I wanted my friends to see the emergence of a new Indian identity in our literature as the result of a dialectic, not a mixture, of the living old and new, which would be germane to the genius of our languages. Kannada writers had such a relationship with Sanskrit literature once, and our achievement in the past was not a copy of Sanskrit; in some writers at least it was unique-although within the context of Sanskritic tradition. In my argument I had assumed that language rejects what is wilfully and artificially imported into it, and discerning literary criticism can distinguish between what is genuine and what is faked without going into the abstract and unsolvable question of how much of western influence is good for us.

Moreover, I argued, the language, Kannada, may have a literary tradition of a thousand years; still the contemporary writer can only use the current language that has become a part of his experience in his own lifetime. The search for the language adequate to one's creation is also a continuous one; it varies from one work to another.

When the writer influenced by western literatures chooses to write in a language like Kannada, he has made a moral choice. If the ideas that are still not of my language are embodied in my language creatively, then it becomes a part of the living tradition of my language.

I said that one uses only the current language of one's lifetime; but perhaps it is even narrower than this. As a writer I have felt often that my essential language is what I acquired during my childhood in a village and what I have been able to add to it—not superficially but experientially—in the process of growing up. In the actual business of writing don't we all know how much of our knowledge and our acquired language is really superfluous and useless? The magic of literary creation lies in actualizing new facets of experience; suggesting the inarticulate while articulating the particular and the given; conquering new domains of experience which are not yet the property of my language. If I should do all these in a language that has become my own only from the days of my childhood, then that language which has roots in me must have roots outside me as well—in its tradition of a thousand years, and what is affecting the lives of the people who speak that language today. If the western impact on us is a reality, how can we wish it away? I will have to relate myself to it with my language, which, if it has to have evocative power, should have its roots in the language of the ancient poets, and its current life in the idiomatic vigour of the illiterate peasant's speech.

As a creative writer I work on this assumption, but I can't wholly silence my literary conscience with that argument. Hence what the painter said, his extraordinary appearance and ability as an artist adding to the power of his argument, deeply disturbed me. In retrospect what he said may seem simple to me now, but the fact that I was disturbed by his argument (and a few other writers were also impressed like me), is an indication of a profound disquiet among the Indian writers today in their search for identity. The painter was travelling through villages in North India studying folk art. A lonely cottage at the foot of a hill attracted his eye. As he approached the cottage, he was puzzled by a piece of stone which he saw inside the cottage through the window; it was decorated with kumkum—the red powder that our women wear on their foreheads as an auspicious sign and flowers. He wanted to photograph the stone that the peasant worshipped and he asked the peasant who was weaving a basket outside the cottage if he could bring the stone outside the cottage into the sun so he could take a picture. After taking the photograph, the painter apologized to the peasant in case the stone he worshipped was polluted by moving it outside. He had not expected the peasant's reply. 'It doesn't matter,' the peasant said, 'I will have to bring another stone and anoint it with kumkum.' Any piece of stone on which he put kumkum became God for the peasant. What mattered was his faith, not the stone. Do we understand the manner in which the peasant's mind worked? the painter asked us. Can we understand his essentially mythical and metaphorical imagination which directed his inner life? Will Lukacs and Bertrand Russell, who influence the structure of our thinking now, help us see instinctively the way this peasant's mind worked? That is why we don't understand the complex pattern of ancient Indian thought, its daring subjectivity, caught as we are in the narrow confines of western scientific rationality. In his simplicity the peasant still keeps alive the mode of thinking and perception, which at the dawn of human civilization revealed to the sages of the Upanishads the vision that Atman is Brahman. Shouldn't we prefer the so-called superstition of the peasant, which helps him see organic connections between the animal world, the human world and the nature surrounding him, to the scientific rationality of western science that has driven the world into a mess of pollution and ecological imbalance? The painter continued: Western education has alienated us utterly from this peasant who belongs to the category of the 70 per cent of the illiterate Indian mass. There is no gap for him between what he perceived subjectively and objectively. As his senses were actively engaged with the world outside him, he had no time to reflect on the luxury of the existentialist problem of whether life was meaningful. If we don't understand the structure and mode of this peasant's thinking, we can't become true Indian writers. Therefore we should free ourselves from the enslaving rationalist modes of western scientific thinking, from which even their great writers are not totally liberated. Only then we will be able to see what connects this peasant vitally to his world that surrounds him and to his ancestor, who perhaps plowed the same patch of land some three thousand years ago. The western modes of perception will not help us understand what sustains this peasant—whether it is liberalism, scientific positivism, or even Marxism—these European-born theories only serve to make us feel inferior and thus turn our country into an imitative copy of the West.

As I said, we were moved by the painter's argument. In the midst of Camus, Sartre, Kafka, and Lukacs, he had stood before us, an authentic Indian who was untouched by the ideas of any of these writers whom we were using as points of reference to define our positions.

In retrospect a doubt nagged me. Isn't the authentic Indian peasant, whose imagination is mythical and who relates to nature organically, also a current radical reaction against western materialism, which has begun to exercise an influence on the educated middle class writers of India? What if these spiritual reactions to the West are their way of keeping fit, and the 'decline of the West' theory is a glibly repeated humbug?

In India, Mahatma Gandhi, who himself approximated the Indian peasant in his appearance, in his mode of thinking, and in his political imagery, still chose Pandit Nehru, the westernized Indian, as his successor. I don't think that the children of that peasant will believe in the magic of transforming the stone into God, nor did the painter work on his canvas that way—he sought an objective form, there, on the canvas, for his perceptions and ideas, and he couldn't ignore the experimentations in western painting.

Still why did the painter move me with his argument? Why do we educated Indian writers of my generation—most of whom now belong to the middle class intelligentsia—suffer from a nagging self-doubt? Why are we all soliloquists and monologuists' stream of consciousness technique is very popular with our novelists—whereas the older generation of writers, who were also English educated and belonged to the upper classes and castes in India, did not think that their perceptions were limited to themselves? Perhaps as they belonged to a generation that was involved in the struggle to free India, they felt a common destiny with the masses of India, which in the post-independent India we don't feel. They did think that they wrote and spoke for the whole country—whatever be the quality of their writing, a good deal of which was sloppy, sentimental and revivalist. I even envy the home-spun plain khadi clothes they wore, which were egalitarian symbols in the post-independent India of Gandhi but which no longer are, because they are the clothes of our corrupt politicians and ministers. We do not think that we can be intensely personal and universal at the same time—a confidence which is important for the creation of great art. As a result we keep reacting rather than creating; we advocate the absurd, or in reaction to it admire the authentic Indian peasant—all of them masks to hide our own uncertainties. In the morass of poverty, disease, and ugliness of India, isn't the westernized Indian inauthentic, and inconsequential, and the traditional peasant an incongruous and helpless victim of centuries of stagnation? Why did it seem to us that to be authentically Indian we should idealize the simple peasant? We had great Indian writers in the past who had a quarrel with the belief patterns of traditional India. In their search for an authentic mode of existence, twelfth-century mystical poets in my language, Basavanna, Allama, and the woman poet Akka, were very impatient with the naive acquiescence and resignation of the traditional Indian mind. They didn't emulate the peasant, but tried to rouse him into an awareness of his inner potential. The great Indian tradition was not merely spiritual and devotional; we had the materialist Lokayata School, the Sankhya System, and Jainism and Buddhism which were atheistic. It is a tradition of an intense conflict of world views, yet our revivalists prefer to select only one aspect of it. Isn't this debilitating romantic strain in us also due to our obsession with the West?

I shall summarily try to pose the question like this: the continuity of tradition of rural India, and the gymnastics of the Indian intellectual which begin and end with him, have remained apart, unrelated. Why is there still no reaching out to each other? Why are we not fully possessed of the vital problems of India? And why don't we have the confidence and desire to affect the thinking of the peasant who, in turn, should become creative as some of them did in the twelfth century in my language? If and when the writers of our country give such immediate responsive attention to our situation, would we not then be less obsessed with the West, and wouldn't much that is happening in the West today seem irrelevant to us? The noble Nehru ran the affairs of the country with his face always turned to the West. What will the post-Nehru generation of writers do? Would Gandhism and Maoism, which have many similarities, create in our countries the situation that necessitates the kind of attention I spoke of? But then, wouldn't our literature become monotonous, burdened with one theme, one purpose, one attitude?

II

I should take a more professional look at the problem and clarify issues as they are, rather than lose myself in wild speculation as I did now. Yet I do not regret revealing to you the tenor and trend of our minds in India today. I don't want to pretend that I have overcome the painter's argument; the peasant does bother me, like Anna Karenina's dream in Tolstoy's novel, and I am worried that the underlying assumption of the literary culture in which I write is potentially capable of making the peasant's mode of existence and thinking irrelevant to me. And a large part of the reality of my country is still him, and he is there in my language, whose vigour of expression has been preserved by him.

Between any two literatures there can be roughly three kinds of relations: first, the relation of the master and the slave; second, the relation of equals; third, the relation between a developed country like Europe or America and a developing nation like ours. The example for the first is the way the white men imposed their culture on the blacks in America. Yet no imposition can be completely successful—as in music, in literature too, the minority culture of the blacks may contain the creative nucleus that will influence the literature of the whole country. The interaction between the English and the French literatures illustrates the second kind of relationship. When a French historian writes the history of English literature, it is possible that he sees a French writer at the back of all the important English writers.

The third kind of relationship is more complex than the first two. I use economic categories to describe this relationship rather than terms like East and West, for the thought patterns arising from the division of mankind into East and West are often simplistic. In my own country, as it must be evident from my talk, it results in either imitation or frigid conservatism. Only because I am born an Indian I refuse to think that it is a crime to respond more to Tolstoy or to Shakespeare than, say, to Pampa's epic in my language. I must also be aware when I say this that the novels of Karanth in my language, although they fall short of the world masterpieces I admire, are much more relevant to me in forming my sensibility.

We are a very poor, humiliated nation now, but with a rich and highly sophisticated culture in the past. This creates many psychological complications in our relation to the West. The influence of western literatures may either sharpen our attention to our own reality, or it may take our minds away from what is most relevant to our situation. This is the heart of the problem—how can we have a mature relationship? Is it ever possible to have a mature relationship of equals, when the relationship is one-sided? America wants our gurus, but will she ever need our poets and novelists and respond to them, as we respond to American writers? And even this response is often out of proportion to the real merit of the writers—which is still another problem of uncritical acceptance of received opinions from the West.

Dr Lohia, a great Gandhian socialist thinker of India, once described Indian intellectuals either as backward-looking, sideways-looking or forward-looking. The backward-lookers entertain the illusion that the solution to our problem lies in the revival of our past. (Which aspect of our past? The revivalists are highly selective; they ignore the skeptical and rationalist aspects of our past.) If this is the typical thinking of the conservative upper castes in India, the cosmopolites in India always look sideways. Shall we be like America? Or Russia? Or France? Or Britain? They too speak very emotionally about the ancient glory of India, yet they seek their intellectual motivations from the West. They can get very upset about the American atrocities in Vietnam, but they don't raise a finger against the burning of the huts of the untouchable castes by the landlords of Andhra Pradesh in India. They admire Ginsberg's protest and ungentlemanly ways, yet when one of our earnestly radical legislators removed his chappal to beat the corrupt ministers in the Assembly, they were utterly shocked by his lack of manners. They wear the hippie costume, but the material is imported terylene.

But if you think that the great scientific and cultural progress of the West, with its exploration of space and its undoubted creative energy, is related to the famine and hunger among the illiterate peasants of the rural areas of Gulbarga and Bijapur in my state, and that these two interrelated phenomena are bound to react mutually as our people are roused to consciousness, then we have to become forward-looking; not only the people of the East but those of the West, too. The forward-looking Indian will then have to work for approximation among mankind, which is possible only through a new technology, and a new political and economic order which are again related. For the writer in India who has such a vision, the famine in an Indian village, a new literary experiment in French literature, the science that has caused enormous wealth in one part of the globe and poverty in another, the ancient mystical poetry of Kabir and Basavanna, which he may read wearing western dress, but which still moves him to the depths, all these coalesce into an immediate contemporary reality. He has to make many more connections than he does now, or more than much of contemporary western literature, which he reads, does.

As a writer, then, he will have to struggle to embody his vision in a language in which you can write like Blake and not analytically like Russell, and which, unlike European languages, is still rural.

I am sorry to have slipped into such a high note again. I spoke of the cliché postures of backward-looking orientalism, and imitative westernization—they are really the same. The great sage of the Upanishads, Yajnavalkya, was not an orientalist; he was not bothered about his Indian identity. Imitation either of our own past or of Europe leads to sterility; and attention to the immediate reality is warped. Also, as I have indicated earlier, the Indian orientalist chooses to uphold a highly simplified version of India, the image of India created during our freedom fighting renaissance, an image again moulded in the narrow Victorian sensibility. Even Mahatma Gandhi was essentially a puritan and lacked the richness and complexity of ancient Indian thought.

In reaction against the orientalists and the westernizers, some of our really intelligent and sophisticated writers have created a new kind of work of art, which, apparently, looks Indian and original. Yet in a very subtle manner these works are also Indian equivalents of western models. The conceptual framework into which the material is organized is western. The material is Indian—the details of life, the myths, the folklore, the legends are all there, but you feel 'Why should I read this after reading Kafka or Camus?' You can't borrow the style or form of these writers without their philosophy, their concept of man; it is not neutral like classical realism. I would say there are some 'mental frames' today in western literature, born out of certain definitions and concepts of man which dominate the literature of the world, and certainly of India, and this has resulted in monotony. Therefore the Indian writer looking for a new mode of perception is certainly attracted by the simple peasant who has remained through the centuries impenetrable to the cultures of the conquerors. It is important to know that he exists; our hypersensitive, highly personal nightmares will at least be tempered with the irony of such knowledge.

The question then could be put this way: in India, what should happen to the whole country so that we will be forced out of the grooves that I have been speaking of?

III

I will not attempt an answer to this big question but will try to take another look at what makes these grooves in our cultural situation. Is there a relationship between what the writer creates and the expectations of an ideal reader? What I wish to say now is based on the assumption that the implicit awareness of his potential ideal reader is one of the important factors entering into the writer's creative process-the embodying process of bringing a work into existence in a particular cultural context. Let me see then what has been happening in my language. In the classical period of Kannada literature nearly a thousand years ago, the ideal reader, who belonged to the elite class forming a very small fraction of the society which could read and write, could presumably read Sanskrit also. Therefore he brought to his reading of Kannada aesthetic expectations formed from his study of Sanskrit. The best of Kannada literature in the past is original within the context of Sanskrit literature. Its departures are important, yet they are departures. No good writer limits himself to the expectations of the reader; he extends them, but within a given context. Even now the literates in my language are hardly thirty percent, and the discerning ideal reader of our literary works is one whose sensibility is formed by a study of English literature. This is the cultural situation in which we are writing; the peasant at the foot of the hill can't read me. His consciousness may enter my work as an 'object' for others like me to read, which will be very different from what would have been if I were aware in my creative process that he was also my potential reader. The socio-economic process that will make him a potential reader may also make him a man of the sideways-looking middle class like us. Is it possible then to have a different context for writing in a country like India? Yet there is literature in India which cuts across this framework. There were revolutionary periods in our history which saw important socio-cultural changes brought about by great religious movements. These religious poets worked in the oral tradition, and therefore in the creative process itself they had before them both literate and illiterate people. Thus when the illiterate masses were not mere objects and themes of literary creation, but participants in the act of communication, our regional literature underwent a change not only in theme, but in its aesthetic structure. In an important way, this literature created in the oral tradition, since it was not conditioned by the expectation of the Sanskrit educated literati, becomes most daring and original in its imagery, metaphor, and rhythmic structures. There is a big gap between the language and rhythm of classical literature in Kannada of the twelfth century and the language I use today. But the language and rhythm of the mystical poetry of Basavanna, Akka, and Allama, who are also of the twelfth century, are like those of the language in which I write today. And these poets were radical in their attitudes too. I must note an important point here. Their audience which cut across social barriers was an immediate one for them. It was not a mass audience to whose taste they catered. The difference is significant.

I don't foresee such a socio-cultural and religious turmoil challenging us to create outside the defined frameworks of the cultural and literary expectations of our highly limited reading public. The oral tradition is still there in India, but the urge to work in it is not found among our English educated middle-class writers. The expansion of the reading public, whether it is brought about by the present system in India or by the kind of Indian Marxists we have now, will again be through a process of modernization and industrialization-and therefore such a literate mass may not create for the writers a qualitatively different writing situation. What we see of the Marxist progressive writing in India is propagandist; its relation with its audience is hackneyed and unproductive; it is not truly a dialogue in Paulo Freire's sense.

I hope you will appreciate why I can't neatly end this paper. What is the best that a writer who has this awareness can do? Perhaps write for himself. But that is not even ideally possible—I would like to add—and yet….

THE CONTEMPORARY SIGNIFICANCE OF LOHIA

I had once rashly told Ram Manohar Lohia that he and D. H. Lawrence were the two great influences on me as a Kannada writer and that I wanted to write about that. I was barely thirty then, still finding my way, experimenting in short fiction and poetry. Lohia had listened with interest to my view on Lawrence and had chided me good humouredly for my reluctance to use four-lettered words, even though I admired Lawrence's reverence for the whole of life, for all the functions of the body. Lohia could see without my telling him why Lawrence was necessary for liberating me from the inhibitions of an orthodox Brahmin upbringing, but where did Lohia come into the picture? He had suggested that it would be interesting if I could write about that. 'Don't bother yourself too much with footnoting and quoting, but write straight from your feelings,' he had advised. I had then gone on to talk to him of the political and spiritual rebellion of the twelfth-century Kannada Vachanakaras, and Lohia probed me with extraordinary keenness for details about the careers of Basava, the Brahmin rebel who got a pariah married to a Brahmin girl, and the woman saint Akka Mahadevi, who asserted her spiritual equality with men by going about naked. Both of them are great poets of the twelfth-century Veerashaiva movement. My own understanding of this movement was deepened that day by Lohia's question and comments.

On the question of why I associated Lawrence with Lohia in my mind, I was vague then, and still am vague. Yet they existed in my mind simultaneously, and they had together given me an angle that made it possible for me to connect disparate strands of my experiences and thoughts. Writing, as I did, under the cultural imperialism of European-born ideas, like many other Indian writers, I was fortunate to have read Lohia, for he rooted me in the Indian soil. Those were the days when, for the Indian intellectual, the unorthodox behaviour of an Allen Ginsberg was revolutionary, whereas Lohia's actions seemed quixotic.

I had read Lohia avidly, particularly his essays in *Interval During Politics* (1965), and yet I could not explicitly state why I associated Lawrence with Lohia. Only in my creative writing such as in my novel, *Samskara*, and some novellas I wrote during the period like *Ghatashraddha*, I feel I did synthesize the creative influence of the two on me. What I could do in my creative writing, I still can't do in expository thought. I can only mumble a few general observations. Lawrence and Lohia were both passionately concerned with the existing state of their cultures and related all their speculations pointedly and concretely to the lived reality. They were both highly and imaginatively selective in what they thought was the living tradition of their countries, and in the mode of their choice, what guided them was a highly developed moral sense of what a living thing felt like. Both could combine love with anger, without the cleansing effect of which love can degenerate into an inconsequential general goodwill. Considering how easily universal love is mouthed as meaningless cliches in our country, Lohia's ability to change these ideas into action was a gift that only moral geniuses have. Lawrence whose intense concern was with personal fulfilment went on, as a natural extension of such a concern, into a daring enquiry into questions of culture and the destructive element in modern civilization—that is, into areas of collective life with an immediacy that reminds you of a visionary like William Blake. There is an excess in him which may make one feel awkward, but the over-insistence is only a matter of emphasis, an emphasis that the age itself necessitated by its moral blindness. Lohia too exceeded, at times, the limits of propriety, which produces in some of his disciples, who are without his moral refinement and keenness of intellect, the effect of a caricature. It is the fate of all gurus to produce caricatures. Lohia chose, in contrast to Lawrence, the political arena as his area of concern but he didn't stop there. He never lost sight of the individual, his craving for privacy and beauty. The moment itself engaged all his attention, and yet he was capable of detachment. He could speak of 'Nirasha ki Kartavya,' a project of 'socialism in one hundred years.' Of the seven revolutions he speaks of, the last, but not the least, 'aims at protecting privacy against encroachment by the collective.' There is another important matter of cultural taste where they were surprisingly similar. Both preferred the immediacy of the artistic expressions of folk culture to those of classicist sensibility. For a certain kind of classicism in music, architecture, and literature with their elaborate and intricate structures and conventions are more often than not products of imperialist and hierarchical social systems, whereas the folk arts are the intimate and immediate expressions of the intuitive 'body' of man that don't require an elaborate shastra.

For a Brahmin like me from an orthodox background, there was a special sense in which Lawrence and Lohia interacted in strengthening my own incipient perceptions. Lohia's caste analysis had helped me to see how the caste system can trap you and thus limit your awareness of life. The Brahmin has intelligence, but without spontaneity, it goes dry and degenerates into mere verbal cleverness. The Shudra has spontaneity, related as he is to the earth, but unconnected with intelligence and capacity for abstract speculation, he doesn't become fully conscious of his existence and his concerns are lost in the trivia of the quotidian. The union of Parasara and Matsyagandha had produced the seer Vedavyasa, and the sterility of our culture could only be overcome again by such a union of the Brahmin and the Shudra. I am putting this idea crudely and simplistically—which, as broad categorization of our complex society, no sociologist would perhaps accept, but that was an emotional drive which guided my creative work in those days and I needed a bold simplification of that kind. Since I worked on a symbolic and poetic, rather than a documentary and realistic, plane the simplification couldn't hurt me. Lohia's Shudra, Jiddu Krishnamurthy's choiceless awareness, and Lawrence's unconsciousness and reverence for all these got mixed up in my mind and helped me clarify to myself what I thought was inadequate in the Brahmin ethos in which I grew up, whose own self-image was one of complacent self-satisfaction (...).

Lohia has continued to influence me, rather indirectly after *Samskara*.

The economic and social reality of peoples' lives is governed by the temple-and the hero, educated in the West, realized that he has no true identity, no true being unless he gets involved in changing the reality of the people around him—which is possible only if the grip of the God is loosened. The God Manjunatha himself was installed over a tribal God, who is made a 'bhutha' in attendance on the Lord Shiva, in an act of cultural colonization. Hence the hero sets out to take the Holeyas into the temple, so that they can recover their own God, and thus set at naught the potent belief that pollution would mean instant death.

There is a chapter in the novel in which the hero takes out the saligram of his own ancestral house and offers it for touch to the frightened pariahs whose consciousness he is trying to arouse. The act is appalling to his relations at home and they gather in the pyol and look on with fascinated fear the hero walking with the Narasimha saligram on his open palm to the pariahs. He wants to prove that it is a mere stone, but the awestruck eyes of the spectators—who include other Hindu castes as well—transform the very act into its opposite. Their intensity of apprehension, which is echoed in the hero's heart, makes what ought to be a stone into a saligram. He goes with the saligram thus charged, paradoxically, to the pariahs, who dare not touch what is offered to them. The stone becomes a saligram, by their refusal to touch it, and the landlord hero is infuriated. He orders the pariahs to touch it and make it into a mere stone, so that they may recover their full humanity and dignity. They do it meekly and the hero realizes suddenly that his revolutionary project has only reduced the pariahs into less than human objects, whereas, to the tradition bound maternal aunt, they are still human for she deals with them in the area of sanctioned relationships.

I think I was probing Lohia's project in his own terms in chapters like these: the distortions, problems and the urgencies that attend upon social transformation, and yet, without which, the individual becomes a nullity, too. My third novel, *Avasthe*, picks up these themes further, enquiring into the distortions of the human essence that a political life may lead to. There can be no personal life, pure and single that can remain outside of politics, but the life of an ideologue given over entirely to politics will also dry up. As Yeats had said it in his poem, 'Easter 1916':

Hearts with one purpose alone
Through summer and winter seem

Enchanted to a stone
To trouble the living stream
(...)
Too long a sacrifice
can make a stone of the heart.

There is dehumanization and corruption either way, whether you are in or out of politics, but the sense of responsibility with which a truly political life is burdened with charges the political man with a rare kind of angst. The ideological preoccupation takes him away from the cares of everyday life, its momentary joys and sorrows that every house-wife knows, and yet he has taken to politics so that this routine everyday reality may take on a meaning. Is the meaning not already there for those who are soaked in it? Is not life something lived here and now? Such questions are at the background of many of Lohia's essays in his *Interval During Politics.* I am not directly referring to any particular idea of his, but the temper of his mind which, even while it pursued the ideal, was fascinated with the life as it is lived in the actual, has been an important factor in my own education as a writer. He saved me very early in my creative life from the two dangers to which I too like many other fellow writers was prone. In India you either end up a pious worshipper of ancient India, mouthing the well-known cliches, or you glibly favour the western imported contempt for India or your superior alienation, also imported from abroad. I have always thought of Lohia as someone who emerged from the great Sramana tradition, the adversary culture that has given us some of the great men in our own century, like Mahatma Gandhi.

From an Indian writer's point of view, I would say that the great value of Lohia's writings lies in his criticism of our culture. The Marxist tends to belittle culture a false consciousness, which arises from a given structure of economic relations and which, in their turn, are determined by the prevalent modes of production. In opposition to this, most of us would tend to take an ahistorical view which often is unhelpful and nebulous. For Lohia who tried to combine theory with practice, both these attitudes were insufficient. I quote him:

> The relation between being and consciousness, between mode of production and expressions of consciousness has not been studied in any detail or in its totality. Why an object may be the same in all the world and yet possess a variety of names in different parts of the earth, all incomprehensible one to the other is a present question. The woodcutter and the axe are same the world over, but they have a hundred different names in different languages… Consciousness may well have a style and a significance of their own and an enduring character….*

The importance of Lohia's mind for us lies in the unique way in which he was open to both Marx and Gandhi, and the creative way in which he learned from both of them. Although I am untrained in systematic political thought, his criticism of Marx has seemed to be of seminal importance. England ruled us not only through its superior technology but through its 'enlightened' liberalism of philosophers James Stuart Mill and Jeremy Bentham, and there are any number of apologists of British Imperialism among us who argue that we needed the British to free us from superstitious practices like sati. The same argument is put forth by Marxist westernizers who condone the Russian invasion of Afghanistan or the Chinese invasion of Tibet, arguing that the ideas of Karl Marx, Friedrich Engels, and Vladimir Lenin would liberate these areas from cruel feudal practices. We forget that a living culture should be able to produce a dynamic of creative internal struggle and evolve on its own, meeting on its way the continuous new challenges of history. Contrary to what we profess, we are truly believers in the iron law of determinism which maintains that human consciousness has no choice except the one of accepting modern civilization. Lohia saw that the fascination of Marxism for many of us lay in its theory that the inexorable laws of development of capitalism would themselves bring in socialism. The struggles of the revolutionary party would only hasten the process. Capitalism was also supposed automatically by its own nature to assure unlimited happiness for mankind. Lohia vigorously attacked such formulations of history and restored to

---

*Rammanohar Lohia, *Marx, Gandhi and Socialism*, Goa: Navhind, 1963, p. 372.

human consciousness and to human culture its rightful freedom and dignity. There are forces which limit our choices, yes, but man can struggle against them. In the sense that it cripples our choices and holds up Europe as a model, Marxism is used as the latest weapon of Europe as against the rest of the world. We succumb to it, not realizing the erroneous nature of its analysis of the growth of western capitalism itself. In the linear conception of history where capitalism is perceived as a higher form of development than feudalism, and which, when mature, gives way to socialism, we in Asia would always be inferior to Europe. The superiority of the West is thus ensured either under the theory of Mill and Bentham or of Marx and Engels. Lohia in his criticism of Marx's theory of the development of capitalism saw that capitalism consisted not alone of an internal circle represented by the West European economy but of two circles—an internal West European circle and an external world circle, from which the west—European internal circle draws its sustenance. Capitalism and imperialism are thus twins. Imperialism is not a tumour of capitalism. They are two circles, one placed inside the other, the rim of the inner circle possessing an enormous porous capacity to suck into itself the dynamics of the outer. There is no use racing with the West, even if you go communist. If Russia is struggling in vain to catch up with the United States of America, China tries in vain to catch up with Russia. We have to opt for an alternative system which is neither Russian nor American. Socialism will be such an alternative when it destroys not only capitalist relations of production but capitalist means of production. The answer is a small-unit machine, and a mode of production that involves man's creative impulse and not subjugate him to its monstrous power.

If the mode of production is the same, whether under capitalism or communism, the consciousness of man remains also the same. Man will forever be driven to seek the spiritual outside the material realities, rather than celebrate the ever-renewing universe of the actual. Lohia, therefore, did not denounce, or look askance at man's effort in history to define the nature of his being in relation to the universe, the most important expression of which is religion. I am quoting him now at length for I feel that what he says is important, and some of his followers in the South in their pursuit of rationalism and attack on religious superstition have not fully grasped:

> While an old time socialism denounced religion as opium to man, the more modern attitude seems to be one of indifference to matters of religion and belief in secularism. This is not a complete attitude. Religion appears in four different ways. It breaks out as quarrels, sometimes bloody, among various religions. It defends and upholds the existing order with its modes of property, caste and woman. It is also an ethical and social training in good conduct. Finally, religion at its best appears as the discipline of compassion and contemplation. The first two expressions of religion are indeed an opium to the people. Instead of making politics religious and thereby softening somewhat the clashes of power, religion itself becomes political and thereby adds fanaticism to intrigue. Such a religion must of course be denounced, but the other expressions of religion cannot be a matter of unconcern to politics or socialism.*

I said that Lohia's main importance for the literary people consists in his vital criticism of culture in which he neither denounces the past nor extols it, but with great flexibility of mind, discriminates between its living and sterile expressions in the present. His test is life, life in the present, and the search for ways in which our stagnant national life may become creative again and not stay satisfied with mere repetition.

*Lohia, *Marx, Gandhi and Socialism*, pp. 374–75.

WHY NOT WORSHIP IN THE NUDE?
Reflections of a Novelist in his Times

The reality for a novelist in India—I am speaking from my Kannada experience—is so complex as to disallow the comforts of either status-quoist acceptance or of revolutionary ruthlessness. R. K. Narayan can afford to say 'India will go on' only as a comic realist in his inimitable low mimetic mode. But when his insightful Indian experience is translated into ideas in a polemical context, it is difficult to defend them. The same is true of V. S. Naipaul's indictment of Indian reality. He can afford to speak angrily and ruthlessly, and plead for a thoroughgoing modernization in India—only in a polemical context. I wonder if he can maintain his position unambiguously in a novel where his imaginative sympathies are fully engaged.

All of us share this dilemma. What we feel and what we think are often in conflict. Even while I am writing this I am engaged in a bewilderingly confusing discussion with my radical friends about an incident in Chandragutti, a village of my district eighty-five kilometres from Shimoga, where every year, in March, men and women of all ages offer naked worship to a goddess in fulfilment of a vow. Early morning they take a dip in the River Varada, wait in the water to get possessed, and then run four or five kilometres to go up a picturesque hill 800 metres above sea level to worship Renukamba. Last month, many young men and women belonging to radical and rationalist organizations went there, with the encouragement of the Social Welfare Department of the government, to plead with these 'backward-caste' worshippers that nude worship was 'wrong' and 'inhuman'. This attracted wide media attention and journalists went there too, with their cameras. Earlier, two weeklies run by rationalist and scheduled caste activists had also carried pictures of nude worshippers on their colourful cover pages. These weeklies published articles attacking what, for them, seemed an inhuman 'superstitious' practice, while they also aimed at increasing their circulation with the nude pictures.

The encounter between the illiterate believers and the educated middle-class rationalists was both fierce and unexpected. The worshippers broke through the physical barricade of the rationalists who stood on the bank of the river pleading with them to wear clothes. And then they ran to the hill in frenzied possession. Some worshippers even turned violent. The deputy superintendent of police was stripped forcibly of his khaki uniform, and forced to go naked in procession with the worshippers. The women-police were also mercilessly stripped by the dancing priestesses, called jogithis. A policewoman, it was reported, felt so humiliated and helpless that she wanted to kill herself. The jogithis, with their matted hair and red-and yellow-powder-smeared faces, danced gleefully, waving police pants and helmets and iron trishuls. The clothed devotees and pilgrims who had gathered in Chandragutti from far and near on foot, on bullock carts, buses and lorries ascribed the mass hysteria to the fury of the goddess Renukamba, even while they felt sympathy for the victims. Nobody seemed to have any sympathy for the photographers whose expensive cameras were smashed like the coconut offerings to the goddess.

In my political action—whatever little a full-time teacher like me can do—I have not wavered all these thirty years. I remain a democratic socialist. But with regard to cultural questions, I am increasingly and agonizingly growing ambivalent. *Bharathipura* was written about a decade ago, at a time which also saw the rise of activism among the Scheduled Caste radicals and rationalists in Karnataka. Some of my intimate friends, whom I respect and with whom, politically, I have a lot in common are among these activist groups and therefore my dilemmas cause me and also my friends bafflement and pain. They often feel very angry and also, naturally, intolerant with my dilemmas.

The papers are full of the Chandragutti episode, and we meet in a committee room of the Central Institute of Indian Languages in Mysore, under the auspices of a journal that I edit, to discuss the happenings. Our small group consists of two anthropologists, liberals of different persuasions, and a woman activist of great courage and commitment who has luckily come back unscathed from Chandragutti. We are eager to hear the anthropologists and the woman activist. We already have some anthropological data regarding the Chandragutti worship. *The Hindu*, a solidly middle-class, even conservative South Indian paper with a Marxist on its editorial board, has published a report with the headline, 'Were the volunteers over-enthusiastic?' (*The Hindu*, Monday, March 24, 1986). The report tells us that we have records of Chandragutti dating back to 1396 CE. It was an early stronghold of the Kadamba kings of Banavasi. The mythological references of Chandragutti date back to the pre-Kruta Yuga days. This was the sage Jamadagni's hermitage, according to legend. His wife Renuka went to bring water from the river as she did daily, but one day she failed to repeat the miracle of carrying water in a basket as she had lost her purity. She had seen a Kshatriya king bathing in the river, and she was for a moment attracted to him. Her husband Jamadagni perceived what had happened, and he ordered his son, Parasurama, to kill his mother. There are several stories about this. Parasurama obeyed his father, and from the pleased father earned the boon of getting his mother back to life, but had to wander round the world in expiation, vainly trying to wash clean the axe of his mother's blood. He also killed all the Kshatriyas and spared only Rama, who, like him, is an avatar of Vishnu. But the legend in Chandragutti is vivid and dramatic. As the son pursued Renuka to behead her, she ran recklessly and in the process lost all her clothes. She hid herself in the Shiva temple, naked. There is still a cave in Chandragutti below which is a rock shaped like two giant hips, believed to be those of Renuka. There is another legend linking Renuka with Matangi, who was Renuka's maidservant. Parasurama, before leaving on his mission of killing Kshatriyas, entrusted his mother to the care of Matangi's son, Beerappa. But he grows into a sex maniac and Matangi, moved by the plight of helpless women, provided them with clothes.

Even today, as the naked women come to the temple of Matangi, they are provided with new clothes. Many of these worshippers are also devotees of Yellamma of Saundatti in Belgaum District. The two are believed to be sisters. There is also a legend that Renuka of Kruta Yuga took the form of Yellamma in Kaliyuga. The radical activists are up against practices observed to propitiate Yellamma of Saundatti. Young girls offer themselves as prostitutes in observation of a vow, and many of them nowadays find their way into Bombay's flesh market owing to commercial exploitation. There are jogithis and khojas in the Yellamma temple, too. Some activists who went to Chandragutti associate the nude worship with the likely enticement into prostitution.

In our meeting, the anthropologists offer proper technical explanations: for the way in which Dravidian culture has interacted with the Aryan in Chandragutti, and for the unique survival of age—old practices like possession—worship, owing to the inaccessibility of the hilly regions of the Sahyadri range of mountains. And, of course, they ask what is the cultural significance of mother worship in general, and what it may mean to the lower castes in Chandragutti. And they offer guesses regarding the private psychological problems of the devotees and the therapeutic nature of the nude worship. They speculate on how some women offer their hair, some others their nudity—whatever is held to be most valuable to themselves, to the goddess. And so on. And finally the anthropologists add: it is futile to attempt to stop a practice until you study in depth what the practice means to the actual believers. But change they must, some day—and their quarrel is only with the tactics employed by the over-enthusiastic activists. They concur with the first sentence of *The Hindu* report: 'Can a deep-seated superstition handed down the centuries be eradicated overnight?'

The woman activist is impatient. We should make a beginning somewhere, shouldn't we? In the name of culture and belief, do we tolerate untouchability and the practice of sati? Have we not legislated against such evil practices? She is also angry with the government that it did not take enough precautions by way of extra police force. Although she didn't actually say so in the meeting, many of the activists are attacking the government that the police didn't even burst tear gas shells, and they had rifles in vain. Some activists suspect the hand of Hindu revivalists in the attack, but one of them also acknowledges that the Vishwa Hindu Parishad, a militant revivalist organization, had published pamphlets calling upon the devotees to give up nude worship.

The woman activist is still under shock from what she has seen, and one of the anthropologists tries to persuade her that the practice of untouchability, which is a social evil, should not be equated with nude worship. Yet he agrees with her that it must go, and that it will go, with education and civilization spreading into the area. Another anthropologist speaks of the practice of hooking oneself up in the air on the back, and being turned round in the observation of a vow, and how the worshipper doesn't even bleed with the hook pierced into the flesh. Such is the intensity of faith in some lower castes, and such is the power of possession.

The woman activist looks on bewildered as the anthropologist goes on to narrate a famous Kannada story by Ananda, *The Girl I Killed*. In the story, the girl is a prostitute from a respectable and rich landlord family. She is given over to the temple in fulfilment of a vow. The story is narrated by a traveller—that he is a superior 'outsider' and a city person is important—collecting historical information on a temple in the vicinity. (Also note that his interest in the temple is aesthetic and historical, not religious.) He stays as a guest in her father's house. The girl in her innocence and gratitude for the affection shown by the sophisticated guest from the city, offers herself to him. He doesn't know what she is. Being a stranger to such practices and a rationalist–moralist, he is shocked by the inhumanity of the practice. He convinces her how despicable the superstitious practice is, only to find her drowned in a well the next morning. The anthropologist implies by his story that we don't have any right to interfere with the belief-pattern of others. But the story also implies a point I feel that the anthropologist has missed that one cannot help interacting—although the result is tragic.

The woman activist is so possessed by her conviction in the rational approach to life, that she is too impatient to pay attention to the subtleties of the story's message. I understand how she feels, and why the cool distance and objectivity that the anthropologist enjoys by virtue of his discipline, sounds somewhat inauthentic to her.

We have in our midst a linguist belonging to the Sikh faith. Only a week earlier he had spoken with great feeling how his people were driven to fundamentalism because of the desecration of the Golden Temple of Amritsar. Today he surprises me with his argument. How can we in India afford to have the objectivity of the anthropologists? The terrorists strike in Punjab because of their faith. Do we merely look on? The jogithis in Chandragutti defend nudity with their tridents. Can we merely look on? The anthropologist doesn't answer him, but argues: don't we tolerate the nude sages of the Digambara Jain cult? When thousands of them congregated in Shravanabelagola, didn't our late prime minister, Indira Gandhi, pay them a visit and get blessed by them? What about the great saint poet, Akka Mahadevi of the twelfth century who wandered naked, and when questioned by her guru, Allama, as to how her nudity could be genuine when she still covered her genitals with her long hair, answered: 'Lest its sight embarrass you. Why do we tolerate practices of pan-Indian communities, and attack only those of small groups of low castes? Why this double standard? Moreover, do we sell anything—a soap, a toothbrush, a screwdriver, a shampoo or even a plastic bucket without the help of a nude today? What about striptease clubs? We get heated up in crosstalk, and the weary woman activist answers that her group has also protested against commercial exploitations of nudity.

As the anthropologists shift from the position that we should preserve what is unique in a culture, to the other position that we must try to change them slowly through sympathetic understanding and education, and as the Sikh linguist argues passionately for a firm position from us who form the national mainstream, which I suspect he will not hold on to firmly, as the situation in Punjab changes, I am reminded of a story by A. K. Ramanujan.

The story is entitled 'Annayya's Anthropology', and had I narrated it in the meeting it could have perhaps induced a deeper self-reflection on the part of the anthropologists present there. Or merely confirmed their own sophisticated scepticism—I don't know. The tone of the narration, as is often the case in Ramanujan's Kannada poetry too, is cool, witty and low-key, and, therefore, its end becomes all the more terrifying. Annayya who had never taken much interest in India while he lived there begins to devour books on Indian anthropology when he comes to Chicago as an economist. He reads with admiration the American academics who write books on Indian rituals with such an eye for detail, and such interest. A recent book by someone called Ferguson fascinates him. Annayya's orthodox parents live in Mysore and he also has a cousin, Sundara Rao, who owns a photo studio in Hunsur. He is piqued to read that Ferguson got much of his material on funeral rites from his cousin. Annayya reads on with an uneasy curiosity and finds photographs of houses and streets that are familiar to him. Could the picture of the burning corpse be of his own father whose death must have been kept a secret from the son, as he lives far away for his studies? Yes, that was a picture taken by his cousin Sundara Rao. Annayya is frightened. The book falls down. He picks it up and opens it to read about 'widowhood' and he sees the picture of his shaven mother in a red sari as a gratefully acknowledged illustration of widowhood. Annayya is aghast.

The story works at many levels and symbolizes much more than Annayya's particular predicament. Annayya is the modern Indian, fascinated by the West, ignorant of his own culture, yet attached to it emotionally. He dislikes India while he lives there, but loves the country when he goes abroad as is the case with most of poetic feeling and objectivity that is all the more remarkable considering his passionate political engagement with the day-to day struggle of the untouchable castes for equality and self-respect. His stories abound in rituals, and intimate description of the everyday life of his characters in their misery as well as their ecstasy. The success of his daring is largely due to the low mimetic mode he employs. The novelette, *Odalala* (1978) by Devanura Mahadeva, where a hungry family eats up a whole bagful of peanuts sitting around a fire without leaving a trace of their theft for the police who search their poor cottage in the morning, is a moving story of the revolutionary potentiality of the untouchable castes even in the midst of their misery. The old woman in *Odalala* who goes in search of a lost rooster she has lovingly reared grows in the story into the proportions of the mythological mother symbolizing the elemental urge of caring. She quarrels, weeps loudly, admonishes her children, tells mythical stories, curses heartily and yet what is remarkable about this earthy woman is that she cares. A young girl in the family draws the picture of a peacock on the wall, a school-going child marvels at his sister's creation, the old woman who has no time for nonsense like a peacock dancing on the mud wall, still tells him a mythical story where the child becomes a potential prince—and at night they all sit and eat the stolen peanuts around a fire forgetting the lacerating quarrels and frustrations of the day. The peanut eating is as intense a creative act—almost a yajna—as the peacock drawing in the story. In this world of simple ritualistic folk life, is also heard the rumblings of the coming change. One of the peanut eaters, who wears a wrist watch, entertains the family crowd with his story of defying a hotelier and demanding respectful service along with others.

Mahadeva can't afford to look on the nude worshippers, many of whom belong to his caste, with anthropological curiosity. Nor can he want them to stay put in a magical world. He wants them to become conscious of their rights in the modern democratic society. Yet I feel he ought to be able—the kind of poetic novelist that he is—to see the grandeur of the souls of the nude worshippers—however necessary and inevitable it is for them to come out of their magical universe—a universe that William Blake and D. H. Lawrence and W. B. Yeats had longed for in the analytical and scientific western civilization. Mahadeva tells me it would have been all right for them to worship in the nude, if the onlookers were also nude, and if some of the girls were not forced or dragged to go nude. I understand what he means. I add sadly that it can't remain the same, particularly after what had happened, and the nude worshippers displayed on cover pages.

I ask myself another question—which is very important for me. How would the Vachanakaras of the twelfth century, particularly the great mystic poets, Basava and Allama, who protested against the 'little' as well as 'great' traditions, have reacted to the nude worshippers? I can only speculate. They would have perhaps pleaded with them for a less magical and a more spiritual God-awareness. And that could have been a more meaningful encounter in our tradition, than between our modernizers and the magical worshipper.

I dare to say 'Yes' in a young poet's ear alone when he accosts me with the question: 'Is Renuka true? Is Yellamma true?' I am alone with him and so I say, 'Yes.' I am surprised at the leap I have taken, but I have hopes of striking a chord in his heart, for he is a poet. He looks uncomprehending at my flushed face. Have I betrayed a part of me, the ever vigilant sceptic in me whom the Baconian-Cartesian epistemology of the scientific West has nourished with a good salary and comfortable working conditions? Haven't I become what I am by demythifying, even descecrating, the world of my childhood? As a boy growing up in my village, didn't I urinate stealthily and secretly on sacred stones under trees to prove to myself that they have no power over me? I remember the terror I had overcome spending sleepless nights, and consequently the ambivalence that enters into my youthful stories and novels. No, I can't be an absolutist, for I am a novelist and not a poet. My dream of combining Marxism with mysticism in actual praxis will never come true. In a literary work, perhaps, but not in actual life. Only as a poet Wordsworth could cry in weary despair, 'Great God, I would rather be a pagan suckled in a creed outworn.' Nor can one be indifferent, or merely curious, or patronizingly tolerant. Chandragutti is no longer inaccessible. There are buses plying from Shimoga, and the once thick forests surrounding the village are now thin, thanks to the greedy contractors and corrupt timber merchants and forest officials. The quick-growing, inhospitable eucalyptus is planted everywhere with World Bank aid for the multi-millionaire Birla's factories. The jogithis, the matted-haired fierce priestesses of Yellamma of Saundatti, are under suspicion of supplying girls for the nourishing flesh trade in Bombay. And Bombay attracts fun-seeking tourists from all over the world.

GANDHI'S TRIUMPH OVER THE FEAR OF DEATH

I have been reading the graffiti on the walls of several buildings of the university I teach in. They are all in red and project the deep anguish of the youth who have written them. These young people write all over the walls, 'We want change, not improvement'. These young people are dreamers. Still not stifled by the monotony of everyday life. It is possible that some of them are prepared for any kind of sacrifice due to their inexperience. It is also possible for quite a few of them to be narcisstic, and even vainly proud. But so long as there are idealists such as these, the relationship between society and individual will find the concern for social justice alive and intact in its scheme. Such people may not find in Gandhi a model to be admired. It is only the desire to make Gandhi relevant to these dreamers that I speak now.

It is true that improvement only means a shoddy patch work. To prevent our system from collapsing totally—similar to the one John Maynard Keynes visualized to save the capitalist system—such an improvement may be necessary and I very well understand the dissatisfaction it causes. Third World countries with all their problems cannot hope for lasting solutions in this. But when these young people ask for change, I cannot but help feeling that they are asking for a social revolution. The revolutions in China and Russia have certainly brought about economic changes in those societies. It would be utterly inhuman to refuse changes in a society such as ours. All said and done, China may not have the kind of poverty and hunger that India has. Literacy is certainly greater there. It is for this reason that the change demanded by these youngsters is far more valuable than a shoddy piece of improvement, for it can shake up our society and introduce reinvigorating changes that can give comfort to many, even if it causes agony to a few. The raging fire of change can even convert negative elements of jealousy, envy and revenge into something positive.

But I must say, with a lot of diffidence, that the change brought about by our youth would be soulless, for the vanguard of change will inevitably have to be heartless. The diffidence comes from the realization that the attempt to check progress would become mere indulgence, if it does not participate in the process of change with conviction. To resist a positive change in the name of idealism can easily become political cunning. The lessons of history cannot be camouflaged even then. One must not hesitate to speak of an alternative to the capitalist and the communist systems, even if no one is interested in such ideas at present. I speak at such a complex juncture now.

Momentous changes took place in China and Russia. But why hasn't the nature of man changed? China desires to go the way of the developed western countries. A revolution brought about a change. But the contentment of the present seems to be dragging China towards the industrialization and the capitalist models of the west. The preoccupation with the strategies of defence and war seems to have gained precedence over social justice. Ultimately, only the American affluence seems to possess the human mind. We are not an exception to this either. Even the revolutionary spirit does not seem to be capable of holding on to its austerity in the face of the comforts provided by an affluent life style.

It is precisely for this reason that those who admire Gandhi seek neither improvement nor change. They ask for transformation—that is, a thorough change of the human soul in a new civilization. Transformation is not necessarily related to the future. It can happen in the immediate present during moments of love, admiration of nature, caring for the universe in a mature manner—moments wherein desire is replaced by contentment in the human heart. Poets, lovers, mad mystics have all achieved this—even if for a fleeting moment—in human history.

There is a photograph of Gandhi that I like immensely. In it, his bald head is slightly inclined to the right, the eyes behind the spectacles are peacefully shut and the body is bare. Not an extra ounce of fat is on his body. It projects a kind of tranquillity that could be ours in a moment of concentrated satisfaction. Nothing could be more difficult than this.

Gandhi desired transformation—of the human soul, and of society.

He made no distinctions between the ills of society and those of the human heart. He even located the evil of British imperialism in the heart of the Indian. If the British looked down upon us, so did we as Indians look down upon our own people as untouchables. Gandhi visualized the imperialist streak within the core of the human heart.

This streak dehumanizes both the master and the slave. The oppressed is capable of realizing his dignity the moment he rejects his low state. But the oppressor cannot do so easily. Gandhi had such pity for those obese with power. He attended on them as a doctor does on the patient. He treated viceroys in the same manner, and had made Lord Mountbatten drink goat's milk.

Who can humiliate a man who has conquered the fear of death? Gandhi had prepared himself to accept this for the sake of truth. The combination of joy and courage that such an attitude produces in one leaves one beautiful—something that can be seen in Gandhi himself. It is said that only Chaplin apart from children could smile like that. For Gandhi, a struggle was not a stern faced affair. The Dandi March is a shining example of how a man who has conquered fear can be lively, cheerful and peaceful. Such a soul can fight the empire with supreme calm of mind. He could stitch footwear for General Smuts who jailed him, and show sympathy to the English Emperor who he said had enough clothing and more for both.

Politically, Gandhi considered imperialism to be the biggest enemy of life. His dislike of it was so deep that he looked into the depths of the human mind as none had done before to remove it from human consciousness itself. He saw the imperialist streak in man's desire to conquer nature, in his sexuality that was unbridled and his craving for material comforts. In fact, he saw in it the modern economic system itself. He saw desire as a demon that would convert man into a demon gradually. A consciousness of death that evades us is also responsible for such a state of mind. His rejection of imperialism was so total that he possessed nothing more than a loincloth. He ate less and worked more, suggesting the possibility of ignoring the master, and the idea of rejecting the all-pervasive state. If we are to control our desires, we would also learn the art of triumphing over the oppressive state. Gandhi clarified for us the truth that life, far from being a rejection of pleasure, was a way of being contented until death.

We would be able to comprehend Gandhi's vision of life if we recognized the dangers of excessive sex and overeating and how glamourous clothing dulls and makes artificial human beauty. He was, in particular, wary of sex, for he was aware of its aggressive and tormenting nature. He was so apprehensive about it that he rejected its soothing joys. Perhaps this rejection was necessary since he also wanted to be a woman. With the well-being of the world in view, Gandhi's idea of celibacy might have wished to direct all desires towards a single aim. He could smile like a child and be a source of comfort, whatever the hostility of the environment and the pressure of the situation.

Gandhi knew that we could realize truth only if we had the courage to push something to extremity. It is for this reason that he was not trapped in the arrogance of ideas or in the duality of desires. The most important book of this century, *Hind Swaraj,* was written by him in 1908 when he was in South Africa. It was in this book that he visualized his ideal man and civilization. His thoughts begin with the thesis that modern civilization is attractive, but evil. The British were able to rule us only because we had a fascination for the values of modern civilization. He questions the wisdom of driving out the British, if we are to continue to admire their civilization. Moreover, if this civilization is bad for us, so is it, for them. Consequently, he takes upon himself the responsibility of freeing the British from its snares too. The search for an alternative to this led him to seek a technology that was opposed to the hegemonizing centralisation of modern civilization, and its accompanying mechanization. The charaka, the simple spinning wheel, was what mattered to him in this deep search. It seems he accepted the sewing machine after the charaka as a tolerable machine. Gandhi was not against machines totally. He was looking for a technology that was part of his vision of man and civilization. The insights of E. F. Schumacher's *Small is Beautiful* are the promptings in Gandhi's scheme of civilization too. The realization is that it is not man alone who has the right to inhabit this world. Even our environmentalists, and those who oppose nuclear energy, have a lot to learn from Gandhi's vision of life.

A man like Albert Einstein with his concepts appears to be beyond us. But the love of life, the vision of oneness that excludes neither birds nor beasts in Gandhi places him amidst us, for those feelings and values are shared and held by us equally. Wasn't Gandhi the ideal for somebody like Martin Luther King who lived in the flourishing Amaravati that America happens to be? He is closest to those who have conquered the fear of death and love life in all its forms. The half-naked body of Gandhi, who brought sex, means of livelihood, dietary habits, meditation, abstinence and politics on the same plane and saw them as inter-related, shone as a symbolic alternative to the destructive appetite of modern civilization.

Translated by N. Manu Chakravarthy

TRADITION AND CREATIVITY

What I wish to talk about is the question of tradition and creativity, and talk about it from the point of view of a particular tradition, and a particular creative writer. And I choose the Kannada tradition and a Kannada writer, that is, myself. This does not mean that I am trying to talk about only a particular tradition or a particular culture; instead, what I am trying to do is to move from the particular to the general. This, I believe, is the only authentic way possible, for you cannot deal in generalities or universals without really addressing yourself to the rootedness of a specific culture.

Let me begin with a great line from William Blake:

'This is mine, yet not mine.'

When you write a great poem, a poem that takes you by surprise, about which you feel so much, the question is whether it has been there all the time—that is, whether the poem was there even before you started writing it. No. It was not there in that form at all. But, Blake says, in the very heart of creativity, in an epiphanic moment, certain things come to him all of a sudden and take him by surprise, because any creativity is also a kind of avadhana—total attention, that which is dark and unspent—which may reveal itself. That is why no creative writer is a creative writer all the time. He can be truly creative only at certain moments when something inscrutable, something beyond definition—call it God, or call it Luck—suddenly makes it possible for him to give that kind of total attention to the bija before him. It is only a seed, this bija, from which everything else blooms forth. If this is what happens in the process of creation, Blake is right when he says, 'This is mine, yet not mine.'

In contrast, T. S. Eliot's theory of 'Impersonality', I believe, is not a happy theory at all. Eliot, here, is basically trying to get into an argument with the Romantics. In any argument, you know, you tend to overstate your case; this is the fate of all polemics, for polemics is nothing but overstatement. Eliot does the same when he says that the writer is only like a catalyst in a chemical experiment, what we call in Kannada, vegavardhakadis—agents which will only quicken the action. So Eliot's theory claims that the poet is there only to quicken the action, to speed it up, to make some kind of reaction possible, without at the same time undergoing any change whatsoever. This seems to me quite wrong. There is reason to believe that the poet is present in his work in a very vital sort of way. Eliot seems to have missed this point, as indeed some post-structuralist critics, who talk about the death of the author, have missed it altogether. Such theories, whether they come from Eliot or some post-structuralist, need not be taken seriously. Blake is much more profound when he says something like, 'This is mine, yet not mine.' It is both personal and impersonal at the same time. The impersonality comes in where he says 'yet not mine,' for it belongs to a whole tradition. I could not have written this but for purvasuribhih (illustrious predecessors), what Kalidasa, describes as manovajrasamutkirne sutrasyevasti me gatih ('in a string of pearls, I am just like the string'). You know, the kind of humility which makes me say 'yet not mine.' Yet, at the same time, it is also possible to say, 'this is mine.' Creativity and tradition coexist in a very existential sort of way.

Now, I should admit that it is very difficult for me to analyse this point any further. If you are creative, you should understand it at once. It is almost like Van Gogh's *Shoes*. When you look at the painting, you immediately think that they are shoes. But they are not the kind of shoes that you find in the showrooms of Bata or Carona. These shoes make you feel that some peasant has worn them. He must have been working in his field for a long, long time, and his shoes are worn out. You can see the sweat, the labour, the anxiety, the suffering of the farmer who has worn these shoes in a particular field, at a particular time, in a particular set of circumstances. Yet they are great shoes, with a universal appeal and significance, universally existing, I should say, though not like in an advertisement. You must have seen a lot of pictures of shoes, making you want to buy them. It provokes a desire when you see Van Gogh's painting. A work which is truly creative and truly in tradition, has that kind of quality: This is mine, yet not mine. It is a general thing, belonging to a specific tradition, but it is not just that either. It has a certain lived-in experience. We have something like that in our own theory of universalisation. A work becomes truly creative when it has what we call a universal quality. You have to feel something like, 'This is my experience also.' But there is a certain danger here: if you begin to give too much emphasis on this quality of universality, it can very well end up as a mere cliche. A lot of creativity, or so-called creativity in India in the traditional way, has tried to achieve sadharanikarana in an easy manner, through cliches, and hence is not at all valuable. It is almost like Van Gogh trying to paint those shoes by copying them from some Bata showroom. Yes, they would be shoes then, but not a work of art. What I am trying to say is this: If the sadharanikarana we accept, where it has a universal quality, belongs to a whole tradition and hence is immediately recognizable as general experience which can be shared by all, it is still not a work of art if it has not that lived-in quality of a particular individual.

It is easy to understand how this facile and cliched accessibility to the universal has contributed to the decadence of Sanskrit poetry in its later years. You should let in the universal only on your own conditions; you should enter the monumental only on your own terms. It should look monumental, but it should also be the experience of a particular individual—like Van Gogh's *Shoes*, again. Sanskrit poetry, in its later decadent age, becomes cliched precisely because the sadharanikarana is achieved all too easily, and is in total agreement with others. Hence, in a way, it does not do anything to the tradition that it seeks to uphold, does not contribute anything to that tradition. You can do it only by trying to keep it alive. But how is this possible?

Some time ago, during a visit to an international book fair in Germany, I had the good fortune of listening to Kapila Vatsyayanji give a beautiful metaphor for tradition. The metaphor is that of a hookah. Someone says:

'This hookah has been in our family for nearly three hundred years.'

'Three hundred years! This same hookah!'

'Yes, but when the bowl became very old and worn out, we changed it. And then, the pipe became too rough and rigid, so we changed it too. But we still have the same hookah.'

Now, in the same spirit as the story was told to me, let me recount an experience of mine. I have a little garden near Mysore. An old man called Ramayya, a Harijan labourer, used to come and work there. I had an encounter with him which I shall never forget. Once I found him removing a big rock. He was a very old man, but he had such dexterity and was so good at using his muscles without really straining himself, that he could lift a pretty big piece of rock like nobody else could. And then I found a little plant growing underneath. I said to Ramayya: 'Look, isn't it wonderful?'

And he replied: 'We Harijans have always lived like that plant!'

Now, he had with him an old sickle which I found quite interesting. In reply to a question, he said: 'We have been using this sickle from my great-grandfather's time.'

'The same sickle? But don't you have to get the iron part sharpened?' I asked.

'Yes,' he said, 'I changed it.'

'What about the wooden part, the grip?'

And he said: 'Oh, I had to change it too, because I found it quite worn out. And there was a beautiful picture of a little bird here which was also getting worn out.'

'A picture?' I asked him. 'Who made it?'

He replied: 'Whenever I don't find any job here—and that is often, because after the harvest we don't have much work—what I do is take the sickle out and draw all these pictures. And when they are worn out, I change the handle and draw them again.'

This is what tradition is all about; this is how you keep it alive, keep it going. Eliot is right—and I value him for this—when he says that tradition is not a static thing, and that every writer who writes something truly creative changes the whole order, or hierarchy of the traditional realm. This is indeed a very valuable point in Eliot....

~

Chandan Gowda (CG): You mentioned you were critical of Adiga, because his loukika orientation would sometimes acquire loukika dimensions. Did your orientation as a loukika writer make you look at tradition somewhat differently than the other writers?

UR Ananthamurthy (URA): If tradition is an entity to which you always look back for correction and guidance, it is a curse. If you take tradition with you to cohabit with the modern, it is one way of keeping your smriti, your remembrance, alive. It's only through a language that we maintain continuity. If you don't maintain continuity, there is no civilization.

The British have a continuity from Shakespeare onwards, because of the English language. We have a continuity, because of Kalidasa, because of Sanskrit, because of our own poets, and hence this continuity has to be maintained, not through worshipping tradition, but through intervening in tradition and changing it.

I was not an anti-tradition writer and Adiga a pro-tradition writer. Adiga was also using tradition to criticize the present. Take a look at his line, 'Purohitara nambi naavu paschima buddhiyaadevu.' It is a very profound line. It means we became westernized, because we trusted only our priests. If we did not trust our priests as carriers of the wisdom, we would not have become westernized for loukika reasons. So, we divided things—this is for worldly good, this is for the other-worldly. That is because we did not understand our tradition correctly. Even our traditional beliefs—Vedas, Upanishads—were guides to live in the present-day world. They were as much concerned with life in the present, at that present. We have to keep that spirit.

CG: I wonder if your own sense of tradition has changed in recent times.

URA: I am very critical of tradition even today, the way its followers see it, because they live in different times without integrating them. They don't test tradition in our own times. They follow it blindly. I oppose it even now.

I want the past to be useful in the present. How to make the past useful is not the concern of traditionalists. How to preserve the past is the concern of the traditionalists. My concern is not how to preserve the past, but how to make the past useful for the present world. That's all. And once you understand this, the Jains, the Buddhists, our variegated tradition—because our tradition is not one, but several—would become useful.

When I began to write, I had great anger against the use of

tradition. The use of tradition was so blind—when you got married, when anything of any importance happened, everything was guided by tradition without examining whether there was some truth in it or not. That is happening even now. Our politicians are fighting for their privileges to make use of tradition. That kind of use of tradition is not to be encouraged, neither here nor in the West.

CG: In some of your recent writings, you have expressed admiration for Navodaya writers like Kuvempu, a writer about whom you were somewhat dismissive previously. What is behind your admiration for someone like him now? Does it relate to what you just said about tradition?

URA: Yes. It was he who began to attack tradition, and also showed how to use tradition within his own Kannada community. He knew how to use Kumaravyasa, Pampa, Ranna and Janna in his own modern Kannada sensibility. And he evolved a philosophical position of poornadrishti* through that kind of an interrogation. I think Aurobindo and Ramakrishna Paramahamsa must have helped him, because his heroes were also from the East. So, our first great writer has put us on the path.

But where I differed from him then, I still differ to a certain extent—his use of language, a certain kind of rhetoric. To write like Kuvempu, one must have belief in one's own greatness.

It's a kind of bhavyata** originating from the self. Deriving your idea of the bhavya through your own experience is limiting. It is like what Keats said when he was critical of Milton: 'I have nothing to say. My attention is all on those two birds which are pecking. I'm that bird.' 'I'm that bird' is a dramatic imagination where you identify with your characters. Whereas Kuvempu's imagination from the beginning was a kind of bhavya originating from his own self. It is something like Tagore saying he was humble enough to be the flute through which God sang. He was a vehicle for something higher to go through him.

CG: Is there anything about tradition that bothers you?

URA: What really bothers me within when we talk about tradition

---

*A whole vision.

**Radiance.

is the caste system. And I am wrong to say 'the caste system'. It has become a habit for us to use that phrase. What I mean is untouchability. How did untouchability come into the whole idea of Indian civilization?

It appears Gandhi was very keen to think that it was not sanctioned in the Vedas. So, he enquired with the great Benares scholars. They wanted to be sentimental and good and said, 'There is no sanction for untouchability in the Vedic period.' And then he went to Tarkatirtha, the great Maharashtrian scholar. He was a very old man. Gandhi asked him, 'Can you find a justification for untouchability in our tradition?' Tarkatirtha said, 'Yes, we will be able to find a justification for it in some text of the Vedic period.' And Gandhi simply said, 'Then I have to oppose Hinduism.' Gandhi's desire was not to oppose Hinduism, but to prove that there was no place for untouchability in it. But if that was not the case, it had to be opposed.

Gandhi was for the truth. What is truth? For him, truth meant something that untouchability couldn't have a place in. What about the caste system? Gandhi was not so opposed to it. He said in a vast country like India, it determined what kind of work you do. And hence, it was a system of decentralization of work and so on. Ambedkar was right to attack Gandhi and say, 'Your own son is not opening a shop. He is working in a newspaper. According to caste, he is a Vaishya.' That is a good answer to Gandhi. Gandhi had problems of that kind.

CG: Gandhi came to accept inter-caste marriages later.

URA: Yes, that was after Rajaji s daughter married his son. Gandhi accepted that. But he was for some kind of decentralization of a society in terms of manual work, and the caste system gave a basis for that. So, Indian society could learn without a government. Even now, for eighty per cent of the people, there is no government. The caste structure tells them what to do. And to a man like Gandhi, who was for vyavastha, and at the same time who, like Tolstoy, played with the idea of...what is that word where there is no vyavastha at all?

CG: Anarchy?

URA: Anarchy. I would say Gandhi was an anarchist. All great thinkers of this world have been anarchists, Tolstoy, Gandhi, Jesus Christ. There is a bit of anarchy in them.

And there is another matter. You get tired and frightened of anarchy and want vyavastha. And when you want vyavastha, you are willing to compromise with many of these things. Caste is one of those things, which gives you a sense of a bhadra vyavastha*. And you see this struggle going on in our debate about tradition and modernity.

I know in my village, during harvest time, there is a certain caste which comes for doing this work, another caste for another work. Agriculture is still based on the caste system. It has such integration. So, to overcome it, there seems to be only one other way, i.e., modernization. Modernization means using machines and modern technology, and handing it over to a corporation and all that. That may also remove casteism. But we are not prepared to do that. Many people like me have a problem talking about tradition and caste because we want pluralism to prevail, but we don't want the caste system which provides the basis for that pluralism. 'I want pluralism but not the caste system'—we have not resolved that question still. And hence, you find this confiision even in Gandhians.

And you can oppose tradition absolutely once you are a part of the new world order, when you begin to teach English to your child even when it is in the womb. If there is an injection that will give the child an American accent when it is born, you will give it! This may not continue for long as the Western economies are not stable.

CG: So you are suggesting that caste inequality should be surely handled, but outside of the frame of modernization?

URA: Yes.

CG: Are there others besides Gandhi whom you admire for questioning caste from within, as it were?

URA: Basava**. He said, 'Kayakave kailasa.' He did not question kayaka.*** Whatever work you did, you were equal to the others.

There were two kinds of attempts in India on this matter. We used to call them the Ramanuja attempt and the Basava attempt. The Ramanuja attempt was to keep the caste, but let castes become equal. For instance, Ramanuja was very particular that Dalits should

---

*Stable system.

**Basavanna: The founder of the Lingayat dharma in the twelfth century.

***Work or labour.

wash themselves early in the morning, chant a prayer (japa), put a holy mark on the forehead (nama), and be very 'civilized'. And then they would be equal to other castes.

But Basava said, 'No, the caste system should be destroyed.' Basava's experiment failed whereas Ramanuja's experiment has been a success.

CG: How do you understand the need for swaraj in thought in India today?

URA: Tm not too passionately involved in what they call the desi, because you won't find the pure desi when you search for it. It is based on Sanskrit; it is mixed with Persian; it s linked with different rulers at different times. There is nothing pure even in folklore. Hence, I am more a follower of Pampa* who wanted to combine the desi with the marga**.

All my writing is a combination of the desi and the marga. I have perhaps more marga in me than desi. But there is something like swaraj in ideas. I have a feeling that we have become second- rate imitators of the West. There has been absolutely no original thought in India, except for Gandhi, over the last two centuries. He was the only original thinker and he had the courage to imagine a world without railways, without technology, without whatever Britain brought to India. He could conceive a world without these, and hence some kind of swadeshi chintane was possible for him—that we can survive without the aid of the West, that we can be intellectual without depending too heavily on Western thinkers. That kind of confidence in your own voice, in your own experience, in ideas based on your own experience, is what I mean by swadeshi chintane. For some people it is not possible at all, because they have been completely overwhelmed by Western modes of thought.

Once Raja Ramanna, a scientist deriving a lot of his insights from the West, told me about an old book he found in a second- hand bookshop in Madras. It was written for early learners by a Sanskrit logician. He said that it shocked him to think there was another logic. The logic we use is based on the Aristotelian logic of either/or, but

---

*A tenth-century Kannada Jain poet.

**'Desi' refers to the local/folk, and 'marga' refers to the classical and mainstream.

India thought of a five-limbed logical system. There is no place for it in the Aristotelian world of either/or. Here, it is not just either/or but this, or this, or this: it has five limbs. And he said, 'You know, if you have a five-limbed logical system, your thought will not run like Western thought.'

We have a Jain way of thinking. We have the Gandhian way of thinking, which is difficult for the West to imagine. I will give you an example of how Gandhi would respond. A British woman, who was a great admirer of his, sent him a birthday greeting once, where she quoted William Blake. Blake has a poem* where he says, 'I have placed in your hand golden thread. Wind it into a ball, it will open the gateway of heaven.' The ball of golden thread is imagination. She wrote, 'You have put in our hand this ball of gold.' And Gandhi writes, 'Blake's imagination is that of a poet. I have also placed a ball in your hand, but it is a ball of cotton. If you take the very delicate thread from it, it will open the gates of heaven here and now.' That's a great way of making use of a poem and writing another poem. Gandhi meant that if we don't depend on foreigners for our clothes and foods, if we can provide them ourselves, there is no need for them to rule us.

They rule us because they get something out of it by selling to us, but if we don't take your cloth, your food, then we're swadeshi, so he changed Blake's imagery into a ball of cotton and also a thread—a simple thread leading you to the gateway of heaven here and now, because we are free. That kind of imagination, leap of thought, etc., going across centuries, is swadeshi chintane.

Gandhi had it much more than Nehru. Nehru's was more a Fabian socialist way of thinking. He had to borrow ideas from the West. Gandhi didn't borrow ideas from anywhere. There is a notion that we shouldn't borrow ideas from the West, but borrow them from our own past. No! Borrowing from our own past is also borrowing. Creating a new thought here and now....

We could do it in a tribal way, because the tribes live an alternate way of life here. If some tribes can live an alternate way of life where

*William Blake, 'Jerusalem: To the Christians', 1815.

they can do without any of the modern amenities and still survive, then that is a great thought available for us. But we don't use it at all. That's why our intellectuals become completely alien, because they don't use modes of thinking, modes of feeling which are available here in India.

TOWARDS THE CONCEPT OF A NEW NATIONHOOD

Languages and Literatures in India

Some years ago, I was in Syria meeting Arab writers from several parts of that country, and most of them asked me this question: 'You have twenty-two languages, but you are one nation, whereas we have one language, one religion, but we are twenty-two nations! How do you explain that?' What follows may provide a tentative explanation of this mystery called the Indian nation. I invoke two names, those of Mahatma Gandhi and Rabindranath Tagore for this purpose. They provide an idea of the nation which is very different from the European idea of one language, one race, and one religion. Hence, although there was an attempt to evolve a European kind of nation, the idea of the nation, evident in all the Indian literatures, was very different. India contains many Indias; one encounters this when looking at literatures in the twenty-two languages of India. Whatever one can truly say about India, its exact opposite can also be maintained with equal truthfulness.

According to the 1961 census, there were 1,652 mother tongues, classified under 105 languages. These languages belong to four language families: the Indo-Aryan, Dravidian, Tibetan, and Austro-Asiatic. But ninety of these 105 languages are spoken by less than 5 per cent of the population and by sixty-five small tribes. There are fifteen languages that are written, read and spoken by 95 per cent of the people in India. From this, the country might seem like a Tower of Babel. However, by knowing two or three languages, one can get by nearly anywhere in India.

In our everyday speech activity, we find that many of us use at least three languages: one at home, another on the streets, still another at our office. We constantly translate from one language to the other. When you narrate to your old mother what happened in your office, you are translating spontaneously. And vice versa. Plurality in language and translation are inseparable.

One of my pet theories is that, in India, the more literate a person is, the fewer languages he or she knows. Those who are literate only in English are tempted to use only English. But in small town where I come from, even one who may not be so literate—a bus stand coolie for instance—speaks Tamil, Telugu, Malayalam, some Hindi, and some English. It is these people who have kept India together, not merely those who know only one language of hegemony.

People in India have always lived, even in the past, in an ambience of languages. Shankaracharya, the great philosopher who wrote in Sanskrit, must have also spoken Malayalam; he was from Kerala. Ananda Tirtha must have spoken Tulu at home and Kannada in the streets, but he too wrote in Sanskrit. Ramanuja, who must have been profoundly moved by Tamil saints—they were non-Brahmin saints, and they wrote in Tamil—took a lot from them, but also wrote in Sanskrit.

These philosophers who propagated the nations of monism, dualism and qualified monism, travelled throughout the country and acquired disciples. They also influenced mystical poets who wrote in regional languages, and whose utterances became myths and poetry in languages of the common people which I call bhashas. With such happenings a profound egalitarian impulse shot through the hegemonic structure of Indian society. The caste system was questioned not after the Europeans came to India; it had been questioned much earlier. In the twelfth century, the great Kannada Vachanakara poet, Basava, got into great trouble for arranging a marriage between Brahmin girl and a Pariah.

The Buddha, on the other hand, chose not to write in Sanskrit, the 'father tongue'. (My friend, the scholar A. K. Ramanujan, always called Sanskrit the father tongue, somewhat like English is today.) The saint-poets of the medieval period in India did not use Sanskrit at all, they used rather the bhashas, the languages of India. They were mystics whose experience of God was immediate and not speculative. But they were deeply concerned with the society. Hence, although they were mystics, they were not apart from society. Belonging to different parts of India, these mystics, by opting to use the language of everyday speech to convey their religious experience, actually began to communicate with their gods in the languages of the streets and of the kitchen. There was indeed a special language to address the

God, but by their use of a familiar language, the mystics brought God to the common people. As a direct consequence, their poetry empowered women and the lower castes for the first time. For instance, in Karnataka, menstruating women are considered impure. But the mystics said: 'No, they are as pure as ever,' defying a commonly held belief of the time. In this sense, the empowerment of women in India goes back to 800 years.

The spiritual insights and philosophical subtleties which marked Sanskrit, the language of the elite classes, thus became the possession of the Indian bhashas. Since the medieval period, these bhashas have been the conduits of egalitarian passion working through the history of India. It has been a continuous process of inclusion, rather than a negation of any language; of Sanskrit in the past, or of the bhashas, or of English later on.

The most recent of these great saints, who may be described as one of the great critical insiders of Indian civilization (I use the term 'critical insider' for many of these people; they are insiders to our tradition, but they are critical of this tradition even if they are within it), was Mahatma Gandhi, who wrote in Gujrati, Hindustani, and also in English.

In our times, English serves the communicative function that Sanskrit did in the past. It was Sanskrit that our writers had to cope with then. A fourteenth-century Kannada writer once remarked that there was nothing left in Sanskrit, as everything is taken away from it. The Indian bhashas, which had earlier digested the essence of Sanskrit, today cope with the challenges of the West. Thus Franz Kafka, Leo Tolstoy, and other European writers have influenced writers in the Indian bhashas.

I do not use the term 'mother tongue' as it is understood by Europeans. For instance, some of the best Kannada writers such as Joseph Conrad, who wrote in their language of adoption. But these cases are very few. In India, however, many writers do not speak the same language in which they may be writing. I once asked one of the greatest Kannada poets, who used the Kannada language magically, just as Blake used English, whether he had always spoken that language. He replied 'No, I spoke Marathi at home, but until I was twelve or thirteen, I did not know that I was speaking two languages!' He was then a very colourful old man. At that point, his daughter-in-law came into the room where we were talking in Kannada and whispered something in his ear. He turned and spoke to her in Marathi, without realizing that he was speaking in Marathi. This kind of shift takes place constantly and quite unselfconsciously.

Shifts in tongue and texts are true of a large number of writers in Hindi who speak Rajasthani, Bhojpuri, and many other languages related to Hindi. The characters in their fiction may be actually speaking these languages, but they are rendered for us in Hindi.

More significant than this in our understanding of what constitutes a text is a unique Indian phenomenon often bypassed. Kalidasa's *Shakuntala* isn't a text in a single language. An early poet of our times in Kannada, Shishunala Sharief has poems where the first line is in Kannada, the second line is in Telugu, and the third in what may be called Urdu. He came from an area where these languages are spoken. As he was a mystical poet of the people, I am sure his immediate audience would understand all these languages and their copresence in the same poem must have made a unique sense to them. They were listening to the silence beyond the spoken word—especially to the silence celebrated in a variety of words.

Along with this free play of languages, which existed in an ambience allowing for shifts and mixtures, and also because of such a free play aside from hegemonic indications that languages carry with them, the poets of the past in Indian languages could acquire the territory of Sanskrit for their vernaculars. The use of vernaculars never seemed to threaten free communication with others, isolating each language group in its own territory. Such a process of cultural inclusion and quiet synthesis has gone on in India for more than a thousand years. First, if it was the language of the Gods making way for the language of the common people, now it is the official domain of English making way, however reluctantly, to the vernaculars in the process of the empowerment of the people. Translation, oral as well as textual, was the principal mode in the past as well as the present for such negotiations.

In support of my ideas, here are some concrete examples. The coastal Karnataka has small town called Udupi, a name made familiar by its inhabitants who have opened restaurants all over India. There are at least three languages spoken in and around Udupi. Tulu is the language of a large number of its inhabitants, the peasants and workers and it is also a language rich in folklore. Not only the lower castes speak it, but a Sanskritized version of it, considered impure by native Shudra speakers is spoken as mother tongue by the Brahmins as well. Next to Tulu is Konkani, mainly the language of the trading castes.

Kannada exists in Udupi along with other languages. One could say it is perceived as the language of high culture, whatever that means. Kannada is also the mother tongue of a large section of people. However, the point I want to make is this. A large body of Kannada literature in the past as well as the present has come from this coastal region. If one encounters a stranger on the streets, the language used for communication is Kannada. But a Tulu or Konkani speaker encountering other speakers of those languages would invariably use the language native to the speaker. Otherwise it would be considered arrogant behaviour. And almost everyone of the native Tulu and Konkani speakers would understand Kannada and if he or she happens to be a writer, most probably the language of choice for writing would be Kannada. Thus *Chomana Dudi*, a celebrated novel in Kannada by K. Shivaram Karanth, is written in Kannada. Choma the hero of the novel is an untouchable, and in real life, he would be mostly speaking in Tulu. In fact, one could say much of the novel takes place in the language of Tulu, and the author Karanth while writing the novel is truly translating from Tulu to Kannada. But is this not true also of the good fiction in English written in India?

EPICS AS LANGUAGE

A thousand years ago, Pampa, another great Kannada poet (the fact that I cite examples from my language should not be mistaken as chauvinism, it merely gives me a sense of authenticity) wrote of Arjuna, his hero. Being a Jain, he could not make Krishna his hero, Krishna being a spiritual figure. He instead made Arjuna the hero of his work, and identified him with his own ruler, the Hindu king Arikesari, who was also his friend. Idealizing Arikesari, he created the

Hindu king after Arjuna. He also did something very interesting: he mixed his own narrative with that of the Mahabharata. He used a new figure of speech, Samasa Alankara, which draws very unrealistic equations between a great epic of the past and a contemporary event. Personally, I think this a great device, one which Pampa used to voice his worldly concerns. It was a daring initiative, to make one's own river flow into the rivers of the past.

Not only have experiences been transferred from one language into another in a continuous and spontaneous act of translation in the course of daily life, but Indians have also lived simultaneously through many ages. The Mahabharata has been used freely for this purpose. Therefore, it is possible to say that apart from the innumerable languages of India, there are, metamorphically speaking, two more languages: the two great epics, the Ramayana and the Mahabharata. Many Indians, I dare say, have never read for the first time this epics. Yet they have encountered them right from childhood, through several modes.

A translator of Indian literature once narrated the following experience. He was collecting oral stories in Kannada language. There are a thousand such stories in Kannada which are sung or narrated from memory by non-literate rural people. In the original episode in the Ramayana, Rama advises Sita that she should stay back in the palace and not accompany him to the forest where he has been exiled. He says: 'You do not have to come with me. You are a princess. Your feet are tender and you have been brought up with such care, so do not come to the forest with me.' But Sita says: 'No, I am your wife, and I should go!' However, in one of the folk stories, when Rama similarly advises Sita, she says: 'In every other Ramayana I know of, Rama lets Sita go with him. How can you deny it to me?' Thus India knit, according to this translator, through an inter-textuality, which occurs not only across the texts which we read, but across oral texts as well. That is why I state that the Ramayana and the Mahabharata could be two languages which knit India together. This rural Sita is aware that there are other Ramayanas without even knowing the names of the authors.

For the modern Indian writer, therefore, there is a confluence of languages: Sanskrit, English, perhaps translations from French and

Portuguese, and certainly Russian, because Tolstoy was read even during British rule. English was used not only to read British writers. I do not think Jane Austen ever influenced an Indian writer, but Tolstoy certainly did. English, being a hospitable language offering many translations, was used to read much of the work from Europe.

I wish to emphasize this element of plurality within India. For instance, there was an attempt in Tamil, the oldest of the modern languages, to develope an alternative to Sanskrit poetics and grammar, and also a theory of poetry that was very different. Great writers like Tagore and Gandhi became much more than literary figures for the people who spoke the languages in which they wrote.

An interesting point may be made here. While there are certain metrical compositions which can only be read, there are also compositions, in a certain kind of rhythm, which can be easily memorized. Some of the great poets used rhythmical expressions that enabled a composition to directly enter the memory of the people. There are wonderful memory devices within those metres, and they are present in the common speech of the people.

Literary figures were however generally in the high mode, which is classical. There are thus two streams entering into India's languages: the classical and the desi, or the indigenous stream. After Kalidasa (this is a daring statement that I make), there had been no great literary figure in India until Kabir came on the scene. Interesting here is the fact that at one time a literary figure could emerge only in Indian bhashas. One of the Indian bhashas like any other, Bengali, which is neither as widespread as Hindi nor is ancient as Tamil, produced a literary figure equal in stature to Kalidasa, a figure who will be emulated all over India. This must have been due to the spirit of nationalism in those days. Since independence, however, we have again become so Euro-centric that we cannot think of any Indian language producing a literary figure for the whole country. Instead, we borrow our literary figures from Europe.

I would like at this juncture to say something about unity and diversity. Dr Sarvepalli Radhakrishnan, the great philosopher, once said at Sahitya Akademi, the Academy of Indian Letters, that since all the twenty-two languages are represented there, Indian literature is one, although written in many languages. The use of the phrase 'unity and diversity' in politics and in culture has now become cliched. In fact, I would shy away from using the phrase myself, until I suddenly realized it could still be applied, if one thought of it as a process.

If you overstress unity in India, and maintain that there is only one India, then diversities begin to appear. This becomes a political phenomenon too. Thus, after Indira Gandhi, who wanted a strong centre, there have been problems in Assam, in Punjab, and in Kashmir. It has been argued that as Tamil is older than Hindi, Hindi should not be imposed on Tamil. This could be stretched to mean that Hindi should not be imposed on Bengali, or on Marathi. So, if one overly stresses unity, diversities begin to assert themselves. On the other hand, trying to emphasize diversity, arguing that Indians are all different, and that they have nothing in common, makes me uneasy and I start to feel that there is something common after all between a Bengali and myself and everyone else. We are all Indians. So unity-diversity appears true only in actuality and in these last fifty years we have seen an ongoing drama of unity in diversity.

As far as diversity is concerned, over the last fifty years there have been many attempts at grasping the postcolonial situation. Paradigms have been tried and given up, communities imagined and been dissolved, traditions constructed and deconstructed, the principles of unity and of difference alternately appealed to. Further, the western presence has been acknowledged and negated, the radical European concepts and models have alternated with a return to indigenous roots, to the classical and folk elements of India's heritage. Decolonization has become a major preoccupation.

Creativity in India has just been released afresh. Literary discourse is marked by the negotiation of the necessary heterogeneity, using a concept of identity that lives through difference and hybridity. Over time, this hybridity enters the languages. There are a number of words of Portuguese and Arab origin in Kannada, and quite often people speaking that language are not even aware that they are using words from other languages; such is the way with the Indian bhashas. The philosophers say that there is a little fire somewhere in the atma (soul) which can digest anything, known in Sanskrit as the jeernagni, the digestive fire. I consider the Indian bhashas the great jeernagnis of India, because they digested Sanskrit at one time, as they digest Europe now. They have been transacting with different languages in this manner right through their history.

A great and new phenomenon in the Indian languages were the Dalits, the untouchables, who wrote, first in Marathi, then in Gujrati and are writing now in Kannada, Telugu and Tamil. Thirty centuries of silent suffering, a whole culture of silence, lay behind their articulations of indignation.* There is a kind of subaltern protest in their writings. They have succeeded in re-drawing the literary map of their languages by exploring a whole new continent of experience, and also in revitalizing language with styles, timbers, words and phrases so far kept out of literary use. The tendency of Indian languages has been that whatever is closest to Sanskrit has been used by the elite groups. When new groups begin to talk, words which have never been used in a literary context enter in the literary texts. I shall have something more to say about this phenomenon a little later on.

In addition to this Dalit literature, India also has a committed feminist literature. Some of the great women writers are Lalitambika Antarjanam, Mahadevi Varma, Mahashweta Devi, and Vaidehi (Karnataka). These are not self-consciously feminist writers, but I shall not dwell further on this.

Last of all, let me make a personal statement, since I am myself a creative writer. I feel uneasy when I write just academically, because I may not be handling the issues objectively and rationally. But when I write in a creative idiom, I am more comfortable. So I will end my observations about Indian literature, and how it makes for a new kind of a nation, on a personal note. I use traditional Indian home, my own childhood home, as a metaphor for Indian literature.

My father and his friends frequented the front yard of the house, which had a raised urban platform under a country-tiled roof, known in Karnataka as Mangalore-tiled roofs. The upper classes usually have

*The subsequent criticism among Kannada literary scholars which engaged the robust folk epic traditions among Dalit communities made him review this view. See his essay, 'Dalit Contribution to Indian Literature' in this volume.

Mangalore-tiled roofs over their homes, while less well-off have round-tiled roofs. In the front yard of my home, caste was not a problem. My father's non-Brahmin friends in the village came to consult him about auspicious days for weddings and other ceremonies and, more frequently, to settle land-related disputes. They sat around him on coloured mats. The very poor who belonged to the same caste sat on one of the steps leading to the platform. This was like a porch, a mat-less, quite cold, but well-swept space.

My father offered everyone palm and betel nut, and even tobacco to chew. This front yard space, framed impressively by massive, well-carved pillars, was a place of authority, yet cheerful and full of tidings of the temporal world outside and the spiritual world beyond. On auspicious occasions, for example, traditional story-tellers would be invited to recite in the front yard. As a child, I came to know of the affairs of the world, I heard even of Edmund Burke and Gandhi, in this man-dominated front yard of the house. My father was a self-taught man, literate in English, Sanskrit, and Kannada, and therefore an unusual and sought-after scholar in the hilly villages around. He spoke enthusiastically to villagers of the freedom struggle, then being led by Mahatma Gandhi. And the villagers would gossip, narrating again and again the same stories about the British government and its officers, whom they admired for their efficiency and generosity. On auspicious occasions, some elder or the other who came as a guest to our house would describe the glories of the Dasara in Mysore. Or he would choose an appealing episode from the Mahabharata and sonorously read it out.

There were only men in the front yard, and if women came at all, they were taken inside to a cool dark hall which was the centre of the house, called nadumane. If the women were Brahmins, they went deeper into the house, to the place for family dining. The spaces of the house had their own meaning, depending on where you were and where you sat. The nadumane had coloured bamboo mats spread on a smooth, cold and swept floor. The family dining space, more private, had wooden planks to sit on.

Adjoining this was the most private place of all, the kitchen, which had a niche for the household god, where an oil lamp burnt night and day. Only my mother had free entry to this space; even my father could go there only after he had bathed and removed his everyday shirt. Next to the dining hall was a big bathroom, and near that was a workshed for the servants. Beyond that was the backyard; the most magical space for me. Had I not frequented it and eavesdropped on the gossip there, I would never have become a writer, because I got my material from the backyard.

Into the backyard came women of the village, either to draw water from the well, or just to talk to my mother, or receive a gift of leftover special food which my mother would give them unsolicited. These used to be gracious moments of kindness and friendship and courtesy among the women. A woman might refuse politely, but my mother would keep talking and say 'not for you, but for your child'! After the exchange of such civilized courtesies, much more would take place in the backyard as the women relaxed and the conversation became more intimate.

My mother was ritually more orthodox than my father, who drank coffee and who knows what else in the town. Yet, in the backyard, caste barriers among women were forgotten and they would confide the secrets of their sexual lives. I heard a lot as a child about the sexual life of women, and about affairs in the village. So I knew that no matter what was presented in the front, the spiritual India, there was something else at the back, even in the village. This is how writers are made, in the backyard, not in the front yard of civilization. The front yard produces professors!

Women would talk of everyday sorrows of the complicated relationships between men and women, and speak of bodily aches and pains that would never get cured and could never be shared with their menfolk. The world of the front yard and the world of the backyard were such different worlds! The backyard world was not only the secret world of women. Here, mother cooked delicious smelling dishes from herbs and leaves that grew beneath the untended bushes. Only my mother knew them by their names, and every small thing that grew had a name which never entered the learned dictionaries of my language.

My grandfather would also venture into the backyard to collect roots and leaves of plants as medicine for the sick in the village. It was taboo to reveal names, which were mostly in Sanskrit, or even identify the plants. Such medicines were effective only if secrecy was observed. Today, I wish secrecy had been observed, because, under globalization, most of those medicines are going to be American medicines and will cost large amounts of money to obtain.

Grandfather used to assure me as a child that he would pass on to me the secret knowledge when I grew up. But I grew up to be a different kind of person because of the influence of my father's front yard, where the use of Sanskrit led to Anglicization and worked on me to make me modern. So the education that began in the front yard of my traditional home finished in England and America, the great front yards of modern civilization.

The Indian literatures in the bhashas have a front yard and a backyard as well. I use the word bhashas since I do not like the word 'vernacular'. It is very condescending word and should never be used. Nor I am happy with the word 'regional language'. One does not call Portuguese a regional language, so I do not want to call any of my languages a regional language. All the languages of the world are also regional languages. Even the word 'dialect' I do not like, for it is of dubious usefulness. For if a dialect has an army and a national poet, then it becomes a language.

Which is the front yard of India's bhashas? I will take the example of Kannada, my own language. The front yard had Sanskrit literature of pan-Indian fame. But it had a secret backyard, fragrant, fertile, and neglected. Here one could find the innumerable indigenous folk and oral traditions in Kannada, the desi traditions. The classics in Sanskrit constitute the marga, the great road. Desi and marga are actually the words used by Pampa a thousand years ago. His genius lay in the telling combinations he made of the two, and what he did had implications for the treatment of his themes; it was not just as aesthetic exercise.

The universal truths celebrated in Sanskrit literature were not only given a local habitation and a name but, cohabiting in Kannada with the folk imagination, they became pulsatingly alive. The two worlds of the front yard and the backyard have been meeting ever since in Kannada literary works. The backyard is inexhaustible. From it, as literacy spreads, more and more people emerge into the front yard of all civilizations, like the dalits and women today, bringing memories and desires to integrate with the mainstream of the front yard literature, the world literature. The backyard, which is still the world of women, of secret therapeutic herbs, and roots and tendrils for the creation of new dishes, keeps literature in the bhashas continuously supplied with fresh themes and stylistic patterns.

Sanskrit as a language had no backyard of its own. It had to admit the bhashas of the backyard to ensure the survival and continuity of its spiritual substance. In the bhashas of India, the front yard contains the classical literature, Sanskrit literature. However, what dominate the goings-on in the front yard of our lives are not just the Sanskrit classics. There is also the powerful presence of English, the language of modernity. But neither Sanskrit nor English have any power if isolated from bhashas, in fact, they are important if they fail to interact with the world of the backyard.

Literatures in the bhashas have also constituted themselves as literary traditions, in search of their own particular royal highways. Tamil and Kannada have searched actively, and discovered their royal highways. A royal highway is meant for those who can compete with the classical Sanskrit tradition. What happens then to the backyard? The linguistics of cultures such as those small, powerless castes and their areas are undermined in the process. Yet while these sub-groups can be undermined, they cannot be destroyed. When the royal highway becomes pompous and loud and artificially rhetorical, and therefore solely a voice of public emotion, it loses the flexibility and truthfulness of common speech. It is at such moments of cultural crisis that the traditions in the backyard make a comeback and revitalize our languages. This was what Blake and Hopkins did to the English language in their own country, and what has been done with much greater consequence for our culture by poets such as Tukaram, Basava, Mirabai, and Kabir. When such people speak the language, they bring new life into the languages.

Women have without doubt been empowered by the great saint-poets of India. So it is misleading to speak about literature in the Indian bhashas without recognizing its intimate relationship with larger political and cultural questions. The tradition of lively dialectical contention between the royal highway and the indigenous in India will be marginalized if globalization encroaches upon everything; if everything loses out to the corporate world. That is the danger in India today.

DALIT CONTRIBUTION TO INDIAN LITERATURE

When I say Indian literature, I don't mean only written literature. In India, written literature is of course alive among the twenty or thirty per cent literate people who read and write books. But a larger number participates in oral literature. Oral literature should include even the Vedas because they were once a part of it.

The Dalits in Karnataka had their own oral literature in Kannada, from the fourteenth and fifteenth centuries onwards. When I talk about Dalit contribution to Indian literature, I am not only including the contribution of those who came under the influence of Gandhi and Ambedkar, but also of those who came under the influence of the great saint-poets of our country. In this talk, I'm mostly dealing with people from Karnataka because this is the area I know. But figures from their languages can be brought into the kind of scheme that I am trying to build up.

For many people, literature is that which is written, printed, and can be read from a book. It was so in Kannada from the tenth century onwards. Pampa is the first to write down literature in that sense, and then Kumara Vyasa. But my first proposition is that literature doesn't mean merely what is written.

If you visit Mysore during certain months, you will hear women reciting an oral epic for seven days, and this epic would go into several thousand pages. They are Dalit women. They also come with big cymbals, they dance and they sing, and it is not merely literature for them, it is a kind of a religious rite also. The major Kannada oral epics have now been collected. Sahitya Akademi has also brought out the English translation of one of them. So let us not hegemonize written literature but think of all literature as basically oral.

Great poets who write down their poetry somewhere belong to the oral tradition. They are poets when they recite their poems, and it happens with a kind of immediacy. A literature which has lost its oral quality is no longer good literature. One of the tests of literature is to see if it has retained an oral quality. When literature dies, it is revived through the spoken word. And, the spoken word is kept alive by the lowest of low in our society. I have sometimes said that Indian languages will live because there are enough 'backward' people in India.

I am not being cynical. They are the ones who will retain the Indian languages. They have kept the languages alive for others to work on and even take it forward. They are creative with phrases, they bring in musical notes, they use wonderful proverbs. Proverbs are like Vedas for the poet. They are also part of Dalit literature. And many radical progressive thinkers do not take the oral part of Dalit literature into consideration, and hence many theories of Dalit literature are mostly based on realistic renderings of Dalit experiences. I am not excluding the latter but including it along with the oral; then it becomes richer.

In Karnataka, there was a movement—a Dalit movement as a result of a very simple political statement made by one of our Dalit ministers, Basavalingappa. He was in the Congress party; he was deeply influenced by Ambedkar and Buddha. Once he said that he got nothing from Kannada literature: 'It is all boosa (cow fodder).' When the cows are fed with boosa, it makes them yield more milk and also fills their stomach but that is all the contribution it makes. The statement annoyed the patriots of Kannada language, and they started to protest against him. It was obviously a linguistic movement, but it turned into a caste movement. The Dalit boys and girls in colleges were in danger of being beaten up.

I wrote a letter to a newspaper saying that if I were born a Dalit, I may also have said what Basavalingappa said, that Kannada literature is all boosa because a lot of Kannada literature is religious literature. I would need to read Ambedkar to get my strength and my conviction. So there is nothing wrong in what Basavalingappa said. And Kuvempu, one of the major writers in Kannada, also came out in support of his statement. Then many Dalit writers began to write and express themselves. All these led to a big movement. The Boosa Prakarana was a very important event in Kannada in the 1970s, and Basavalingappa was instrumental in it.

At that time, there were two important Dalit writers in Kannada.

One was Siddalingaiah, who wrote poetry of a progressive kind. It is not essentially Dalit in that sense because we had a progressive literary movement, based on Marxism and communism which was called bandaya (protest). But the Dalit movement was different. It had bandaya, but it also had an idiom that the Dalits use in everyday life. A new movement is not only a new movement in content but also in the idiom. It changes the idiom.

Devanura Mahadeva was the first Dalit writer to use a Dalit variation of Kannada, and not the Kannada of the well-to-do and the middle classes. He wrote a very poignant story.

The Dalit experience of humility and humiliation has been expressed in different ways by three great writers. One is the high mimetic way. Much earlier than Devanura Mahadeva, a great Kannada writer, a Brahmin in south Karnataka named Shivarama Karanth had written a novel called *Chomana Dudi*—Choma's Drum—which later became a film. The story of *Choma's Drum* is: Choma wants to own land, but his landlord cannot give him any land to own because he is a Dalit. He can only work on the land, but not become its owner. But he goes on dreaming of owning land. One of his sons becomes a Christian, and he is also enticed to become a Christian so that he could get land. But he is as wedded to his old deities as he is to his desire for land. He expresses himself through beating a drum. The most important character in the novel is the drum.... Choma is almost like King Lear, losing his children and his self-respect, and in the end, he dies beating the drum. Karanth's novel is in the high mimetic mode.

Now I come to *Odalala*, a story by Devanura Mahadeva, a Dalit writer. In this story, which is written in a low mimetic mode with a humorous side, a poor Dalit woman finds her cock missing and thinks someone must have stolen it. She goes in search of it. She goes from house to house, sniffing to find out whether they have made a curry with her cock. In that very process is a detailed description of a whole community. She is a very strong woman. She does not find the cock anywhere and comes back home. She has a small hut but it is still property for her. She does not want her daughter-in-law to take away anything from her but stay there and be obedient to her. There is a quarrel between the daughter-in-law and mother-in-law, where they mime the quarrel of the richer people, as if a hundred acres of land was at stake. They share the notions of property and ownership of the upper classes.

She also has a school-going grandchild. This child draws a peacock on the wall with a chalk—this has been done so well in the story—and then the peacock begins to dance. Something new has been created, a new creativity. The grandmother's grandson comes to her. She talks to him and tells him a story where he is a king. This is her daydream. All this while they are hungry; they haven't eaten. There are many brothers in this family. One of them goes to a rich man's field in the dark and steals a few big bags of groundnuts. He brings these bags home and they shut their door, build a fire, and all of them sit around it and begin to eat the groundnuts, throwing the shells into the fire. This is a great metaphorical event. It is like a yagna being performed for the god within themselves. They are hungry. They eat the groundnuts and throw the shells in the fire. And each one begins to tell a story, a story of a conquest in the past. In one story, someone goes to a hotel, but is denied a cup of tea because he cannot drink from the same cup as the others. And, he says: 'Go to hell, I don't want your tea.' He might not have said it then, but here he says that he told them so. All the potential of each one's rebellion comes through in a humorous way while they are eating. The rich man finds out that his groundnuts are gone. He calls the police. When the police come, these people who have been eating the groundnuts, close the door and throw the groundnuts into the fire and see to it that not a single groundnut is found anywhere. When the policeman opens the door, and finds nothing, he scolds the rich man. 'You lodged a complaint and you brought us here. We found nothing here.' The police officer comes and sees the cock that has come back and says, 'Amma, why do you want it? I'll take it,' and takes it away. So, finally, she is cheated by the police officer. This is the story.

The story has such deep insights of different kinds. The story of rebellion is not narrated in a high mimetic mode, but in a deeply inward tone. Dalit literature is not the same kind everywhere and it is different in Kannada for some reasons. I do not know what reasons, but that is what I want to find out.

But it has taken a different direction in Kannada and it came into the mainstream immediately. Although it was Dalit writing, we never thought we were making concessions because it was written by a Dalit, because it was as good as or even better than what others were writing, because it was deeply metaphorical and went deeper into social reality and said many more things than realistic literature could have said. With realistic literature you either agree or disagree; with this there is no agreement or disagreement but only participation. That is how Dalit literature came to us.

Now I will go into why this was made possible. This happened because some Dalit literature is still alive in the oral epic mode. There are the two epics of *Male Madeshwara* and *Manteswamy* from the fourteenth and fifteenth centuries.

In the twelfth century, there was a movement in Kannada called the Veerashaiva vachana movement. The great figure of this movement was Basava, a Brahmin, who rebelled against the Brahmanical rules and led the movement, and for the first time in Kannada's history, you found writers from almost every community. They perhaps could not write and could only speak; that is why their poems are called vachana. Vachana is that which is spoken. In the vachana movement, there was a revolutionary figure called Allama. We do not know which caste he belonged to, but he was a strange character in the movement. He does not even believe in Shiva. He even makes fun of him because he worshipped only that which had no form or essence. He is a leader of the movement but the others consider Shiva as their lord. Therefore, there is a conflict between him and them. There is an attempt on the part of the Veerashaivas to institutionalize their religion in the twelfth century. But this is difficult to do because each one of them is unto himself or herself.

Sule Sankavva, a prostitute has left behind a vachana. She is not ashamed of being a prostitute. She says: 'Basava said work of any kind is worship of god. You don't have to be ashamed of any kind of work!' It was a revolutionary movement but it degenerated very quickly within three centuries. The Veerashaivas became another caste containing within it almost every caste. They had inner problems within their own communities because the upper-caste converts would not accept the lower-caste converts. So, they developed different mathas. They are now a ruling community in Karnataka. They may commit atrocities against Dalits but their own theory has no place for it. Since they believe in an ideology very different from what they do, degeneration sets in.

The fifteenth-century *Male Madeshwara* is a story of rebellion against the degeneration of the Veerashaiva movement. Madeshwara, the god, destroys a king, who has Shiva's blessings and has become dangerous. Destroys him how? (Mistaking him for a cobbler), the king asks Madeshwara arrogantly, 'Make me a pair of chappals.' 'All right, my Lord, I'll make you a pair of chappals.' He makes him a pair of chappals, and when the king slips into his chappals, they are on fire. So, he dies. This is an example of how an oral epic tries to go against the epics which have the destruction of an asura as a theme by giving it a different type of a treatment.

According to a Veerashaiva story, when Allama goes on travel, his disciples become so arrogant that they don't recognize him when he comes back, looking almost like a hippie, his hair knotted, eyes red, and clothes torn. He looks like a beggar, and his disciples cannot recognize him as their guru. But he has achieved the highest of wisdom. The only man who can recognize him is Basava. So also here, Madeshwara and also later on Manteswamy, when they go back to Kalyana—Kalyana is the place where all the great discussions happen—but in the Dalit re-rendering of this, all the great people in Kalyana are cobblers, lower-caste people who have become great saints. When they are not honoured there, they leave and re-establish the order somewhere else. That is what is narrated for seven days, a reassertion of the values that the Veerashaiva movement has forgotten but remembered by these people who are illiterate. So, for three centuries something is not forgotten but redone. Allama is now grafted onto Manteswamy. How does Manteswamy make his entrance? Manteswamy comes with a pot of toddy in his hand and a dead calf to be eaten as beef on his back. His devotees recognize that Allama has come this way, and he is to be respected and revered. It is a religious ritual for them and so they do it to sing about their own community.

There is a big difference between the literature of the upper castes who have the mahakavya, and the literature of the lower castes and Dalits. The difference is this: in the mahakavyas, the country is sung about. In the epics of the lower castes, it is not the country, but the community that is sung about. The bahujana kavya does not talk about the country but the values of the community. While only the mahajana kavya talks about the country.

A friend of mine, D. R. Nagaraj—he is no more now—has written a very profound book on this whole movement*. There he uses a Rainer Maria Rilke poem where what has become the golden coin, and accepted in the nation as a coin, suddenly has a desire to go back to its origin, and become the ore again. Now, many of these kaavyas have the desire to become the ore again. They know that what has become the naanya (coin), which is used in everyday life, no longer contains the original value of they stood for. Hence, they want to go back to the ore. There is that kind of a pull within Dalit literature in Karnataka. Because it has a past of this kind in the fourteenth and fifteenth centuries, the modern writer no longer has to go to the oral literature of this kind for his inspiration. He has within his own tradition an inspiration of a kind where you can turn your social rebellion into a metaphorical rebellion, a deeper kind of rebellion, a universal kind of rebellion, and is as deep as anything that upper-class literature can ever produce.

On the whole, the gist of my discussion is: When you think about the Dalit contribution to Indian literature, we need not think of only our time of enlightenment where they have asserted themselves, but of a longer time in India, from at least what is called medieval India. The medieval in India is not like the medieval in Europe. Medieval India was much more alive than medieval Europe. It was in medieval India that the Bhakti poets empowered women. In the Lingayat movement, a woman need not sit outside when she menstruates. She can take a bath and she is accepted in society. She can also wear the lingam. And the Dalits have made many transformations. Let me give you a few examples. The Lingayats speak of ishta linga on the palm, but the

---

*D. R. Nagaraj, *Allama Prabhu Mattu Shaiva Pratibhe* (Allama Prabhu and Shaiva Creativity), Heggodu: Akshara Prakashana.

Dalits speaks of a fire in the palm. When they say fire, they do not mean merely the fire you see in the sun or in the sky, they also mean the firefly, which has light. In other words, they go into the everyday details and find their source of inspiration. That is one difference between the Dalit epics and other epics. The details are all quotidian in the Dalit epics. That is why Allama comes with a pot of toddy and a dead calf. The everyday life is glorified in Dalit literature, but grafted on to the older poets; grafted not because they want to imitate the earlier poets, but they want to debunk it. And hence it does two things at the same time: one, you begin to belong to the greater tradition; and, two, you assert your own identity. These twin jobs are done in Dalit literature. That is why I think they are something unique and very important in our own times.

—Transcribed and excerpted by Chandan Gowda

HINDUTVA OR HIND SWARAJ?

How did Gujarat produce a pan-Indian hero? The Gujarat massacre took place when he was chief minister. To say that he tried to prevent it but failed would mean he was weak. Nobody can say that. One is reminded of an image used by the poet Adiga. When yajnas are conducted, everyone present is involved in some task or the other. But a mantrajnya, an expert in the mantras, does not participate. He is known as the 'brahma', and is crucial to the ritual. The brahma does nothing.

Modi was the brahma. Whatever happened has happened. Raskolnikov was tormented by the thought that he should not have committed the murder. A hapless prostitute teaches him love. Modi also feels remorse. But of another kind. A remorse that says if a pup gets run over by a car, what can be done? One could say, 'Oh, poor thing. If the car had stopped, would the puppy have lived?'

Here I will dare to express a thought. Maybe this is why the people of India appreciated Modi; see how he silenced the minorities. On *NDTV 24x7*, Barkha Dutt invites a prominent Muslim and encourages him to praise Modi. We no longer see the harsh-sounding Modi. This is a Modi beloved of all. Who is this Modi created by everyone, including the media?

We are bombarded with images of Modi offering flowers, paying homage to a small photograph of Gandhi. All our apprehensions are dispelled, and what emerges is the image of a new-age leader with foresight, who works without sleep, wears attractive clothes, a turban, holds a mace in his hand—transformed from the outside but unchanged within. He has kept his wife away, he has liberated himself from his past and his caste, has become the new-age Shivaji and Patel. So what if the country is clouded with the smoke of forgetfulness? So what if we forget Gandhi? Why, we could even erect a statue of Gandhi in London's Westminster if a trade deal is struck.

I feel an urgent need to talk to myself, both because of the nationwide humiliation that came my way when I rejected Modi and because of Modi's overwhelming victory that left me astounded. So also Modi's backing by corporates. And the advertisement-like support given by the media, and how that softened our critical awareness. Television channels we admired for their commitment to the truth actively worked to enhance Modi's public image. They acted in bad faith. While these channels may appear to be suspicious of Modi, they hesitate to criticize him or remind us of the Gujarat massacre. Modi's fluent oratory—in Hindi, which has a pan-Indian appeal, and in a manner that allowed no room for introspection—was among the reasons for his victory. Equally responsible was the corruption in the Congress, the bland and expressionless face of Manmohan Singh, the organizational disarray of a befuddled party that, despite its many achievements, believed there could be no leadership outside the Nehru–Gandhi family, its bankruptcy of intellectual thought, and Rahul Gandhi's unfocused search guided by sentiment rather than conviction. Mesmerized by the visual media, even the sceptics among us turned mere spectators, and are as much to blame.

No funeral rites were performed for those who died in the communal violence in Gujarat. Their ghosts don't seem to be haunting anybody. As our leader Modi calmly says, their death was like that of a puppy run over by a speeding car.

Perhaps the massacre was not at Modi's behest. But I have said it earlier and I repeat it here: Modi, who sat like a brahma at the sacrificial yajna in his cut-sleeve kurta, was transformed into a broad-chested gallant. Modi became the mask that his adoring fans greeted him with wherever he went. Like Krishna in the *Ras Kreeda*, Modi was everywhere.

∽

A foreigner went to Ramana Maharshi and said, 'I have come to be converted to Hinduism. This is my punyabhoomi.'

Ramana Maharshi replied, 'Is it right to say that, in the whole world, all of which is God's creation, there are only some punyabhoomis?'

One of his disciples told me this story. For Ramana, the Arunachala mountain where he dwelt was his punyabhoomi. There was blistering hot sun there. If he sat under a tree, there were swarms of honeybees that would sting him. The undulating land with its ups and downs would exhaust him. The place was also a hideout where he could stretch his tired limbs on smooth, well- worn rocks. Ramana, who loved all animals, built a tomb for the crow who used to sit on the well in his backyard. When he was dying of cancer, the peacocks he used to feed began to screech for food. Even as he took his last breath, Ramana told his disciples to feed the birds, as he would on any other day.

Kashi is a punyabhoomi for all. When Gandhi returned from Africa and went there on a pilgrimage, he found it unbearably filthy. How is it possible to call this a punyabhoomi, he asks. He sets up his ashram in the sweltering hot town of Wardha. In 1940, when St Paul's Cathedral in London was bombed, Gandhi writes that he felt as if the bomb had fallen on Kashi. Thus the concept of punyabhoomi is not confined to one country, it could be any place. While Savarkar, the rationalist, fervently praises the supporters of Hindutva, the religious Gandhi offers a liberating text to all humanity in his *Hind Swaraj* (1909).

Vinayak Damodar Savarkar's ideology is based, in essence, on the concept of Hindus who share 'blood ties' and acknowledge India as punyabhoomi. As opposed to this, Gandhi through his conversation in *Hind Swaraj* presents two different perspectives of a modern concept of civilization that would appeal to Indians. People like Dadabhai Naoroji and Gopal Krishna Gokhale were dear to him. While he respects the eminence of Bal Gangadhar Tilak, he has a fondness for the moderate Gokhale.

During one of the huge satyagrahas Gandhi had called for, an Englishman was killed because of the mean-mindedness of the people. He called off the satyagraha, although his followers felt that withdrawing a rapidly growing struggle was not right. Gandhi calls his failure to recognize that there were still some people who were not ready for a non-violent struggle 'a Himalayan blunder'.

In another essay, 'The India of My Dreams', Gandhi writes that no army can vanquish India, which is made up of innumerable small, independent, self-ruled villages. This porcupine-like India, even with a small army, will remain unconquerable.

In this way, two visions of India emerge at the beginning of the twentieth century. One was an all-inclusive India that was local and decentralized in the form of panchayats. The other emotionally charged vision denied its multilingual, multi-religious nature and was limited to those who considered it their punyabhoomi. Hitler did the same in Germany. The whites in Germany were deemed Aryans. The Jews, non-Aryans. The Jews were sent to concentration camps and exterminated. The Germans made rings and bangles from their charred bones. Even as the Jews were being exterminated, Germany widened its roads. Industries that fed the war flourished. People exulted in the arrogance of their superiority.

In the time and the context in which it was written, Savarkar's argument was not as extreme as Hitler's, but it had all the potential to incite cruelty. Inspired by him, people were willing to sacrifice their lives. Nathuram Godse was one of them. That the Congress was capable of the same sort of brutality was evident in the massacre of Sikhs after Indira Gandhi's assassination.

It is a mindset. Gandhi's life was a rejection of that mindset. Even his end refuted it. In the neo-nationalist discourse that prevails today, people believe that it is possible to cultivate this mindset without any associated guilt. The Muslims of India light the fire of resistance only to get burnt themselves. The seeds of hatred which Gandhi's Noakhali yatra could not suppress continue to grow as trees of death in Pakistan with encouragement from its military.

While Savarkar's writing stems from a heightened emotional state, Gandhi's passes through the sieve of introspection.

Deliberation is not a characteristic of modern civilization. The visual media thinks in a rush of relentlessly moving images. It is quite natural then for present-day Savarkarites to think that Gandhi's writing, which looked for the violence within to reject it, amounted to timidity. But Gandhi asks himself some tough questions.

Why are the British here?

Because we too love modern civilization.

Why should we oppose modern civilization?

To liberate not only the Indians but the British as well.

The fact that he wrote *Hind Swaraj*, which makes this argument in his mother tongue Gujarati, is important.

Nehru is critical of *Hind Swaraj*. In a letter that Gandhi writes to this dear disciple of his in 1945, here is what he says: 'You are going to be the leader of independent India. But you don't seem to have read my *Hind Swaraj*.' Nehru's affectionate and respectful reply was, 'I read it long ago. I do not agree with your views. India's villages are hellholes of superstition.' (B. R. Ambedkar also believed that Indian villages were hell.)

The term 'modern civilization' was used sarcastically by Gandhi. When he visited Britain for the Round Table Conference, a journalist asked him, 'What do you think of modern civilization?' Gandhi replied, 'It is a good idea.'

Gandhi was not one to regret the past. His vision of Sarvodaya, more relevant today than ever, included every individual—no matter where he lived and thrived and flourished. He believed that it was possible for a person to instantly change into this ideal citizen. Such a citizen will also evolve continuously throughout his lifetime.

Gandhi asked only his ashramites to follow the code of the ashram in their daily lives. There was always coffee for Rajaji and cigarettes for Maulana Azad and Nehru when they went there for meetings. He did not succeed in ridding Kasturba of her coffee addiction. (I for one would not willingly live in Gandhi's ashram.)

In this context, I am reminded of Rabindranath Tagore's *Gora* (1910), a canonical text. The hero of the novel subscribes to an extreme form of Hinduism. He clings to his faith and denounces the Brahmo Samaj, which has a flavour of Christianity, a love for the English language and an arrogance in its superiority. The light-skinned Gora was not aware that he was born in a stable to an Irish couple who were fleeing from the rioters during the Sepoy Mutiny, and the woman he loved and looked up to was his foster-mother. His foster-father was a selfish man and a sanatani, an orthodox and ritualistic Hindu. To hide the fact that Gora was not his son, he even performed the boy's thread ceremony. And yet, when he was performing a puja at home, he would not touch Gora. Later, Gora—brought up as a staunch Hindu—discovers that he is an outsider. He adopts his mother's humanism as his religion and becomes a vishvamanava (universal man). Transcending the inhibitions of a sanatani and the anglicized cosmopolitanism of the Brahmo Samaj, he becomes an Indian.

When the Babri Masjid was demolished by the Hindutvavadis, I was the president of the Sahitya Akademi in Delhi. I tried to encourage everybody across the country to discuss *Gora*. This work is critical to my study of Hindutva. I urge the readers to study *Gora* in order to understand my brief thoughts on it.

What has emerged from our study so far is this: It is not cowardice that counters Savarkar's egocentric aggressive standpoint or Gora's sanatani faith. It is selfless compassion. It is the path of the Buddha who in his time took shelter under the Kshatriyas.

In our times, Gandhi followed the path of egoless fearlessness. He respected the moderates but was extreme in his own way.

Even today, there are many people who practise a Hindutva that is not articulated clearly even to themselves. Among them are both upper-caste and lower-caste Hindus and those who fit Savarkar's definition of Hindutvavadi. In their view, the cosmopolitan Congress leaders appear as escapists who not only cannot stand up to the Muslims but also pander to them for their votes. In this situation, it seems like only Modi has the kshatra quality to rule this country with chaturopaya, by silencing the Muslims of this country and appeasing the avaricious ones among them. They don't see this trait in the well- mannered Advani who inadvertently praised Jinnah. The person who seemed to rival Modi for a brief while was Arvind Kejriwal, who did not hesitate to be seen as a practising Hindu and posed for cameras with his bare, vibhuti-smeared body after a dip in the Ganga. In these elections, Kejriwal alone countered Modi's Hindutva intellectually as well as through simple Hindu rituals. Rahul Gandhi, with his liberal European mindset and a half-baked cosmopolitanism, speaking some Hindi but better English could not weather the storm of Hindutva. The low-caste leader from Gujarat became the ideal, like Shivaji, for Indians who had a deep-seated longing for kshatra qualities. He rekindled memories of Vivekananda.

It was possible, in ancient India, for a low-caste individual to become a ruler. A Shudra with his bravery could climb the caste ladder and become a Kshatriya. Shivaji was crowned like this. I believe that this egalitarian dream, so dear to many of us, is realized today in Modi—not because of the Sangh Parivar's ideology, but because of the environment created by Gandhi, Ambedkar and V. P. Singh. This environment became necessary for the Sangh Parivar as well.

When I was in Kerala, I invited V. P. Singh to our university. At breakfast I asked him, 'When you were in the Congress for so long, you did not think about the upliftment of the "Mandal" castes. What you are doing now, is it political?'

After thinking for a moment, he replied, 'It is not only my politics. All political parties will have to bring it into practice.'

~

After Modi came to power, it would appear that all leftist ideas have been decimated. One of the reasons for this is that, gradually, mouthing leftist ideas has become easy. As for secularism, it was little more than a convenient term. Yet, because India is a democracy, the right to information and schemes like the midday meal in schools have kept our self-respect intact.

On leftist words becoming mere sounds, Gopalakrishna Adiga has written a humorous poem. It begins like this: 'Leaning to the left, flashing their left eyebrow, they are coming, they are coming, the land surveyors are coming.' Now changing it slightly, we can say, 'Leaning to the right, flashing their right eyebrow, they are coming, they are coming, the brazen crooks are coming.' For whether it is the highly eloquent English media or the Hindi media, they are learning a new language, one that is acceptable to Modi.

Translated by Keerti Ramachandra and Vivek Shanbhag

FASCISM AND THE BOURGEOIS WRITERS*

A complex of reasons, sometimes even apparently contradictory, have to be considered when accounting for the attraction of Marxism and the Communist Party for bourgeois writers like W. H. Auden, Christopher Isherwood, Edward Upward, and Cecil Day-Lewis. Left-wing sympathies did not necessarily lead every one of these writers to join the Communist Party. Auden, Isherwood and Louis MacNeice, despite their sympathies with the progressive ideas of Marxism, never expressed a total faith in the political creed of communism. Orwell's indictment that 'politically they are almost indistinguishable', that communism of these English intellectuals was simply 'the patriotism of the deracinated' is a typical Orwellian exaggeration (1940: 168), both unjust and indefensible: the writers associated with Auden are varied in talent, and their communism was never of the purely orthodox kind; they never toed the Party Line slavishly during the brief period they were associated with the Party. Stephen Spender, for instance, who was a card-holding member of the Communist Party for a short period of time, held his reservations even at the time he joined the Party. As the title of one of his books suggests, communism for him was a step forward from liberalism—an attitude which makes him a typical figure of his group. He hoped that communism would make the idealist achievements of the liberal state real:

> Liberal democracy is like a dishonest pair of scales heavily weighted in favor of industry, which has the real power...to make and unmake governments and control their policies when they are made: nevertheless, the scales do work, and with great resolution, energy, and an enormous popu lar increase of political realism, it would be possible for socialism to tip the scales.... (1937: 22–3)

*This excerpt is from URA's Phd thesis titled *Politics and Fiction in the 1930s*, University of Birmingham, 1966.

But liberalism had failed everywhere in Europe to stem the tide of fascism. The bourgeois writers, who came largely from a liberal background, were eyewitnesses of the quick and dramatic happenings in Germany:

> The poets had travelled and, on the whole, the politicians had stayed at home. 'Wake me up when that's finished', Baldwin used to say when foreign affairs were discussed. But John Lehmann, Christopher Isherwood, Wystan Auden, and Naomi Mitchison were eyewitnesses of Nazism. They had been present at the birth of the beast. Spender and Isherwood in particular had identified themselves with the victims of Versailles, the fragile children, emaciated men, and the young people who were so spiritually crippled that when the time came, in 1933, they could actually welcome Adolf Hitler and Herman Goring (Blythe:106).

More than any other reason, it was the threat that fascism held for the future of human civilization, and the failure of liberalism to stem its tide, which made writers like Spender, Isherwood, and Auden sympathetic towards Marxism. It seemed to them that the only way to care for literature, and the human civilization which made imaginative writing possible, and on which the whole edifice of the values that inform literature rested, was by fighting against fascism. Spender speaks of a remark a great German writer once made to him: 'You are lucky to write in English. It is no longer possible to be a German poet.' (1937: 67)

It was not only that books were burnt and writers were exiled from Nazi Germany. As Sartre had observed, a blacksmith will be affected by fascism only in his life and not in his craft; whereas a writer will be affected in both, 'and even more in his craft than in his life.' (46)

Fascism was not merely a foreign phenomenon that could be ignored; it had affected the English writers too. As Orwell remarks, 'The people who have shown the best understanding of fascism are either those who have suffered under it or those who have a fascist streak in themselves.' (1946: 88).

And writing about W. B. Yeats, he observes: By and large the best writers of our time have been reactionary in tendency, and though fascism does not offer any real return to the past, those who yearn for the past will accept fascism sooner than its probable alternatives (1946: 119).

If the threat of fascism was regarded with a sense of intense personal urgency by writers like Spender and Isherwood, it could have also been because they discovered in their own attitudes a fascist streak. There were moments, Spender confesses, 'When I felt that there was a conspiratorial relationship between the evil passions of the Fascists—which I so profoundly understood and my own anti-fascist virulence' (1951:191).

Isherwood has also confessed that the fantasies and longings of his youth, centered on the idea of 'The Test'—of your courage, of your maturity, of your sexual prowess' had a fascist streak about them (1938: 75). Edgell Rickword writes that Auden's failure to analyze the social movement which so profoundly affected his work led him into making irresponsible statements. In particular, he finds Auden's following couplet nearly fascist in attitude:

> All of the women and most of the men
>
> Shall work with their hands and not think again (New Verse, Nov. 1937: 21–22).

That at some point in the early 'thirties, both communism and fascism might have seemed equally attractive to some writers is probable. From this point of view, Wyndham Lewis's answer to the New Verse questionnaire is very significant. Politically, he said:

> I take my stand exactly midway between the bolshevist and the fascist—the gentleman on my left I shake with my left hand, the gentleman on my right with my right hand. If there were only one (as I wish there were) I'd shake him with both hands (No. 11, Oct. 1934: 7).

Later in the thirties, when communists were forming alliances and popular fronts in support of democracy and against fascism, Christopher Caudwell as a Marxist theoretician felt suspicious of the motives which led some bourgeois writers to support communism.

Writers like Day-Lewis, Auden, and Spender, he said, often glorified the revolution 'as a kind of giant explosion which would blow up everything they feel to be hampering them' (Caudwell, 1937: 319). Therefore, it was the wild and destructive part of revolution that seemed most picturesque to these writers. The source of their hate was 'petty bourgeois suffering from bourgeois development.' In many cases, it was evident that 'a revolution without violence would be disappointing to them.' Therefore, Caudwell concluded, the motives which brought these writers to communism gave 'even the revolutionary element in their art a fascist tinge.' (1937: 320). This only means that the communism of the creative writers is necessarily more complex than it seems, and so must be gone into in greater detail taking into account a number of reasons—psychological, political, and literary.

For further reading of the texts mentioned in this essay, refer to:
Christopher Caudwell, *Illusion and Reality*, New York: Macmillan and Co Ltd, 1937.
George Orwell, *Critical Essays*, London: Secker and Warburg, 1946.
George Orwell, *Inside the Whale and Other Essays*, New York: Gollancz, 1940.
Ronald Blythe, *The Age of Illusion*, London: Hamish Hamilton, 1963.
Stephen Spender, 'Oxford to Communism,' *New Verse*, No.31-32, 1937, p. 9–10.
Stephen Spender, *Forward from Liberalism*, New York: Gollancz, 1937.
Stephen Spender, *World within World*, London: Hamish Hamilton, 1951.
Wyndham Lewis, 'Response to Questionnaire', *New Verse*, No.11, 1934, p. 7.

MEMOIRS

SURAGI

MYSORE

After passing my intermediate I decided to go to Mysore. My father agreed. I travelled a full day and night, for the first time in my life. I took a bus and then hopped into a third-class train compartment. But this was not to see the Dasara celebrations. My desire was to study at the historic Maharaja's College, under the tutelage of professors like M. Hiriyanna. Hiriyanna was not as famous as Sarvepalli Radhakrishnan but was more erudite. Kuvempu, who spoke against state authority, also taught there. Influenced by the socialist movement in the Malnad region I reached Mysuru to study under Kuvempu. By the time I saw my first Dasara, I was perhaps too old to experience the charm of the stories of our acquaintance Ballala. Peering into the Bombay Box bioscope was no longer interesting. For us socialists, taking the maharaja out in a procession was a sign of feudalism, backwardness, and superstition. Socialists had decided to protest the convention. Under Gopala Gowda's leadership, youthful socialists such as J. H. Patel arrived in Mysuru, gathered some activists, and planned a black flag demonstration. It was customary for the maharaja to go by in a procession, dressed in all his finery, sitting on a caparisoned elephant. For the socialist activists this was a risky protest: people loved the maharaja and the procession. If we marked an inauspicious start to the procession with black flags, there was a good chance people would turn into protesters and assault us. We sought police protection and carried out a symbolic protest, waving black flags. This continued year after year.

CDN'S GUIDANCE

Bharat Raj Singh and C. D. Narasimhaiah were from Cambridge University. It was my desire to meet them and ask if I could join the Honours course. Rajagopala, communist activist G. H. Krishnamurthy's brother, used to run People's Book House adjacent to the Jaganmohana Palace in Mysuru. He took me to Bharat Raj Singh, who was on the faculty of Maharaja's College and requested him to admit me as a student. I had scored well in English and had no doubt I would make it. 'So you want to join English Honours? Let me see how many of these books you have read,' Singh said, handing me a list that comprised George Eliot, Jane Austen, Walter Scott, and several other names. 'Not Walter Scott, sir. Because my father asked me not to read him,' I said. 'Oh, this is very strange...your father telling you not to read. What is your father?' he asked. 'My father is not college-educated but he has read all these books. I have not read any of these but I will tell you which ones I have,' I said, telling him about Gorky and the others. To which he remarked, 'You have read something on your own. This is very strange. Boys don't read anything like this, you have read many things. We need a student like you.' He had come to English on the royal path, whereas I had taken a side lane. Singh was kind. He had liked the way I conducted myself. Yet, despite his deep knowledge, he did not impress me as much as Professor Narasimhaiah did.

It was true I was well read but I did not know as much English as those who had studied in English medium schools. I ended up making silly mistakes. We had a professor called C. D. Govind Rao. He told us to write an essay on a novel by Jane Austen. In it the father is on the verge of getting his daughters married off. I wrote, 'The father wanted to marry his daughters.' Govind Rao came to class and said, 'Whoever wrote this stand up.' I did. 'Better go and join Kannada Honours. What are you doing here?' My confidence about being well read got a big jolt that day. But the thought also entered my mind that one day I would prove how different I was.

Narasimhaiah, who had just returned from Cambridge after studying under the guidance of the famous literary critic F. R. Leavis, influenced me deeply. His teaching was unique. We would gather in his small room. He gave no lectures—his classes meant constant debate. Anyone could say anything in class. An hour would go by without our being aware. Humour was allowed even in the middle of serious discussions.

If CDN taught us in a manner that helped realize the true meaning of literature within ourselves, Professor Ranganna, his senior, peered into his well-structured notes and spoke in a soft, firm voice about Aristotle and other great philosophers. I learnt a lot from him. When I completed my Honours, I was floored by the certificate he handed me. It read: 'He has studied under extremely difficult circumstances and shaped up. I am impressed with his original thinking.'

The two professors invited us home for lunch at least once a year. Ranganna would not only give us a hearty meal but also perform Saraswati puja, and make an hour-long didactic speech in his soft voice. We would listen to it out of devotion to the goddess and gratitude for the fulsome meal. Under the modernist C. D. N.'s hospitality, on the other hand, we could sing. We were even allowed to step aside and have a smoke. Dr Gopalaswamy was the principal of Maharaja's College then. He was a celebrated psychologist. He gave Akashvani its name when he started it in Mysuru. He was simple, liberal, and a thinker who spoke little. In those days Gayathri Talkies showed good English films. We would buy the cheapest tickets and sit on the benches. I was surprised sometimes to spot Dr Gopalaswamy among the students at the cinema. During his tenure, Maharaja's College celebrated its centenary year.

Siddalingaiah, then a renowned sculptor in Mysuru, had carved an image of Saraswati for the occasion, and to our delight it was placed in a nook near the staircase.

GRAND COLLEGE TRADITION

Maharaja's College was not like other colleges. When we started as freshers, seniors showed us around, pointing to the rooms of the great scholars. Kuvempu came in a tonga, for which Mysuru was known, wearing a kachche panche and white jubba. His practice was to alight at a distance and walk towards the college, his gaze turned upwards. He mounted the stairs, strode directly to his room, and took his seat. We would watch all this respectfully. D. L. Narasimhacharya held his umbrella like a stick, oblivious to its handle. With his slim nama and turban, he was a picture of profundity. Ta. Su. Shama Rao, who spoke to all students with warmth and familiarity, was a favourite. We had heard with awe that poor students got to eat at his house.

Professor Purushottam, who taught philosophy, had made a name as an orator. We clamoured to hear his lectures in English. Professor L. Srikantaiah, who had returned from England, became a lecturer in the political science department. A staunch Marxist, he had once countered Purushottam's idealism with Marxist realism. He had a law degree. Soon after returning from England he resigned from his position at the college. After giving up his job, he won a term as an MLA. Incapable of crafty manoeuvres, he remained an ideologue, and mingled with us freely over the years. He influenced me deeply.

Mitra Mela, the theatre group was born; it staged many plays. Vishwanatha Mirle, Sindhuvalli Ananthamurthy, Na Rathna, and P. Srinivasa Rao were among those who came into their own with the help of Mitra Mela. They became close friends, and I spent long hours with them at the canteen. The handsome and youthful C. D. N., who was the cynosure of all eyes, was the president of Mitra Mela. Some mischief mongers, who couldn't bear to see boys and girls mixing freely, made allegations of sexual misconduct and ended up destroying Mitra Mela.

LOVE AND MARRIAGE

I must say a few things about relationships without attempting any self-justification. It has been fifty years since I got married. My wife says, 'I have lived with him for fifty years.' She talks of it as an accomplishment, as in putting up with hardship. I could say the same. She knows I think of it the same way. When we mutually think this way, we have no bitterness. When the bitterness goes away, intense love doesn't stay back either. Perhaps what remains in a marriage is for the couple to adapt to each other within the confines of a family. They just have memories of love.

I have such memories. My wife was a young girl sporting two plaits when I saw her as a student in Hassan. She came over to my house for private tuition. When she sang a film song at an event, it brought tears to my eyes. She sings well even today.

I had given her class an assignment: Describe someone you like or dislike. She had written about me, making fun of my gestures and teaching style. A girl in plaits who could write so candidly about her lecturer had ignited my curiosity and interest.

The first door of my romantic world opened when I realized she could speak about me with such abandon. I didn't want a girl who would adore me; I wanted a companion. I fell in love with the girl who had come to me on the pretext of tuition. She was then just sixteen or seventeen. I developed no physical intimacy with her. She was at an age when she didn't know enough about the world's ways, or about right and wrong. She interacted with me in all innocence. When she invited me over to her house I felt I was entering another world.

Everyone in her family liked me. Esther was among the many students who came to me for coaching. While the others paid me a fee, Esther gave me her guileless love. I was fond of fish. A student had brought me some, which I had placed in a glass bowl. I was often engrossed in watching the swimming fish. This would annoy Esther. 'What are you doing there? Can't you come here and do some lessons?' she would snap. She was outspoken even in those days.

One of my grandmother's sisters lived with us. She used to observe us closely. She sometimes made us sit next to each other and served us lunch. My brother was supportive of our romance. One day my aunt said something that made me furious. 'Ey, Ananthu, keep her as a mistress. Stay out of marriage and all that.' I was seething but replied calmly, 'You shouldn't speak that way, aunty.' My sister was yet to be married. I knew it would be difficult to find her a groom if I married out of caste.

A few days later my father told me he had found a match for my sister. I knew he didn't have enough money for the wedding. I began giving more classes and earned some money. The father of one of my students, a Muslim, ran a cloth shop in Hassan. He provided the clothes for the wedding at cost price.

My father had found a boy in haste and fixed up the wedding. When I went to the village, I found my sister unwell. I sat by her side and asked her affectionately, 'What's the matter, Kumari? What's wrong?'

She couldn't hold back her emotions. She said, 'I don't like this match.' But the family had given its word. The news had been shared with our relatives and friends. The only thing left was to have the invitation cards printed and distributed. My mother panicked on hearing Kumari's words.

I stood strongly by my sister. 'There is no question of prestige in this. Kumari doesn't like this match. This wedding shouldn't take place.' My father was enraged by my words. He paced up and down the stairs in a huff and said, 'You are destroying me and my name.' I tried to reason out, 'Appa, it's nothing like that. Just say your son opposed the wedding.' My father trusted me. He didn't want his daughter's life destroyed because of a decision he took. He agreed and called off the wedding. I knew my father needed such pressure in critical situations. I am happy to this day about the firm stand I took that day. A few days later we found another match for Kumari in Mattur. She is a mother of four now, happy to this day. Mattur is a town that prides itself on speaking Sanskrit for its everyday transactions. My niece recites Naranappa's *Kumaravyasa Bharata* fluently. My brother-in-law is a Shivalli Smarta Brahmin; my father, a Shivalli Vaishnava Brahmin. I must mention here that my father was liberal enough in those days to look for a groom in a sect other than ours, as inter-caste marriage was not common in those days.

I had to wait for a long time even after I had decided to marry Esther. I moved to Mysuru after teaching in Hassan for some years. My mother was with me then. She was disturbed when she came to know about my relationship with Esther. She would suddenly become weak and slump to the ground. She also complained of pain. When we took her to a doctor he diagnosed it as a mental illness. She was tormented during this period. As a little boy, when she went to the hills for her morning ablutions, I would scream, 'Amma, are you dead or what?' and keep crying till she called back. Her agony on my account was something I couldn't handle. My mind became turbulent.

RAJEEV'S ADVICE

After years of learning sarod under Ustad Ali Akbar Khan, Rajeev Taranath had returned to Mysuru. He was thinking of doing a PhD.

We became close during this period. He instilled confidence in me and said I should marry Esther. 'If you don't take a firm decision, everything will break, Ananth,' he said. Rajeev got married around the same time Esther and I got married. His wife Madhavi was beautiful and older than him; she had a son from an earlier marriage. She hailed from a reputed family. Polanki Ramamurthy was a close friend to both of us. He was a sentimental creature who used to whistle film songs to himself. He was great at arguments. He fell in love with Anuradha, and married her later. Rajeev told Ramamurthy, 'Look, you sat inside your room just whistling and got to marry such a charming girl. I struggled hard to learn the sarod and ended up marrying a girl older than me.' This was a popular joke among us.

I was under no pressure from Esther or her family to marry her in a hurry. She had then joined a college in Bengaluru to do her BSc. I would occasionally visit her there. I remember the first gift I gave her, when I first met her in Bengaluru, was K. S. Narasimha Swamy's *Mysuru Mallige*, a book of love poems. I had dilly-dallied enough. I sat with my mother one day and said firmly, 'I am marrying Esther.' We went to a registrar's office and got our wedding formalized. The registrar happened to be film actor Ambareesh's father. He took care of the formalities. He said we could marry if no one raised objections within a given date. My father got wind of this and took my mother away to the village. He didn't say a word to me about the wedding. He went to Tenginakere, near Beguvalli, and became a sharecropper on a piece of land belonging to a matha. He took up a hut there, got its roof tiles fixed, and started living there.

I didn't know how to react to these developments. Esther and I were not living together. I had applied to be an NCC officer and was selected. I went to Hyderabad to train as a pilot officer. I put myself through a life of discipline, listening to lectures on flying and weather monitoring. The training included cross-country walking, running, and shooting. I tried to douse my inner turmoil with this regimen. I woke up early and had things to do all day. I spent three months this way. The notice period had passed. The moment I returned I married Esther.

Was it just my morality that made me marry Esther? Was the love as intense as before? I suspect most love marriages are like this, and I wish they weren't. Perhaps the intensity of the love is lost by the time a couple finds the courage to marry. But Esther had no such dilemmas. In this sense, she is more honest to life than I am.

She thinks pragmatically. We got married in a simple ceremony in Bengaluru in April 1961.

I suffered several embarrassments soon after we were married. We hadn't gone through any religious rites. When Esther's family invited us over, a priest dressed in a suit walked in. He stood up just before the meal and said, 'Let us pray.' He muttered some prayer in his Kannada-mixed English. All of this made me uncomfortable but not because I am Brahmin. It went against my attempts to transcend caste. 'What am I doing here!' was a question that nagged me. My friends were teasing me, saying things like, 'Ananthu, let's change your name to Anthony Martin.' By being around for Esther and me, and bantering away, they prevented the grimness from overwhelming us.

T. G. Raghava signed as a witness at our wedding. I had to buy things for the house. He gave me five hundred rupees from the money he had earned by giving tuition, and we made our purchases with it. Tejasvi spoke to a relative and got us a house on rent in Mysuru. Tejasvi, Shamanna, and Dr Shamsundar—a friend who could drink up half a pot of water!—came home every day. We chatted about literature, Tejasvi's experiences in the wild, and the boyish mischief of Tejasvi and Shamanna. Tejasvi's sense of humour had the power to change our bookish perspectives, and served as an antidote to my frowning self. I read and wrote a lot. My salary was two hundred and fifty rupees, and I sent to my mother the fifty rupees I got for being a pilot officer. My father wouldn't take anything from me. When I ran out of money for my monthly purchases, I borrowed fifty rupees from Polanki Ramamurthy, and paid back when I could. Esther did all the household chores. My shirts were an immaculate white, thanks to Esther beating them on a stone and washing them thoroughly. Our house was tiny. Boregowda, student and relative of our socialist friend, Kalegowda, also lived with us. He would go to the village once a week and return with butter and eggs. He remains like a brother to me to this day. He runs a rice mill in his village and is well off. A grandfather now, he calls Esther 'sister'.

Rajeev's mother-in-law was a painter. When Esther was pregnant with Sharath I would take her on my bicycle, drop her off at Rajeev's house, go to Coffee House, and pick her up on my way back. Rajeev's wife Madhavi was pregnant at the same time. His mother also lived with them. A couple of days after our son was born, Rajeev and Madhavi had a son too.

The discussions with Gopalakrishna Adiga at Coffee House inspired many of my writings. We had created a world of our own there, amid shared cups of coffee and the haze of cigarette smoke. We were busy ushering in modernism in literature when a jukebox, which we saw as a symbol of modernism, arrived at Coffee House. Attracted by its loud music, young people thronged the cafe. Modernity had snatched away the comfortable cane chairs that encouraged discussions about modernism. We went to the parks, looking for space under the trees. Without coffee our discussions lost charm. We didn't have money for beer at the pubs. And in any case Adiga wouldn't drink even though he was a modernist!

I had remained vegetarian even after marriage. Esther loved fish and longed for it when she was pregnant. A restaurant near the railway station was famous for its fried fish and I would bring her fish from there. She was unhappy about eating it all alone, and, to give her company, I started eating fish. After a year of blissful domesticity, Sharath was born on 6 November 1962. He developed a whooping cough soon after he was born. People said children who developed a whooping cough so young would find it hard to survive. Dr Kini, Kuvempu's physician, was known as a good doctor in Mysuru. When he treated Sharath, the cough gradually subsided. Ram Manohar Lohia visited our house when Sharath was unwell. He had a meal with us and enquired about his cough. He spoke to Esther, standing in the kitchen, for as long as he had spoken to me.

Lohia was in Mysuru, and was staying at the Krishnaraja Sagar Hotel. Gopala Gowda took me along to meet him for breakfast. Lohia was a courteous conversationalist; he enjoyed talking. It is difficult to find anyone as hospitable as Lohia when it comes to serving at a meal. He first persuaded me to eat my fill of papaya. The vegetarian Lohia made a concession for eggs. He ordered omelette and toast for the two of us. Our conversation turned to languages. Lohia remarked, 'You are a writer. You must write and propagate this. All of us must learn English as a language of grasping knowledge but not as a language of expression. I don't know if Max Mueller, who translated the Vedas and the Upanishads into English, knew how to speak Sanskrit. But he was able to do such wonderful work because of his grasp. We must similarly be able to understand European languages. But we need our own languages for expression. I have a suggestion. Use Kannada for education till the graduate level. I suggest you use Hindi for postgraduate studies.'

I then said something that occurred to me that instant. 'Sir, if a language is unfit for postgraduate education, we must assume it is unfit for primary education as well.' Lohia heard this but didn't offer a counter argument. 'I completely agree with you. But India needs a common language. I say this because that language shouldn't be English. India is a country of many languages. All languages are national languages. When people come from our provinces to Delhi to sit in Parliament, we should have several people translating between languages. That is when swarajya comes naturally in all languages.'

In those days I was wracked by guilt on many counts. I was troubled to think I was growing while no one in my family was keeping up with me. I had assumed, after I was married, that I would be the one to help my brothers study. In 1966, soon after I returned from England, I invited them over to Mysuru to live with me in a house I had taken up in Saraswathipuram. My wife didn't like the idea of looking after my brothers, besides our two little children, Sharath and Anu. She came from a Christian nuclear family; perhaps she could never understand the idea of a joint family. My salary was meagre. All this was new to her. She didn't know how to live in difficult circumstances. When I couldn't take her nagging any more, I called her father and told him to take her away. The writer Chaduranga, dear to both of us, intervened then. He pacified me and gave Esther a word of advice. There was no way I could abandon my brothers. Looking at all the commotion, my brothers said they would go back to the village, but I didn't agree.

Much to my surprise, Esther, who doesn't hold any grudges, changed gradually. She started working as a schoolteacher and added to the family income. She had worked when we were in England and earned her fare. When we returned from England it wasn't easy to afford even cereal for our children. And now we also had to think about Anil, studying for his MBBS, and Gururaja, doing a BA. Esther managed the house amidst these difficulties without ever getting us into debt. She wasn't a graduate when we got married. Facing such difficulties at home, she joined Sharada Vilas College to do her BSc. She took coaching from Lakshmana Rao and Srinivasan. She was able to do all this with help from my brothers. They took care of the children allowing Esther to do an MEd and take up a teacher's job. Esther's achievements are inspired by her Christian family. She overcame the attitudes of the nuclear families that we see everywhere these days—why bother about educating brothers?—and my brothers became her brothers. She put in effort, and my brothers did too.

If you were to ask if our married life has been successful, an annoyed Esther will sometimes say no. But she suddenly turns cheerful. In 2011, after getting both her knees replaced, she toured Jordan and Israel, places hallowed by memories of Jesus, with her sister. With little religious fervour, she had a good trip and returned longing for home. The one who told her about the legends of Christ was me, not her Sunday school priest. She accompanies me wherever I go. The desire to look beautiful hasn't left her. I wouldn't blame her: at eighty, I haven't lost my enthusiasm for life and I refuse to wear faded clothes.

Esther is past seventy but her face retains its youthful charm. She refuses to heed my advice to this day and talks back to me. The Esther of the photogenic face is an extreme miser who has saved me from getting into debt. She would never hire an auto or a jutka, preferring to walk home all the way from the railway station. She takes after her father. Her mother is fashionable and generous.

Esther doesn't like me being immersed in my own world. Left with no choice, she puts up with it. Lost in doing the dishes and looking for dust and cockroaches in the corners, she also worries about whether the sapling she planted has dried up, her son's lunchbox is ready, and the tea she made for me has gone cold. This woman, so worldly as to seem unable to renounce anything, is the same girl I pursued and married, isn't she? Perhaps I needed someone like her as an excuse for my failures. This woman—who never gives away anything to anyone, and makes me and the children constantly fight with her—is a wonder.

She won't even donate ten or twenty rupees, forget thousands. She has become accustomed to getting gifts from my admirers but won't give away a thing. For all that, she has never sought things beyond my means or pressured me to become corrupt. My relationships with friends bother her. Yet she spends every moment for me and our children. If you ask whether this marriage has led to anything positive at all, I would say yes. It has given me delight and resulted in many happy things. When I was in Kerala, Esther was diagnosed with cancer. My diabetes then went out of control and pulled me down. We have two loving children. Esther looks after us with so much concern that it is sometimes annoying. I believe a family brings, besides a sense of security, many things: quarrels, selfishness, dilemmas, anxiety. We long for both security and love. That is a paradox of life.

SPIRIT OF OUR TIMES

Let us take my marriage to understand our yugadharma. A hundred years ago, if I had given up my caste and married outside, the mathas would have boycotted me. This continues till date but not as often and is not as cruel as before. (However, the situation hasn't changed for the Dalits: they still suffer in a pathetic manner.) I remember a Brahmin in our village who had been cast out by the matha in Bheemanakatte. I forget the reason. No one would invite them to a community lunch, or have any relationship with the family. He tried hard to rid himself of the stigma. I remember my father speaking in his favour and arguing the boycott had no grounds. He conducted rituals and brought him back into the community. If widows become pregnant, they are ostracized. In my story 'Ghatashraddha', Yamunakka suffers because she is thrown out, and thereby cut off from all relatives and relationships.

A woman had suffered this way. After being ostracized she had grown her hair back and worked as a midwife. Since she was an outcaste, she was served her meals in the backyard or in front of the house. But times have changed now. No one boycotted me when I married out of caste. I was not harmed physically. Of course we had psychological difficulties. If we had married in a village, the story might have been different. Even if we marry within our caste, problems of compatibility remain. When we marry out of caste, we are not obliged to attend other weddings. In India a love marriage could be a trick to beat poverty. The couple doesn't have to host a poor sister's daughter who wants to study. These days some marriages within the caste also turn out this way.

In a so-called love marriage or a nuclear family, a couple lives for itself, true. In such a set-up one can simultaneously follow one's convictions as well as one's selfish ways. Words cast a spell. When nuclear families talk about their success they generate envy, and seem to believe everything they say. On the other hand, a marriage within the security of caste provides the couple the strength to pay donations for their children's engineering seats. Vermilion and turmeric appear on mango-leaf festoons made of plastic. But the magic of true love evaporates in such a marriage. Everything is showy, dismissive, and meant to create envy. Here is something that anyone we like could be saying. What speaks here is love burnished by money:

> My father has always been independent. But he cannot live without mother. We take them out to a homestay in Coorg when we have a long vacation. Father loves a drink when he is not at home. You know the secrets of the orthodox. He is happy that I chant the Gayatri mantra every day. He still wears his old college tie at his official functions. And mother never misses the Gowri festival. My wife never forgets to buy her a traditional sari, which she wears only for the festival.

In the absence of bad faith, speech becomes forthright and cutting. When I said I would marry a Christian girl I recall my father's first reaction. 'If I come to your house at an odd hour, you will fetch stale food from a hotel and serve me, won't you?' he said. Eyes welling up, he turned his face away. It was mandatory at home to make cucumber *huli* and serve a meal to our guests. As hosts we would bring a pot of water for the guests to wash their hands and feet and refresh themselves.

Initially my mother was hurt for material reasons as well: the eldest son, who earned well, was lost to an infatuation. This comes from a personal, family perspective. She was the sort to spice up her talk with tales: as she had done about a man in Basrur who had married a girl recommended by his elders but also kept a mistress. She would gossip about the design of the gold chain he had gifted the mistress. While pounding rice, after she was done with singing Purandaradasa songs and talking about the glory of God Venkateshwara, she would take up these local stories. My father was not bothered about such things. My mother used to save the extra money I earned as an NCC officer, something my father wouldn't touch.

I was anguished that I had to go against the wishes of my parents, and afraid I was stepping into a world whose ways I could not understand. I was caught between my love and my secular convictions. My loathing for the inhuman caste arrogance of Brahmins was growing. I had come under the influence of Gandhi because of my father. I couldn't tell what made me stand firm: my ardent love or my egotistic pride in my convictions.

The moment he learnt of Sharath's birth, my father drew up his horoscope, smeared it with vermilion and turmeric, sent it to me, and then called me over. I took Esther and the suckling Sharath to our village. My mother and my sister Kumari performed an arati and welcomed us. In later years, my father grew close to Esther.

This is today's yugadharma. My brothers accepted my relationship. My children didn't have to face any caste discrimination. My daughter fell in love with a Gaud Saraswat Brahmin and married him. My son-in-law Vivek's conservative grandmother did say, 'How are you compatible? She is born of a Brahmin and Christian, isn't she?' But all this was just conversation, and didn't translate into major suffering.

I have been a socialist since my college days. Several friends were similarly inclined. When we decided to wave black flags as the Mysore maharaja went by in a howdah mounted on an elephant, we sought police protection. In those days we had to suffer a bit for our socialist struggles. Protesters were jailed but released soon. That involved some suffering. These days things are much easier: it is not so difficult to obtain bail. Those truly suffering in today's yugadharma are people like Binayak Sen, the jailed paediatrician, and Aung San Suu Kyi, whose equanimous mind has no hatred. In our times she is the one who has fought for her convictions and suffered for them. Nelson

Mandela of South Africa spent many years in jail. Once he came out, he said he had forgiven the whites who had incarcerated him, and campaigned for a ban on nuclear bombs. His suffering is genuine. Martin Luther King, who fought for the blacks, also championed his cause by suffering for it. Coming back to India, during the Emergency, a few from Karnataka went to jail. Snehalata Reddy was jailed for taking part in George Fernandes's agitation and trying to blow up a bridge. Soon after she was released, she died of a heart attack. In Kannada literary circles none of us, Lankesh and myself included, suffered. We were part of Jayaprakash Narayan's agitation against the Emergency, and helped form a government after Indira Gandhi was defeated. Several student leaders and followers of Jayaprakash Narayan went on to become chief ministers. The landlords and the middle class who opposed Indira Gandhi, besides the chattering sorts like us, grew in strength. It is pointless to discuss who was corrupted more by power—the socialists or the Sangh Parivar—or even if the Congress was a role model to all of them.

Ambedkar is not alive in Mayawati's time. In the era of Mulayam and Lalu, Lohia and Jayaprakash Narayan are not alive. Madhu Limaye is not around to see George Fernandes's misadventures. Nor is Gandhi anywhere in sight. Manmohan Singh is a well-wisher of America. We are delusional creatures who refuse to recognize this. Our yugadharma is reflected in the bad faith of our personal relationships, the hypocrisy of our public life, and the cynicism we share in close circles.

My rebellious friends have acquired cabinet-rank positions. The connection between our words and our inner lives is broken. This was not so a hundred years ago. People went to jail for their convictions and lost their homes and properties. In our times few have paid so dearly. Some made token gestures, that is all. Karanth gave up his Padma Bhushan but that didn't affect him. People did face injustice at the hands of Indira Gandhi's son, Sanjay. He evicted the poor. He thought it was essential to curb population growth among the Muslims, who believe children are their wealth. But people of my class were not affected; such fears don't bother our class. We abort foetuses so that girls are not born at all. I believe if we must respond to the times, we must experience 'intellectual suffering'. This is way different from the physical suffering our ancestors experienced.

Many of us had invested our faith in the Soviet Union, believing it was a good system of governance. For the Leftists it was the ideal. One day it just crumbled. But people who called themselves communists didn't suffer. They didn't introspect why and how this happened. When the Europeans sent their tanks and occupied Hungary, many communists in Europe I knew opposed it and quit the party. They became orphans. For them the Communist Party had been like a caste. All their relationships and dealings took place within it. Quitting the party was a difficult act. Edward Upward, whose work I had researched, was among those who quit to oppose the occupation of Hungary. He remained a Marxist though. Such people suffered intellectually. The incredible book *The God that Failed* (1949) was published against this background. In it, major writers have written about how the God they had trusted was defeated.

Bhisham Sahni was in the Soviet Union when it collapsed. He didn't write a single word about its wretched system, or about Stalin killing people. I once said, 'But why? Why didn't you write about what you saw with your own eyes? Writers in Europe have written so much about it.' He didn't reply. His wife called me aside and said, 'Don't ask him such questions. They cause him pain.' His suffering was confined to such pain. Many who visited the Soviet Union came back without writing a word about what they saw.

When Darwin's theory of evolution was published, faith in Christianity was eroded. The major writers in England were in a dilemma. Doubts arose about the Bible when it was said that the world had evolved not from Adam and Eve but from the apes. Matthew Arnold said we should read the Bible not literally but as a work of poetry. His reasoning was that it would survive if we read it as poetry but become a lie if we read it literally. T. S. Eliot responded that, if read as poetry, the book would not influence us as profoundly as it had as a religious text. So how do you read it? Literally or metaphorically? A comprehensive debate took place about whether what was said in the book was right or wrong. This is what I call intellectual suffering.

RAM MANOHAR LOHIA

I first saw Lohia at the Shivamogga railway station. He was the only one awake in the Sagar–Bengaluru coach. I handed him my mother's filter coffee and hot idlis from a nearby eatery. He must have been on a protest fast, and so declined my hospitality with a smile. I must explain the background. During the Kagodu satyagraha, Lohia had tried to plough land and was arrested like the farmers. He was known as one of Nehru's best friends. The government had locked him up not in Sagar, but in Bengaluru. Even when he was arraigned, he used his native idiom, calling the magistrate 'Magister'. He justified it, saying that was the way he used language. He was to travel to the USA. There was speculation that Nehru had intervened and secured his release. Several stories about Lohia floated around. One of them was that Indira Gandhi was fond of him. The newspapers had reported that Nehru's daughter Indira had sent him a basket of mangoes when he was in jail.

Lohia had come down to participate in the Kagodu satyagraha. Kagodu is a village near Sagar. Karnataka's first ever farmer satyagraha took place there. I was in my second year of college then. I missed many classes and immersed myself in learning socialist ideology. Some of us had formed the Students' Socialist Club and I was its secretary. Young boys and girls from all communities were its members. I had read Karanth's literature, and in my youthful enthusiasm invited girls involved in prostitution to join the club. Gopala Gowda was instrumental in taking the decision to launch the farmer satyagraha.

I remember a meeting on the terrace of the Socialist Party's office. C. G. K. Reddy, president of the party and managing editor of the daily *Prajavani*, had come over. The well-built, six-foot Garuda Sharma, who had stayed for a month in Kagodu and studied the problems of the farmers, was also present. He later became a staunch follower of Vinoba Bhave. Speaking first, Reddy placed the Marxist proposal that the socialist agitation be initiated by workers. But Gopala, born in a village, had argued like a Maoist. Our party was full of lawyers who debated the prospects of our satyagraha for hours. The gigantic Sharma then stood up, and in his stentorian voice said, 'This will be like pulling a hill with a strand of pubic hair. If we win, we get the hill. If we don't, we lose nothing!' Without as much as a smile he sat down. The rest cracked up and piped down. The meeting resolved to launch the satyagraha.

Lohia assigned Sharma the job of ensuring the farmers did not get violent. He must have felt there was no man better suited for the job, given his build and voice. Sharma carried out his responsibility well. The satyagraha was simple. The landlord there, Odeyar, was cultured. He had studied in Shantiniketan and was a Congress leader. He was an orator with a smiling face. But all said and done, he was a landlord. He had gradually increased the size of the vessel used to measure his share, and the farmers came to know about this and refused to part with the crop. Odeyar threw them out of their sharecropping land. The moment the farmers carried their ploughs to the land, the police arrested them and took them away. Lohia was similarly arrested. Several socialist youths from other parts of Karnataka took part in the satyagraha and went to jail. I was a student then, and my job was to visit them in jail from Shimoga, seventy kilometres away, and deliver whatever they loved to eat.

WITH LOHIA AGAIN

I had returned (to Mysore) from England then. I got an opportunity to meet Lohia again. He asked me about my thesis. I told him about the writer Christopher Isherwood, who had gradually moved away from the idea of revolution and become a devotee of Ramakrishna Paramahamsa. Lohia, who had criticized Achyut Patwardhan's spirituality, was intrigued, and sought more details about Isherwood from me. The same day, I read out to him the poems of Basava, Allama, and Akka Mahadevi, where spirituality turns into revolutionary politics. Gopala Gowda must have done this before me. Lohia, who thought deeply about the emancipation of women, was attracted to Akka....

Another incident concerns Lohia's anger. Gopala Gowda persuaded Lohia to address the students of political science at Mysore University. A professor there had brought pressure on Gopala Gowda to arrange the lecture. The reserved Lohia agreed and arrived at the campus. By then he had declared he wouldn't use English in public. He was determined to speak in Hindi, and had become unpopular among South Indians. He had said a South Indian should become prime minister, which made him unpopular in the North. However, that day, pressured by Gopala Gowda and the professor, he spoke in English. The essence of what he said is this: Shankaracharya was India's last great thinker. After him, no thinker of such calibre was born in India. The reason: people are living like frogs in their own caste wells. Unless this country witnesses a major intermixing of castes, no new knowledge will be generated.

When Lohia sat down after this speech, the university professor displayed his knowledge. He ended his speech lamenting that Lohia, who used to be Nehru's right hand, had become so pessimistic. Lohia, who had been listening to all this quietly, walked out and sat in a car. Gopala Gowda, the driver, and I were at the spot. That was the first time I witnessed how furious Lohia could be with his companions. 'Gopala Gowda hasn't graduated from any university. He is under the illusion that people with university degrees are great scholars. He took me to meet an idiot. I had to break my vow to speak in wretched English. Instead, I could have stood at a street corner and spoken to the people,' he said, with a frown. Gopala Gowda was also upset. But he thought Lohia's criticism was unfounded. In a deep voice, he said, 'I've had enough of serving you' and became quiet. Lohia broke his gloominess, put his hand on Gopala Gowda's shoulder, and said, 'Let's forget all this.' Gopala Gowda broke into tears.

WHAT MARXISM MEANS TO ME

At the outset we must recognize the difference between the Communist Party, with which we have disappointments, and Marxism. Initially I used to suspect Marxism, thinking it places all our problems in an economics context. Once, in Kottayam, when we were chatting, the novelist, Thakazhi Sivasankara Pillai winked conspiratorially and said, 'When I was young, I found the arrogance of Marxism, which offered solutions to all problems of the world, attractive. It had given me a key that could open all locks. I suspected the arrogance but I lived in its shelter and became a writer.' When he said this, he had in mind both Marxism and the Communist Party, which had brought about a certain awareness in Kerala. Even when his faith in the party had diminished, he continued to be in love with the ideology. In Birmingham I remember what Raymond Williams said at a meeting attended by some of us. 'If a Pope does something despicable, we can use the Bible he believes in and criticize him. Similarly, we can use Marx's writings to criticize the wrongs of the Communist Party. But in the case of Hitler his actions are cruel, and so is his text.'

Another point about Marxism, which Lohia had observed, has troubled me. Marxism explains that the capitalism in Europe later turned imperial. Lohia contests this, saying Europe has always been imperial, its imperialism helping capitalism grow. In the absence of territory, the land grabber cannot grow big. Lohia questions the essence of Marxism. A country that establishes its authority by expanding its empire continues to grow, and its rival nation grows similarly, just a step behind. In other words, although Marx questions the supremacy of European culture, he implies it is supreme in impact. But Lohia rejects the linear theories of Hegel and Marx, and upholds Toynbee's circular view of history. Rome and India, which were once in the forefront, were pushed back. Europe, which was backward, surged forward. This will change again. The course of history, as Tagore says, is a continual rise and fall.

Over the years, I understood that two Marx-es exist. I came to understand the second Marx thanks to my reading of F. R. Leavis. The Marx used by the Communist Party focuses on exploitation and profit. Its objective is the dawn of a new order from the conflict of the capitalist class and the proletariat. Contrary to what Marx had predicted no revolution took place in Germany, where capitalism had grown strong. The revolution actually took place in the economically-backward Russia. In fact the Marxism of the younger Marx, who had spoken of alienation, is difficult even for the Communist Party to digest. A potter finds the clay, seasons and mixes it, shapes a pot on his wheel, dries it, and finally sells it. He feels no alienation from what he has created. But when big machinery comes into the picture, the final product and the labourer have no connection. The separation of humans from what they create becomes a source of deep sadness.

Only Tolstoy and Gandhi can understand this Marx. That is the reason Marx seems like a great poet when he talks about money. He borrows such a vision from Shakespeare.

This Marx does not come in so handy for party building because such insights come from introversion. It is not possible to turn them into slogans. But it was Lenin who found a Marxism useful for political mobilization: this is found in his idea of the vanguard of the proletariat. The workers cannot carry out a revolution; instead, the Communist Party carries it out on their behalf. Those in the vanguard are initially many but, in reality, the plural becomes singular. Stalin killed all his colleagues and ran a terrifying monogarchy. In China something similar happened with Mao, and eventually only he and his girlfriend survived. But he vanished too. Thus, Marxism, with its theory of exploitation and profit, became a trick to usher in capitalism in backward countries. It remained a means to bring in industrialization. I believe it is important to be closer to the alienation theory than to the exploitation theory. But I am also aware this could seem like escapism in situations that call for action.

MY DIFFERENCES WITH LOHIA

While I love and respect Lohia, I have also been critical of him. He once told his followers, 'Be free in speech but disciplined in action'. Contrary to this our politicians show no freedom of speech and do as they please. Lohia ended up breaking his party each time he insisted people be free in thought and disciplined in action. Since Lohia was also a politician, he sometimes relaxed his expectations and joined hands with anyone practising non-Congress politics and opposing Nehru. 'I like Nehru. Why do you sometimes criticize him so harshly?' I had once asked him. My question was prompted by what Lohia had said soon after Gandhi was assassinated. In a speech he had referred to Nehru sitting at the forefront of Gandhi's funeral procession. Lohia said only Gandhi's family had the right to sit there, and Nehru had taken their place to show he was the rightful successor. As one finding my feet in the Nehru era, I was shocked, and thought he was being needlessly cruel. Lohia heard my complaint patiently and replied, 'I have many good things to say about Nehru. I will say them after it becomes clear his family doesn't succeed him.' Lohia continued to say things that displeased many. Jayaprakash Narayan, who hadn't been able to continue with Lohia, said towards the end of his life, 'Only two people tried to build a genuine opposition party in India: Rajaji and Lohia.' In other words, J. P., dear to Nehru, had implied no opposition party could be built without Nehru being opposed. That is because only two streams of thought were in vogue: Nehru's and Gandhi's.

Even the communists, who support industrialization, are Nehru's men. That is the reason Nehru appeared to Lohia as one who had completely abandoned Gandhi.

When I mentioned this to Ramu Gandhi, he didn't agree. 'If Gandhi had named Patel or Rajendra Prasad as his successor, the country wouldn't have accepted them after his time. The entire nation was hungry for the fruits of modernity. And Gandhi knew Nehru was the only one who could meet such demands. That is why he chose Nehru. He thought Nehru would in any case hold him close to his heart, and not jettison his dreams completely. When Nehru thought spiritually, he was close to Gandhi; when he thought materially, he was close to the West. By being Indian in feeling and Western in worldly matters, Nehru didn't appear weird to Gandhi. Being a visionary, Gandhi believed his ideals, despite the pressures of the age, could be stashed away and preserved in someone.'

Gandhi chose Shudra culture to govern the country. It was not his practice to chant mantras every day. Instead he would clean latrines and spin the wheel. The work of Shudras and women was sacred to him. [...] Lohia brought Karpuri Thakur and Kishan Pattanayak to power from among the Shudras. This set a precedent. If his health had been good, Gopala Gowda would also have become a leader like them. My friend J. H. Patel didn't become personally corrupt but he compromised with the corrupt. This is a tragedy, as far as I can see.

The times are such that we all say bygone days were better. A story illustrates this. A boatman is known as heartless. He rows the boat to a point where the water is knee-high, and tells his passengers to get off. As he is dying, he tells his son he wants a good name. Taking this seriously the son starts dropping passengers further away, where the water is waist-high. People then say his father was better.

To those like me interested in politics, this is the blight of ruling families. But a blight eventually goes away, as we can see from the history of USA and England.

Lohia attempted to give momentum to such a history. When the wheels are bogged down they call for extra force to get them going. That is why Lohia criticized even someone like Nehru in a tone that sounded extremely harsh. One extreme remark I still cannot accept—when India had been humiliated in the war with China, Lohia said we should get a bomb from Kennedy. Even as hyperbole, I cannot accept this.

∽

Midwinter spring is its own season
Sempiternal though sodden towards sundown …
—'Little Gidding', T. S. Eliot

When I suffer extreme ill-health, and my pain is unbearable, some experiences liberate me. I was admitted to hospital in Manipal with no strength, and doctors said I should undergo dialysis immediately. 1 was terrified. My mind suddenly remembered a phrase from Eliot: 'Midwinter spring in its own season.' The reason is bizarre. The line acquired astonishing meaning. I had read about midwinter spring somewhere: in an extreme winter, when it is so foggy that it is difficult to make out day from night, spring makes a sudden appearance. This is a unique phenomenon of time moving backwards. A season that peeks into another is neither this nor that.

I tried to recall the second line but couldn't. I thought I should call Manu Chakravarthy and ask him about it. What is the second line, the third, the fourth? In what context does it appear? It occurred in a flash that a new energy was rising in my body, like 'midwinter spring is its own season'. This is not just my ailing body. I am not just a suffering man. I am nothing. I have let in another season into my body. This is springtime that dazzles in winter and then vanishes. Such a season has risen in my hurting body. But then this is not the only reality. Another season truth exists. It is the truth of winter, with a glow of eternal spring. Sempiternal though sodden towards sundown. The second line suggests the chill, unsettling moisture of sunset, the uncomfortable stickiness of slush, and eternal light. The adjective 'eternal' turns into 'sempiternal', filling up the mouth. I read the rest of the lines not as a divine experience but as a poetic experience accessible to mortals.

Translated by S. R. Ramakrishna

A LIFE IN THE WORLD

BIRMINGHAM AND AFTER

Chandan Gowda: What was your dissertation research on?
U. R. Ananthamurthy: My thesis is called *Politics and Fiction in the 1930s: Studies in Edward Upward and Christopher Isherwood.* I wanted to work on D. H. Lawrence. But Malcolm Bradbury, the novelist, who was initially my PhD guide, said that a lot had already been written on him and suggested I find a subject nobody had worked on. When I couldn't think of such a subject, he thought of one that suited my interests in socialism and social transformation. In the 1930s, there was a crisis in European civilization because Hitler was rising to power. Mussolini was rising to power. Democracy didn't seem to be working. In Germany, after the war, things became so expensive, you had to carry a load of money to the shop just to buy a pack of cigarettes. All this is wonderfully described in Goodbye to Berlin by Christopher Isherwood, who is one of the subjects of my dissertation.

Country after country fell to fascism. Some writers abandoned writing. And then some writers felt: We should now fight the fascism within us, but how do we do it? We can't do it with our resource of writing. We are all middle-class writers who write about the middle class only. Some writers wanted to change their consciousness and become part of the working class. People like George Orwell became working class. He went begging. His *Down and Out in Paris and London* is a great story.

Some writers stood on street corners, and wrote down what people did the whole day in a notebook. These writers thought of themselves as passive observers. Isherwood said, I am a camera, I can't write anything. I can only take a picture of what is, because the whole thing is very confusing.'

Hitler also attracted quite a few people. There were some writers at least who thought that there was an answer in his kind of ruggedness and forcefulness rather than in the liberal rhetoric of democracy. Even Yeats was attracted to it, though only for a while.

The 1930s attracted me, because there was some such feeling in all of us: Because we do not know the life of the common people, we can't write about them. What we write becomes sort of elitist.

Bradbury suggested I work on Edward Upward who had influenced W. H. Auden, Christopher Isherwood and many others into joining the Communist Party and had written two great stories. These stories were Kafkaesque though he hadn't read Kafka. Since Kafka was not accepted by the Marxists, he thought it was a sin to write like that and abandoned writing and became a recluse. He was a great friend of Auden and Isherwood. Auden has a poem on him.

I wrote to Upward's publisher, who then sent my letter to him. Upward wrote back to me: I'm coming to Wolverhampton to see my daughter. I can meet you there. I'll come to the Wolverhampton station wearing a working man's cap and holding *Encounter* in my hand. There are many Indians in Wolverhampton. I won't be able to find you easily. You also bring an *Encounter* with you.' So we met. And then a long friendship grew between us.

Upward then resigned from the Communist Party and became a schoolteacher in the Isle of Wight. He resigned from the Communist Party only when the Soviet Union attacked Hungary, but remained a Marxist. He had also lost faith in the British Communist Party, which had misled the Indian Communist Party due to the influence of the Stalinists.

Upward gave me all his written manuscripts. He has written me several letters. I wrote a thesis on morality, writing and social change.

I began to write on his earlier works—how they were very distinct and very important. Realism was not just about reality. There is something like symbolism which Marxist theory doesn't accept. That's how I began to argue against Andrei Aleksandrovich Zhdanov's theory of socialist realism, which killed many writers.

Upward wouldn't agree with me on many things and would agree sometimes. And later on, when I finished the thesis, he told me, 'You have made it possible for me to write again.' He died only a few years ago. He lived to a hundred.

I worked on Isherwood also. Upward and he were friends. They had gone to the same public school and were together at Cambridge. Upward became a Marxist; Isherwood become a Ramakrishnaite. There was a theoretical question for me here: How a certain frustration with Marxism and the Communist Party led Isherwood into Vedanta, whereas Upward gave up the Communist Party but remained a Marxist until the end.

I wanted to also examine the liberal style, the liberal imagination of Isherwood and the socialist realism that was opposed to it.

Before I started doing my thesis, I had a guide in the university who looked after all the foreign students. He'd had a very bitter experience with foreign students who were not able to write a thesis. Sometimes the guide himself had to finish the thesis. So, he called me and said, 'Why do you want to do a thesis? I would recommend that you study the English language. Learn the language well, how to enunciate it well.' I said, 'No, I have come here to do literature, I will do nothing else.'

'You are a fool,' he said. He was very affectionate. 'Look at Rajan. He is India's representative in the United Nations Organization. Why? Because he speaks English well, and you should also learn to speak it well. They have a two-year course.'

'No,'I said and argued with him.

Earlier, he had asked me what I wanted to do my thesis on. 'Edward Upward,' I said. He replied, 'It is not Edward Upward, it is Ed-ward Upward. Ed, say E.' At some point, he said he had met 'Eyengar'.

'Say Iyengar,' I told him. 'If you can't say Iyengar, why should I learn to say Edward Upward with the right kind of pronunciation? I won't. It will make me look like a monkey back in India. Sir, thank you, I am resigning from my Commonwealth scholarship.' I came home. Esther was sitting with Sharath. I said, 'I'm going back to Mysore. I'm not going to stay here to learn perfect English intonation.'

Richard Hoggart heard about it and said, 'He is a good man. He means well. I'll talk to him. You go ahead. But to be safe, we will give you one paper in English. Do it well. Nobody can then object that you can't write a thesis.' So, I studied Shakespeare and wrote a paper within three months. I passed with a first class. The man who had started it all said, 'Thank you. I think you will do your thesis well.'

I began to do my research. Malcolm Bradbury went away to another university soon after. Alas, he is not alive any longer. He was my age, a very bright man. He wrote extensively on the form of the novel, and on E. M. Forster. He also wrote very humorous novels. After he transferred to another university, Richard Hoggart put me under David Lodge. He was also a novelist. He wrote on Catholic themes. He was as humorous in person as he was in his novels. He defended H. G. Wells. He was fond of Henry James. It was great fun working with him.

CG: Tell me more about your relation with Richard Hoggart.

URA: I belonged to a group called Centre for Contemporary Cultural Studies, which was started by Richard Hoggart. Stuart Hall was his colleague. And since their discussions were open to all, I began to sit in on them. That meant I read a lot: the old English classics, the social and political discussions on Mill, Bentham, etc. Richard Hoggart was even interested in the kinds of curtains being used in recent times. For him, nothing was irrelevant so far as the study of culture was concerned. Culture was not just literature. He was a hero because of his book, *The Uses of Literacy*. He wore a working-class cap and also spoke working- class English at times.

So, when I told him about the man who wanted me to say 'Edward Upward' correctly, he said, 'He wouldn't admit me too, because I used to speak working-class English.' So, I had a real great friend in that very wise man, Richard Hoggart.

He was profound. He used to teach Yeats. I attended his lectures. One day in the classroom, he couldn't find the meaning of a certain line. He stopped. 'I will ask David Lodge.' Then he put down his gown and went to David Lodge, who was the youngest teacher, and came back after ten minutes and explained it to us. There was that kind of atmosphere.

CG: Looking back, what did you think was intellectually exciting about this interest of theirs in studying culture?

URA: I became the kind of literary critic I am because I was a member of that group. Literature didn't mean just literature; it meant several other things. I was not only doing my PhD, I was part of the group's discussions, I was writing my own novels. At no point in my life have I been as active as I was in those three years.

CG: Did it strike you as odd or interesting that Raymond Williams or E. P. Thompson or Richard Hoggart weren't concerned to the extent you would expect them to be with the question of colonialism and its relationship with British literature, with the making of British culture?

URA: These words were not used very often. People like Richard Hoggart were more worried about the dominance of the elite classes in their own society, in their view of literature, in their view of culture, in their view of life, in their view of politics and so on. You should know that England in the days of Matthew Arnold and in our own days has had a continuous struggle against the dominant classes and they were right to be involved in that.

I never thought about colonialism because my worry was how we treated Dalits. We were never into the study of neocolonialism and things like that. They were not urgent. What was happening to you in your own land was urgent. And it was so with the British intellectuals whom I respected. They were having a perpetual quarrel with their own newspapers, with their own media. They had a battle of their own.

CG: No, since you were there with your own experiences....

URA: You know, I was better off than a working-class boy in my own university.

CG: But your second novel, *Bharathipura*, is a deep rejection of the validity of certain kinds of intellectual orientations for understanding India, mainly the liberal egalitarian tradition, within which, I would think, their concerns with culture were also being articulated, which is why I asked my question. You mentioned you taught at the secondary school.

URA: They were schools for very poor children. I was a supply teacher.

CG: What is a supply teacher?

URA: A supply teacher is one who fills in for a teacher when he is on leave. The teacher on leave, in my case, had had a nervous breakdown. Not being able to teach, he used to come to class with a little whisky inside him. I took over his classes. It was really a big thing for me.

I worked as a schoolteacher because I didn't have enough money.

I had to deal with difficult British boys and girls in two high schools. It was an experience by itself. I will tell you about one incident.

I taught in a secondary school where the teachers were harassed by the students, some of whom came drunk to the class or on drugs. There was a British teacher who was in charge of sports. I had to take all my students to a field to play football. We had to pass through an apple orchard along the way. A Pakistani boy who was very naughty picked an apple. I hadn't seen it, but the teacher who was waiting for us, an Englishman, had. So, as we reached, he called that boy. 'Where did you get the apple?' He made him bend, took off his shoe, and hit him. Hitting with a shoe was common, but when he hit him, he said, 'Remember, you are in England. You are not in your bloody country!' I lost my temper. I held him by his collar and said, 'Punish the boy, but don't punish the whole country. There was a train robbery in your country, you should know!' And then all the students there got confused, because of my sudden anger and my holding that man by his collar. He said, 'I am sorry, Ananthamurthy, I didn't know what I was saying.'

I was shaken. Because I thought that I was angrier than I should have been, because that teacher was humiliated in front of many black students and students from British and Irish backgrounds. He took his cycle and went away.

I went back to the school and met the headmaster to say sorry for losing my temper. But he replied, 'I have already come to know. The teacher came to me to say he was very sorry for what he did. He was grateful to you for pointing it out then and there.' I was very moved. And the next day, at the prayer meeting, the sports teacher said, I have a statement to make. I said wrong things and Ananthamurthy was there to stop me. I am very grateful to him.'

I was able to act quickly. I had this tendency for a long time. I wouldn't wait, I would say what came to my mind. As I grew older, I lost it. Richard Hoggart said, 'I am very happy that you could say such a thing.' So, I had that kind of truly liberal background when I was in England.

I had many experiences of this kind—the British decency. As a matter of fact, if there is another country 1 love after India, it is

England. I have some admiration for England but also feel angry when I read about how the British created Israel. They were the most cunning rulers of the world. I don't know how they have been able to combine a certain kind of fairness for people who live in England and its total opposite when they rule a country. I had to face this later on. I faced it not with prejudice against England, but with a certain kind of sympathy for England. Because every writer I read, whether it was Wordsworth, Shelley, Keats—they were all against imperialism. I learned the language of anti-imperialism through British writers.

After I defended the Pakistani boy, the West Indian, Irish, and other students began to like me because they had not seen a teacher take another teacher to task.

So, in a way, I was quite happy. But the students wouldn't learn to read, to write; they were very difficult. Milk used to be supplied to the whole school. They would throw away their bottles of milk and not use them. And I had to take them to lunch and there would be a prayer. Once, a Muslim boy said, 'I can't say the school prayer.' I had to intervene, go to the headmaster, and pick a different kind of prayer for him. These kinds of problems were there. Many Pakistani and Indian boys came to that school.

I used to be paid every week for my work. And when I was leaving England, the headmaster offered me a full-time job! I was a supply teacher in three or four schools like this one.

CG: You had encountered the literary West before you came to England. How was it to encounter it in England?

URA: Not much difference. As a matter of fact, I waited for the daffodils to appear in England. I would look for them. Wordsworth's poem, 'Daffodils', had moved me in my first year as a student of English in Mysore. I loved England before I went there. My father's influence also had something to do with it. He was a great admirer of the British sense of justice. He admired the great speech of Edmund Burke which attacked Warren Hastings. He made me learn it by heart. I have written somewhere that it was not the Purusha Sukta which I had to learn by heart, but the impeachment of Warren Hastings.

CG: Did your understanding of the West change after being there for three years?

URA: Because of the way they were dealing with Rhodesia, I became very critical of the British governmental policy. And fortunately, when I went to England in 1963, Harold Wilson became the prime minister. He was a pipe-smoking man. He was very articulate. A conservative member of parliament from Birmingham had got elected on a slogan, 'If you want a nigger for a neighbour, vote labour.' Wilson had addressed him in Biblical language inside the Parliament: 'Thou shalt abide here as a leper.' Even conservatives were ashamed of him and made him resign.

I went campaigning for the Labour Party once. When I got involved in political questions, I had many problems with British dominance in the world.

I had some admiration for British theatre. I went to so many plays. Birmingham was very close to Shakespeare's birthplace. It was great.

England was poor. There was no cooling or heating in the rooms. We had to put a coin in a little stove, and then burn it for warmth, or use a hot-water bag to stay warm enough in winter. That England I remember, particularly a little shop run by a woman and her husband. She was lonely. Their children had gone away. As I would open the door, she would come and say, 'Oh, my darling, what do you want?' and sell me things.

I was cheated only once. I had come to London from Birmingham. I got down from the bus and found my new long- coat missing. There was an old coat in its place. A British woman looked at me and said, 'One of your countrymen took away your coat.' That was the greatest insult, I felt. I lived in somebody else's coat for a long time.

We had very little money. The Commonwealth fellowship gave me some money and a little money for Esther. But the healthcare system was excellent. The Labour Party was committed to the healthcare system.

The cultural gap between Indians and the British created a lot of problems for us as students. For instance, when Indian homes drew the curtains during daytime, people walking by would feel a little anguished, because you drew the curtains only if somebody was dead. But Indians didn't know that.

And Indians would buy expensive curtains with one side being very nice and the other plain. They would put the nice side inside and the plain side outside. The British used to do the opposite so that others would know that they have a very nice curtain.

But this didn't go on for too long. They somehow accepted Indians and the Indians also began to accept the British ways. The British also could not do without Indian labour. It was to their advantage. My friend, Martin Green, used to tell me, 'Go to any public library. Who do you find eagerly reaching for a book there? An Indian or a Pakistani, not a British boy.' Their schools, their medical services had many Indians.

CG: Any other friendships you remember?

URA: Gangadhar Chittal was a very close friend. I used to read his poetry. I spent a lot of time in his house. He looked after the accounts section in the Indian embassy and was quite a big man. The man who wrote that great book on West Indian cricket was another friend.

CG: C. L. R. James?

URA: Yes. C. L. R. James. It was a political book also.

CG: *Beyond a Boundary*?

URA: Yes. I got to know him because I had West Indian friends. Whenever I went to London, I would spend some time with him. I had long talks with him. He would say, 'Who are the great people of our century? Mahatma Gandhi. Nkrumah because he danced with the Queen. And Mao Tse-Tung because he got the peasants to rebel. Gandhi was the greatest of them all.'

I remember once talking to him about M. N. Roy. He said, 'I know M. N. Roy, I will never forgive him. We worked together. He was close to Stalin, he was close to Lenin, and when we were fighting for Trotsky; he said he was a Trotskyite. He betrayed us. He was not a Trotskyite. He was a Stalinist.' I tried to say that he had changed. He didn't listen. 'Nonsense! He was a Stalinist!'

And then he would say, 'We West Indians have an advantage. We know cricket. We know the English language. We can do better than the English. You don't know English. It isn't your language. But, look, there is another side to it. We have a problem of identity because we speak their language, we eat their food. Whereas you have kept your identity through your language. You should stick to your language.'

He used to be a very alive mind. He would either be ironing his clothes while talking to us or making tea in a small flat in England.The

West Indian students were very fond of him because he propounded the idea of negritude in those days.

I used to know Raymond Williams, Stephen Spender, and writers of that kind, but they were not my friends. I did not move only in the Indian crowd. I could easily make friends with the British. They would have some trouble with my accent, but if they liked me they would understand.

CG: Did you like living in Birmingham?

URA: Oh yes! I don't know about the present situation in England, but I liked that country. It had a certain sense of fairness. I liked going to pubs, talking to the working-class people, and they would wonder at me, because here was a black man, a coloured man who knew Shakespeare.

∽

CG: What are some of the things you cherish most about our society?

URA: What I cherish most in our society is our family life. In a poor country like this, where there is no system of public support, children, no matter what caste or how poor, get educated and come up in life. This is wonderful, and this comes with another fact, which is almost a curse: our personalities are never developed in a close-knit family. We never develop the way young people in Western societies develop. That's what I used to feel. I would envy them. They have an independence which our boys and girls lack because they have to adjust with their families. So, there is a plus side, an enormous plus side, and a minus side. The minus side doesn't come in for bitter criticism, because the lack of independence and so on also results in some kind of control over our own very selfish pursuits. Our young people go berserk but not as much as teenagers do elsewhere. And we easily criticize the minus side in public, but in our homes, we are very cautious with our own children. So, there is a hypocrisy in our family life. But it's a hypocrisy with which we have lived for a long time and we have survived and we have done well.

Second, what I admire most in India are the festivals. The people of India, whether they can read or not, know exactly when the festivals come. People living in huts and so on, they somehow know the almanac better than we do. And there is a feast; however poor you are, there is a celebration. And so India has never been dull despite all the poverty, because of all these great festivals and pilgrimages.

Everyone, even the poorest of the poor, wants to go to Tirupati or to Kashi once. And they do go, or at least to their own temples some hundred miles away. They make a visit. Once I went to a Tirupati temple in Mysore district. They call it 'Second Tirupati'. I found a long queue there. If you can't stand in the queue to get a glimpse of the deity, you will find another Tirupati inside. Somebody has put a stone there and put kumkum on it and made it another Tirupati. A little stone chosen by people becomes a Tirupati. So, you don't necessarily have to go to Tirupati. There is a second Tirupati, and that Tirupati has another Tirupati inside. It's amazing, the Indian imagination. I cannot think like that, but I salute those who can.

CG: Any other likes?

URA: Our streets. Our streets are alive. I miss Indian streets when I go abroad. There are just cars and cars and cars and bikes, but the Indian streets are amazing. People selling their stuff on the pavements, cows grazing, cars honking, women and men going about their own business, stopping traffic: the Indian streets are a wonderful sight.

You curse them when you are here, but if you go and live in America or Europe for a long time, you will miss the Indian bazaars. There is an absolutely wonderful market in Mysore. Whenever I had guests from abroad, I would take them there and show them the row of vegetable stalls.

CG: The Devaraja Market?

URA: Yes. And behind the vegetable stalls, there is a row of flower stalls, and then there are papads and fried snacks in one row. I used to take my guests to a very proud man who sold the Nanjangud banana (rasabale). If you asked him to charge one paisa less, he would say, 'Go away. I won't sell it you.' His was the authentic rasabale. The whole market had its own character. I found a market like that in Paris. Our villages have their own markets. So, that kind of living together is something I have always liked.

CG: And the things that you do not like about our society?

URA: Sophisticated people like you and me, we have a tendency to backbite. Once you turn your back, if there is another person, he is going to make a remark against you. There is a lot of backbiting among the middle classes in India, which I don't like, because it is a class which is forever competing, one against the other. So, that class has come up as a result of modern development. It has no genuine feelings, and no genuine festivals either. They end up having only a Satyanarayana puja [smiles] once in a while. So, it is a lacklustre middle class.

The British middle class in the eighteenth and nineteenth century was not like that. D. H. Lawrence called the British middle class a responsible class. They fought for all political reforms. They were very aware. I'm very critical of the Indian middle class. I dislike it. And nowadays, the absolute lack of morality over money, corruption. That greed has become acceptable is shocking. It was not acceptable at one time.

I remember a story from Kerala. Pattom Thanu Pillai had become chief minister. He was from the Praja Socialist Party. It was in a minority. Because no party could claim power, a minority party was allowed to rule. He found that one of his ministers had bought a lorry. He went to Jayaprakash Narayan in Bihar because J. P. was the leader of the party. 'My minister has bought a lorry. What should I do now?' he said. That used to be the story in Kerala. Buying a lorry could get you in trouble. No longer. There was a time when it was very shameful to have a corrupt father, a corrupt mother. No longer. That's something about India—it's a phenomenon of our times.

Thirty years ago, the African writer, Chinua Achebe, told me, 'You don't know. In Nigeria, we are more corrupt than anyone in the world.' I don't know what I would say now. Are we as corrupt as them or more corrupt than them?

CG: What are your attachments?

URA: My attachments are to my friends really. I have great friends, friends from my childhood, from my school days. I can still joke with them and play pranks with them, forgetting that I am old, that we are old, and we begin laughing over very silly things. That's possible for me. A silly joke shared with a very dear friend can make you laugh, because there are other sides to the joke. I am lucky that I have had friends from all castes and all groups all my life. I have shared different kinds of lives with them, which is what made me a writer, I think. There's another. I used to love good food. I used to be an enormous eater at one time. My mother used to say that nobody should see me eating as that might portend negative effects on me.

CG: What is your favourite cuisine?

URA: They are all vegetarian, but I learned to eat non-vegetarian very reluctantly after my marriage. I eat chicken if I can have a whisky along with it.

CG: Your favourite drink?

URA: Whisky. It used to be beer, but now my sugar level is so high, I can't take beer. So, the body has denied me many things which I like. My body itself is my enemy now.

CG: What do you find most enjoyable?

URA: Talking like this with you. And reading a book, discussing it. This is great fun for me.

CG: What are your favourite books?

URA: My favourite books? I have been talking to everyone who comes here to meet me about *Agnatanobbana Atmacharitre*. Hanur Krishnamurthy has written it. I am fascinated by that book.

CG: Your favourite writer?

URA: I have no favourite writer in India now. I used to. Nirmal Verma was one of them. Dilip Chitre was one of them. Purnachandra Tejasvi, P. Lankesh, and Yashwant Chittal in Kannada. There are younger writers whom I like: Jayant Kaikini, Vivek Shanbhag. And there are some very fine poets, who are not great poets yet. There is a lot of good work going on. I feel that Kannada is alive. I feel happy about that.

CG: Western writers?

URA: I read all of Shelley. I read all of D. H. Lawrence, Yeats and T. S. Eliot. Also Sartre, Camus, Dostoyevsky, and Leo Tolstoy. I did do a lot of reading. I don't read many of the contemporaries now. I have no time.

CG: What about theatre? Your favorite playwrights?

URA: I don't see many plays. My favorite playwright really is

Shakespeare, and to some extent Brecht. And in Kannada, I like Girish Karnad and Chandrashekhara Kambara. Theatre is good, but I am not awed by it.

CG: Favourite films?

URA: When I was very young, I used to like V. Shantaram's films very much. They used to inspire me, move me. I am very fond of Raj Kapoor, and also his father, Prithviraj. I liked cinema which was like theatre. I used to go on a cycle from Shivamogga to Bhadravathi to see a film. I would do that in those days. I began to like Rajkumar in my younger days, and some Tamil movies. I like Satyajit Ray a lot. In Kannada, I enjoy Girish Kasaravalli's films.

CG: Any actresses that you liked?

URA: I used to like Kalpana very much in those days. I really liked her. She was a new face for me. I love Nargis even now. The way she lifts her nose.

CG: Any favorite directors?

URA: Very difficult for me to say, because directors became important only when I began to see new kinds of films. Regarding theatre, the notion of a director making a very big change didn't exist until B.V. Karanth came on the stage. It was he who made the director important. Otherwise, it was actors and plays, and not the director. I like Bergman a lot. His religious imagination appeals to me deeply.

CG: Are there any prejudices that you do not want to let go of?

URA: I have a prejudice against people who live in India but don't speak in Indian languages. I can't really like them. If they pretend they don't know the language, and they have lived here for a long time, they are either deaf or dull or unintelligent, or so egotistical that they think they know the world because they know a European language. I am deeply prejudiced against that kind of person. I can't stand a person who drops names, who boasts about his relationships with the top players of society. I don't like that kind of thing at all, and I've never done it myself.

CG: Are there places you wish you had visited?

URA: Africa. I've never been to Africa. This lifetime is not enough. If I didn't have the burden of English, if I had learnt other languages,

I would have enjoyed India more. I deeply regret that I can't speak Hindi. I am not an anti-Hindi man, because if I knew Hindi well, then large parts of India would have been close to me.

CG: Does it matter to you that people like you?

URA: I enjoy being liked. Although I am ill, I forget that I am ill because of the affection and warmth I get from young people who read my writings, who remember what I write, who write me letters. I like it very much.

CG: Can you recall an embarrassing moment?

URA: Only one [smiles]. When I became vice chancellor, I had to be saluted at the gate, and somebody had to come and get my bag. When my children saw this once, they said. 'Are you not embarrassed, Appa?' I felt deeply ashamed. And then I told the staff that there was no need to take my bag at the gate, no need to salute me either.

After a few days, my private secretary came to me, saying, 'Disaster, sir. Disaster.' I asked, 'What disaster?' 'Come. I will show you,' he said. He took me to the room of the man who was supposed to salute me. He was sitting down in his dhoti, with a paan in his mouth. My secretary said, 'Look at him. Nobody has any discipline in the department. There was some discipline, sir, when he had to salute you.' Then I suddenly remembered that I can't be different from the others. So, I told him to start saluting me from the next day. This was embarrassing and a kind of defeat that I experienced, where one can't be totally different from the organization in which one lives.

CG: What is your idea of a day well spent?

URA: I wake up, read something, go for a walk, come back, talk with friends, and then go for a walk, come back, have a drink, chat for a long time and go to sleep. That is a good day. And if a stranger drops in and becomes a friend and you start a dialogue, that's great. A new face acquired every day is a joy. In the past I didn't forget their names. But now I make friends and then if he or she comes after three or four days, I will have forgotten their names because of my old age.

CG: You earned fame very young, your first novel got you a lot of attention. How do you handle fame?

URA: Very easily, because it is no longer my book. If somebody praises the novel, I can see that it has some quality. It has just come out of me. I had to struggle like a mother giving birth, but once it is there, it has a life of its own. I feel it is something like the grace of God that I can create, that I can go a little beyond myself.

CG: My last question: how would you like to be remembered?

URA: As a Kannada writer. For having made a contribution to Kannada through my work. There are many younger writers who will get something from me, because I have brought whatever I could from my own past, from my Brahminical past, from the European world, from my various experiences, and from my probing of my own self in the Kannada language. It might be a threatened language in the modern world, but I have worked against the threat and that is an achievement. I would like to be remembered as a teacher, as a writer.

CG: Thank you.

ACKNOWLEDGEMENTS

We are grateful to Esther Ananthamurthy, Vivek Shanbhag, and Sharath Ananthamurthy for their constant support towards bringing out this book. Rajaram Tolpadi shared a copy of URA's essay on Lohia, which was valuable to include in this anthology. We are thankful to him. We remember with gratitude the assistance of Y. V. Harisha and K. Srinivasa in scanning and processing several of URA's writings at the library at the Institute of Social and Economic Change, Bengaluru. Pujitha Krishnan and Karishma Koshal at Aleph Book Company lent terrific editorial support. A big thanks to them both. While every effort has been made to locate and contact copyright holders and obtain permission, this has not always been possible; any inadvertent omissions brought to our notice will be remedied in future editions. Grateful acknowledgement is made to the following copyright holders for permission to reprint copyrighted material for translation in this volume.

The short story 'Ghatashraddha' from *Indian Literature*. Originally published in Kannada in 1962.

The short story 'Akkayya' from *Stallion of the Sun and Other Stories* (1999) has been included with the permission of Penguin Random House India. Originally published in Kannada in 1995.

The short story 'Mouni' was originally published in Kannada in 1966. The short story 'Jaratkaru' from *Stallion of the Sun and Other Stories* (1999) has been included with the permission of Penguin Random House India. Originally published in Kannada in 1995.

The short story 'Stallion of the Sun' from *Stallion of the Sun and Other Stories* (1999) has been included with the permission of Penguin Random House India. Originally published in Kannada in 1995.

The short story 'Kamaroopi' has been included with the permission of *The Book Review.* Originally published in Kannada in 1995.

An excerpt from *Samskara* (2012) has been included with the permission of Oxford University Press, New Delhi. Originally published in Kannada in 1965.

An excerpt from *Bharathipura* (2010) has been included with the permission of Penguin Random House India. Originally published in Kannada in 1974.

An excerpt from *Avasthe* (2020) has been included with the permission of HarperCollins India. Originally published in Kannada in 1978.

An excerpt from *Bhava* (2000) has been included with the permission of Penguin Random House India. Originally published in Kannada in 1994.

An excerpt *Hindutva or Hind-Swaraj*? (2016) has been included with the permission of HarperCollins India.

An excerpt from *Suragi* (2017) has been included with the permission of Oxford University Press, New Delhi. Originally published in Kannada in 2012.

Excerpts from 'Birmingham and After', 'Tradition', and 'In Conclusion', from *A Life in the World: U. R. Ananthamurthy in Conversation with Chandan Gowda* (2019), have been included with the permission of HarperCollins India.

The essay, 'The Literary Situation in India: Search for an Identity', was originally published in 1976.

The essay, 'The Contemporary Significance of Lohia', was originally published in 1984.

The essay, 'Why Not Worship in the Nude?', was originally presented in1986.

The essay, 'Gandhi's Triumph over the Fear of Death', was originally published in 1990.

The speech, 'Tradition and Creativity', was originally delivered in 1990.

The speech, 'Towards the Concept of a New Nationhood: Languages and Literatures in India', was originally delivered in 2006.

The speech, 'Dalit Contribution to Indian Literature', was originally delivered in 2010.